Structure

SPELLING:

and Strategies

Paul R. Hanna
STANFORD UNIVERSITY

Richard E. Hodges
UNIVERSITY OF CHICAGO

Jean S. Hanna

HOUGHTON MIFFLIN COMPANY　　BOSTON
NEW YORK　ATLANTA　GENEVA, ILL.　DALLAS　PALO ALTO

Printed in the U.S.A.

LIBRARY OF CONGRESS CATALOG CARD NUMBER: 78-139212

ISBN: 0-395-04565-7

PREFACE

We, the authors, have prepared this volume with two groups of readers in mind: (1) the preservice, elementary schoolteacher enrolled in college courses on content and method in the language arts, and (2) the in-service, elementary schoolteacher or supervisor who wishes to update his knowledge of the spelling curriculum and increase his competence in organizing and teaching it.

The text consists of two parts. Part One, titled "Theoretical Foundations of Spelling," presents the general background knowledge, logic, and research findings in linguistics and psychology (learning theory) which in the current decade have contributed significantly to our understanding of the spelling principles of the American-English language and which base the new strategies for organizing a modern, more effective, level-by-level (grade-by-grade) spelling program. Part Two sets forth these new strategies. Pupil-teacher oriented, this part, titled "Strategies for a Spelling Program," suggests methods of choosing the raw materials (groups of spelling words) by means of which pupils may discern and utilize the principles on which our American-English spelling system is built. As much confusion has come with the initiation of the new spelling programs as occurred at the outset of the new mathematics programs a decade ago. Until now no attempt had been made either to present systematically the research findings and logic that support the new linguistic theories and their application to spelling or to translate these theories into a school spelling program. Part One, as we have noted, is dedicated to the first objective; Part Two to the second — to explaining the "what," "how," and "when" of the modern spelling programs.

To assist teachers in understanding the rationale of the new spelling programs, this volume provides a glossary of professional-educational terms that are fairly new to the elementary teaching field but are in general use among linguists, psycholinguists, and educational psychologists.

For decades spelling has been considered a rote-memory subject with lists of words taught by eye and hand techniques. This approach stems from the widely held notion that American-English spelling is so erratic and unpredictable with so few general principles or patterns that these are insufficient to aid the pupil in learning to spell. Therefore, the learning of each word has been treated as an independent act.

From linguists and from contemporary studies of our orthography, we have become aware today that such a view is exaggerated, that the spelling of our language is for the most part quite predictable, that it is largely based on patterns or principles, and that a pupil can learn how these principles function. By means of the new approaches, an elementary school pupil can learn to spell not merely a list of 3,000 words but a vocabulary limited only by his individual needs and abilities. The recognition of these possibilities has stirred the imagination of many teachers and spurred them to study this modern spelling theory and its method of application in the classroom. Hence the name of this volume: *Spelling: Structure and Strategies.*

A study of this text can be approached in several ways. One might begin by examining the presentation in Part One of the theoretical foundations of the spelling of our language and then continue on to Part Two to see how the theory is translated into classroom strategies. Or one might begin with Part Two and observe the sequence of classroom spelling activities from grades, or levels, 1 through 8; then after this overview of a modern spelling program, one might turn to Part One and learn the reasons for such a program.

Another person might wish to begin with the chapter in Part Two that deals with the spelling program for the level he is teaching and then skim through the other seven levels presented in that part, finally turning to Part One to study the theory. There is no single road to gaining an understanding of what we, the authors, are propounding, but we hope that one route or another will help teachers discover the American-English language and its orthography and enable them to impart their understanding to their pupils.

We wish to acknowledge the help received from the many researchers and writers whose works we have consulted, which the reader will find listed in the Bibliography. We wish particularly to express gratitude for the research of Professor E. Hugh Rudorf and Professor Sidney R. Bergquist. For critical reading of the manuscript we express our appreciation to Miss Marie Dickinson, Professor Robert A. Hall, Jr., and Professor Jack Kittell.

Final responsibility for this volume must, of course, rest with the authors. We fervently hope that it will contribute to the development of an effective spelling component of the language-arts program in the elementary school.

Paul R. Hanna

Richard E. Hodges

Jean S. Hanna

CONTENTS

PART ONE

Theoretical
Foundations of Spelling

CHAPTER ONE

Spelling
Is Language Encoding

Whenever we wish to set down our thoughts and feelings in writing we engage in the act of spelling. By placing graphic marks on some writing surface, we are able to make visible the spoken words with which we ordinarily would communicate these thoughts and feelings to others. For most of us, spelling seems a commonplace activity, a skill we have long since mastered despite occasional skirmishes with the seeming vagaries of our spelling system. And because our daily lives abound with written communication, it is easy for us to take for granted this brilliant achievement of man — *writing*, which has permitted the accumulation and transmission of knowledge and has been instrumental in the development of civilization.

The ability to acquire and use the skills basic to written communication is a requisite in modern society, and indeed it is to some extent basic to all forms of human communication. *Orthographies* (writing systems) permit man to record his thoughts and feelings for use at a later time or to communicate with others who may be beyond the range of his voice. In short, written communication extends the functions of human speech over space and over time.

The historical development of written communication is, in its own right, a fascinating story. But, more important, an under-

3

standing of the nature and development of written communication has great significance for the effective teaching and learning of this important social skill. Such knowledge helps ensure that what and how spelling is taught reflects the structure and functions of our writing system.

Language: the oral–aural communication system of human beings

Every language has the ultimate purpose of enabling man to communicate information to others; it is a means by which man's personal experiences with his environment can be systematically symbolized and related to others. Speech is, therefore, a kind of *code*. And, like all codes, it must be understood by both speaker and recipient in order to achieve this purpose.

The code of speech is composed of selected sounds produced by the human voice, sounds which singly or in combination can be used to provide names for the concepts man has of the world around him and the feelings that he experiences. The "words" of speech are in effect sound labels that help man make sense out of his environment. He uses these words as vehicles for communicating his concepts and feelings to others and for keeping a mental record of his experiences.

Language is an *oral–aural* form of communication, utilizing primarily the organs of speech and of hearing. But oral communication has two stringent limitations. First, it is ephemeral; its existence lasts only as long as the sound waves of a particular act of speech persist (although what is communicated may long be remembered by its recipients). Oral communication is therefore limited by the factor of *temporality*.

Second, speech has a spatial limitation; before electronic mechanisms, a speaker normally could convey his thoughts and feelings only to persons within the range of his voice. Thus, information that might be important had either to be passed on by "word of mouth" or not passed on at all. Oral communication therefore suffers the limitation of *space*.

Modern society has, of course, overcome these limitations by the development of electronic sound-recording and transmitting devices such as the telephone, the tape recorder, the phonograph, the radio, and the television. But these are instruments of modern technology, very recent inventions when considered in relation to the length of time in which man has communicated oral sounds without benefit of mechanical aids.

The recording and transmitting of information by means of visual symbols does, however, largely transcend the spatial and temporal limitations of language. And it was to systems of visual communication that man eventually turned in an effort to record and transmit his experiences to others from whom he was separated by time and distance.

Visual communication: a surrogate of language

One way of conveying and recording information by visual means is through the use of concrete objects. A pile of stones at the fork of a path can, for example, serve to indicate which way to follow. Pebbles can be used to keep a record of the number of animals in a herd. A bone or a stick can be notched to keep a tally of the number of days that have passed since the last rainfall.

Concrete objects used in this way, of course, are hardly more than simple "memory aids" and certainly do not fall within the realm of written communication. Yet, such modes of visually recording and transmitting information have long been employed by humans, sometimes with quite elaborate inventiveness.

For example, notched sticks were employed by certain early California Indian tribes for the purpose of recording business transactions such as the amount of labor performed, the passage of time, and the trading of horses and cattle. Squared sticks about an inch thick and about two feet in length were notched on one side to denote numbers through nine, while a long cut was made across the width of the face of the stick to denote groups of ten. In order to record *what* items were being counted, the Indians cut different shaped notches into the end of the stick — a V-shaped notch representing horns, to refer to cattle, and a U-shaped notch resembling hooves, to refer to horses. By notching with crosses and squares, the Indians were able to indicate other kinds of animals or objects.

A visual memory aid even more complex than the notched sticks was the *quipu,* developed by Peruvian Indians. A quipu was a looped cord from which were hung thinner strands of cords of various colors. By combining colors and by tying knots in predetermined positions in the suspended cords, the Peruvian Indians devised an elaborate system for recording the numbers and kinds of objects of which they had reason to keep a record. Thus, the colors red, yellow, and white were used to refer to *soldiers, gold,* and *silver,* respectively; and the numbers and positions of the knots tied in the cord were used to indicate the number of objects being tallied.

Forerunners of writing

The advent of true writing did not stem from the collection or manipulation of concrete objects as visual records of important events; but rather, the writing actually began with the inscribing of visual symbols *upon some surface.* We can only imagine, of course, what inspired primitive man to begin to record his experiences in this way — whether it was some innate artistic urge or the true desire to communicate over distance and time. Shells, pieces of bark, stones, cave walls, anything that could be used as a "writing tablet" became the material on which early man's simple pictures recreated his experiences.

The success of a hunt for food, for example, could be recorded for the inscriber's own personal pleasure simply by replicas of the animals he had killed. But equally important was the fact that others of his group could view his drawings and thus learn of his success. Such *pictographs,* or picture stories, were actually stories without words, representations of objects and animals that could

Figure 1–1

Source: Arthur B. Allen, *The Romance of the Alphabet.* Copyright © 1937 by Frederick Warne and Company, Ltd., London. Reproduced with permission.

be understood without recourse to language itself. These picture stories required literal translation, however, and could be understood only by persons who had themselves experienced the event or had encountered the pictured object. A pictograph was, in short, a visual substitute for direct experience much in the way that a photograph is a literal record of some aspect of our environment.

Pictographs like the one in Figure 1–1 have been found on ancient cave walls. They served primitive man's need to record his experiences and possibly, too, his artistic urge. But pictographs cannot convey such abstract concepts as life, death, morning, and winter, concepts for which no tangible objects exist. To record and communicate these concepts, man needed to draw pictures whose meanings go beyond the mere pictured objects themselves, pictures whose referents are not items but *ideas.*

An *ideograph* is also a picture, but one that communicates something more than concrete reality. The picture of an ox, for example, can denote the more general concept of *animal* or of *food.* Like pictographs, ideographs are not true writing; the visual symbols tell stories without words and therefore are not symbols representing language itself, even though a "reader" of an ideograph may translate the idea into his language. In a very

Figure 1–2

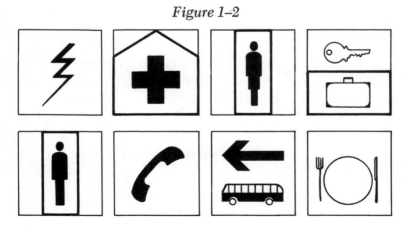

Source: *Official Guide to "Man and His World."* Published by City of Montreal, 1969. Reproduced with permission.

real sense, then, ideographs transcend language, for the communication between artist and "reader" takes place without necessarily having recourse to verbal symbols.

The capacity of ideographs to transcend language makes them useful for many purposes. Figure 1–2 shows some ideographs used at a recent international exposition. They surmount the language barrier and convey important information to visitors from many lands.

Such modern uses of ideographic representation are a common part of our environment. Highway signs that signal "curve ahead" ⟨↯⟩ or "intersection" ⊕ are further examples of how ideographs have important uses even in advanced cultures.

For primitive cultural groups who had not discovered that language — the spoken word — could be represented through writing — graphic symbolization — ideographs became a principal means of visual communication. Figure 1–3 shows some ideographs that were employed by certain American Indian tribes. Notice that the ideographs often suggested hardly more than the bare rudiments of the original pictured objects, and that their interpretations sometimes required associating visual symbols with concepts other than those the symbols seemingly represented.

Figure 1–3

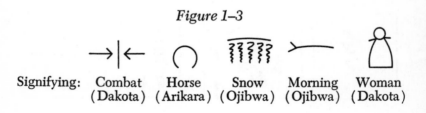

Signifying: Combat   Horse   Snow   Morning   Woman
             (Dakota) (Arikara) (Ojibwa) (Ojibwa) (Dakota)

Source: Walter J. Hoffman, *The Beginnings of Writing*, Macmillan, London and New York, 1895.

The beginnings of true writing

Two great civilizations, Chinese and Egyptian, developed perhaps the most extensive systems of ideographic representation in the history of visual communication. Their importance, however, lies not in their extensiveness but in the fact that each led to true writing, the use of visual symbols to represent speech itself. Let us briefly examine each of these systems, beginning with the Chinese ideographic system.

In the development of the Chinese graphic system employed today, the same evolution from pictographic to ideographic representation occurred that we have noted earlier. Pictures representing concrete objects became associated with abstract concepts that could not be directly represented by pictorial symbolization. Over time, these graphic characters evolved toward symbols bearing little relationship to the real character or quality of objects that they once represented — their original "meanings" unknown except to scholars knowledgeable about the historical development of Chinese ideography. Here, for example, is an ancient Chinese ideograph representing the concept "hermit":

Ṁ.[1] Can you detect how the lower character resembles a mountain while the upper character suggests the outline of a man kneeling as if in prayer? The two symbols in conjunction indicate a "man on a mountain," that is, a hermit.

Most contemporary Chinese graphic symbols owe their heritage to such ancient ideographic characters as that represented by the symbol for hermit. But contemporary Chinese writing is more than ideographic representation, since the characters employ additional graphic signs indicating the pronunciation of the word in spoken Chinese. Figure 1–4 illustrates some more Chinese ideographs and the meanings they convey.

The origins of our own writing system evolved from the Egyptian ideographic system. Like all ideographic recorders, Egyptian scribes employed characterizations of concrete objects to symbolize abstract ideas. Thus, 𓁹 was used to refer to "weeping," while 𓅬 symbolized "child," possibly on the analogy that a goose and a male child were highly prized. Here is a simplified rendering of the Egyptian ideography for "king" 𓎽. It is likely that this graphic character stemmed from an

---

[1] Walter J. Hoffman, *The Beginnings of Writing* (London and New York: Macmillan, 1895), p. 108.

Figure 1–4

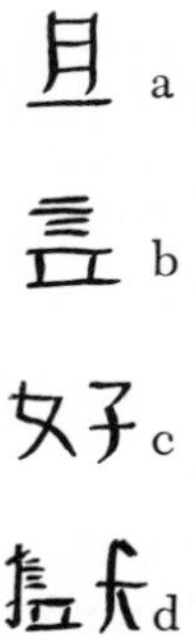

a

b

c

d

In each case illustrated, the signs (characters) are composite, and consist of two, or three, constituent signs. Part (a) means "dawn": the sun (the upper character, which was originally circular) is seen over the horizon. Part (b) means "words, speech." The rectangular character is a pictograph for "mouth," and the horizontal lines show vapor issuing from it. Part (c) is "happy." The two characters stand for "wife" and "child" respectively, and their conjunction suggests the state of happiness. Part (d) is "litigate." The first and last characters both stand for "dog," and in the center we have "speech," as in (b). The whole puts forward a view of legal procedure as an argument like a dispute between dogs.

earlier pictograph for "bee," an insect noted for its capacity for organization.

The early Egyptian *hieroglyphs* ("priest writing") were hardly more than simple pictographs, visual symbols representing concrete objects themselves — symbols such as  (leg)* or  (hand)*. In time, however, these pictographs developed into ideographs such that  * could be used to symbolize visually the concept of "work" or "power," and  * could represent the concepts of "run" or perhaps "fleet (of foot)."

Egyptian scribes never completely gave up the use of pictography and ideography, but their symbols set the stage for the emergence of true writing, the graphic symbolization of speech. This important step occurred when hieroglyphs became utilized as "sound pictures," or *phonograms*. Thus, the ideograph

* Source: Illustrations by the author from *The 26 Letters* by Oscar Ogg. Copyright © 1961, 1948, by Thomas Y. Crowell Company, New York, publishers. Reproduced with permission.

〰〰〰used to represent "water" became a symbol for the Egyptian spoken word *nu,* (water).

Egyptian orthography was indeed complex, a blend of pictographs, ideographs, and the rudiments of true writing. But from this complex system there also emerged an even more crucial development in the historical course of modern writing, the use of some of these graphic symbols to represent the syllables and individual sounds of words. Thus, 〰〰〰 was used to represent the speech sound that our alphabetic character *N* also represents. In like manner, ⬭ , which was a phonogram for the Egyptian word *ro* (mouth), became a representation of the sound of an initial *r.*

Egyptian scribes never fully accomplished the development of a complete system of true writing. But in this conglomerate system of visual symbolization we find the various ways in which all true writing systems represent language — symbols representing whole words, symbols representing syllables, and symbols representing the individual sounds of which syllables and words are made.

Figure 1–5

Ra

Source: Illustration by the author from *The 26 Letters* by Oscar Ogg. Copyright © 1961, 1948, by Thomas Y. Crowell Company, New York, publishers. Reproduced with permission.

The Egyptian hieroglyphic system often required some artistic ability, particularly in the re-creation of some of the more complex symbols such as that for *Ra,* the name of the Egyptian sun deity (see Figure 1–5). As a result, a simplified script was devised, called *hieratic;* this system of writing, still used by priests, was an abridged and somewhat cursive form of hieroglyphics which could be transcribed on papyrus. Hieratic writing eventually developed into *demotic* script, an even further simplification of the hieroglyphic system which came to be used in the recording of business transactions and in the preparation of books.

The development of hieratic and demotic writing promoted the practice of writing *upon* some surface rather than the cutting or pressing of symbols *into* some surface. Yet, among the Akkadians and other cultures of that time, a writing system was devised which continued the practice of incising marks into a surface such as stone or clay. This system, *cuneiform* (wedge-writing), also used graphic characters as ideographs and as symbols for sound features of the oral code. Figure 1–6 contains some examples of early cuneiform.

Figure 1–6

Original pictograph	Pictograph in position of later cuneiform	Early cuneiform	Classic Assyrian	Meaning
				ox
				cow
				barley grain
				sun day
				to plow to till

Source: David Diringer, *Writing.* Copyright © 1962 by Thames and Hudson, Ltd., London, and F. A. Praeger, New York. Reproduced with permission.

Contemporary writing systems

We have seen how man has developed visual communication systems to augment his use of language. And we have seen that these systems, despite their functionality, do not permit the flexibility of communication that speech provides. Yet in these restricted beginnings of true writing lie the nuclei of all modern systems of writing, of *orthographies.*

All languages are man-made systems whose purposes are to communicate man's thoughts and feelings to others through the medium of sound. Although languages may differ considerably in terms of what sounds are used and how these sounds are combined, each language has two features: 1) From the wide range of sounds which the human voice can make, particular sounds are selected with which to construct that language code; these particular speech sounds are the *phonemes* of that language. 2) These selected phonemes are combined in systematic ways to form the syllables and words that a specific oral code uses.

All languages, then, are systems which combine particular speech sounds (phonemes) to make units of sound which in turn become the vehicles for expressing man's thoughts and feelings. Sometimes these meaning-bearing sound units (words) are only single syllables, as is largely the case in modern Chinese, and sometimes they are made up of several syllables in combination. But what is important for our understanding of contemporary orthographies is that each of these elements of language — phoneme, syllable, and word — can become the basis for the creation of written communication.

Logographic orthographies

Any writing system, orthography, that employs graphic characters to represent the words of a language is called a *logographic* (word-writing) orthography. We have seen that Chinese orthography utilizes this principle and that the ancient Egyptian orthography utilized it in part. The principle underlying a logographic writing system, then, is that a unique graphic symbol must represent each meaningful sound unit (word) of language. And since there can be literally thousands of words in a language, a logographic orthography can become quite unwieldy because each spoken word requires its own unique graphic character.

The principle of logographic writing can be illustrated in our own writing system. For example, when we set down the symbols $2 + 2 = 4$, we are writing graphic characters that represent the words "two plus two equals four," which in turn are linguistic ways of representing mathematical concepts. In the same manner, the graphic symbols % (percent), & (and), and ¢ (cent) are logographic characters which are widely used in graphic communication.

Such graphic symbols, of course, serve limited purposes in our personal writing. But imagine instead an entire writing system composed of unique graphic symbols for each word in our own language; our imaginations would be strained indeed to devise unique visual symbols for all the orally produced words we use to express our thoughts and feelings. It is for this reason that mastering Chinese orthography (which contains about 40,000 characters, although about 4,000 of the characters will suffice for most written communication) is an extremely difficult and time-consuming process requiring a lifetime of concentration. In the past this has been one of the major causes of the low rate of literacy of the general Chinese population. Great efforts are currently being made to transform the Chinese writing code in order to make written communication more widespread.

Syllabic orthographies (syllabaries)

A second way of expressing language in writing is to employ graphic characters to represent the syllables of speech. Just as a logographic writing system uses unique graphic symbols to represent the meaning-bearing sound units (words) of a language, a syllabic orthography (syllabary) uses unique graphic symbols for each syllable of the language it expresses.

The advantage of a syllabic orthography stems from the fact that there generally are fewer syllables than words in languages (except for languages, such as Chinese, that largely use monosyllables and tonal change to express meaning). In a hypothetical language, a vocabulary of 10,000 words may have no more than 1,000 syllables which are used over and over again in different combinations to form polysyllabic words. Consequently, a syllabic orthography requires fewer graphic symbols to represent language than does a logographic orthography.

American-English orthography does not contain graphic characters to represent syllables as is the case in syllabic writing, except for such manufactured spellings as "bar-b-q." We can imagine what such a system would be like in our language, however, if we were to write the words *essay, before, any,* and *why* as follows: *SA, B4, NE,* and *Y.*

Syllabic writing was an improvement over logographic writing primarily because of the reduced number of graphic symbols to be mastered in learning to write and to read. The principle of employing graphic symbols to represent spoken syllables was known to ancient Egyptian scribes and employed to some extent in their writing, as was mentioned earlier. And syllabic orthographies are still found among some of the world's current writing systems, such as Japanese katakana.

Toward alphabetic orthographies

As with most of mankind's great discoveries, the development of writing systems has been neither a fortuitous nor a widely scattered series of independently derived inventions. To the extent that scholars have been able to reconstruct the past, it is clear that the great majority of contemporary writing systems are products of the forebears which we have been considering in this chapter.

But what about the development of our own writing system, American-English orthography? What is its ancestry? On what sound principle is it based? The answers to these questions form the basis of the next several chapters and will help you to see that in addition to its fascinating history, our orthography has an underlying graphic principle, the alphabetic principle, that marks one of mankind's great intellectual accomplishments.

CHAPTER TWO

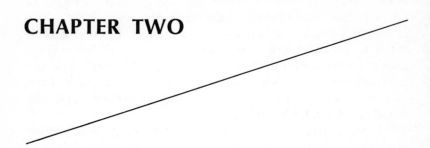

The Alphabetic Principle

Chapter One sketched man's progress in communication from the spoken word through the several early major methods for expressing language in visual forms that were designed to overcome the limitations of time and space which, until recently, have been characteristic of speech.

As we have seen, the foundations of all languages are particular speech sounds (phonemes) which, in various combinations, compose the syllables and words of oral communication. The number of phonemes used in any language is a somewhat arbitrary matter. Hawaiian, for example, uses 13 phonemes (8 consonants, 5 vowels) as the basic building blocks of speech. This is a relatively small and simple set of phonemes in contrast to the phonemic sets employed in many of the world's languages, such as some of the Caucasian languages found in the southern part of the Soviet Union. American English employs 40-plus phonemes,[1] which is about "average" for most contemporary languages.

Regardless of the number of phonemes contained in an oral code, the fact that words and syllables are made up of phonemes can be used as the basis for the development of orthographies

---

[1] The number of phonemes in American-English speech varies in accordance with the system of classification of speech sounds employed by various linguists. The 40-plus phonemes used here include consonants, vowels, diphthongs, and semivowels.

whose graphic symbols (graphemes) represent the individual speech sounds in language.

Alphabet: its origin and spread

The principle of assigning graphemes to represent phonemes (the alphabetic principle) has been in existence since about 1000 B.C. Where and when did the principle of the alphabet originate? This is a question that archeologists, linguists, and anthropologists have pondered for some time. It may be the end product of efforts of widely separated societies to perfect their graphic communication facilities; the *system* of using alphabet letters could conceivably (though highly improbably) have been the brainchild of a single man whose genius was never recognized or recorded. It is most likely that the alphabetic principle originated with the Sumerians and the Egyptians, either simultaneously or in collaboration. It *is* known that both the Sumerians and the Egyptians were working on a system of encoding their language; that the Sumerians did not progress much beyond the cuneiform system of using characters to represent words and syllables; that the Egyptians were never quite able to free themselves of their dependence upon hieroglyphs to represent sounds. Hieroglyphic writing was not alphabetical (⊔ for ointment), but the phonogram (the sign for a meaningful combination of sounds) carried the germ of phonemic writing in such representations as:

⌇⌇⌇ for *lion* and for the consonant *l,*

⬭ for *mouth* and for the consonant *r.*

Researchers are continuing to seek a definitive answer to the mystery of the origin of the concept of an alphabet. As far as we know, a seafaring people known as Phoenicians were the first to *use* extensively a coding system composed of letters for sounds.

From Phoenicia to Greece

The Phoenicians were a Semitic people who lived at the eastern end of the Mediterranean Sea (now Syria, Israel, and Lebanon);

their city-states flourished around 1200 B.C. The Phoenicians were artisans and tradesmen whose great fleets of ships carried merchandise not only throughout the Mediterranean but as far west as the Atlantic coast of Spain and as far south as the tip of Africa. It is possible that the Phoenicians' occupations as traders and merchants led them to use a system for keeping records and making contracts which was less cumbersome and more accurate than the pictographic-hieroglyphic systems used by neighboring societies.

Regardless of whether the Phoenicians invented the alphabet, they must be given credit for introducing it to Greece during the 11th century B.C. There, in a much refined form, it became the basis for our modern Greco-Roman alphabet.

The true alphabetic principle requires that each phoneme of a language shall have its own unique graphic counterpart in the orthography. But the Phoenicians had no separate graphic character for each vowel sound. Rather, the Phoenician alphabet contained about 22 graphic characters — graphemes — each representing a consonant. When spoken Phoenician was transcribed into writing, the vowel sound was understood to be combined with either the preceding or the following consonant, so that the resultant grapheme represented both consonant and vowel. For example, the Phoenician letter *aleph*, $\times$, which is similar to our *A*, supposedly represented a consonant-vowel combination pronounced somewhat like *ha*.

The Greeks apparently accepted the alphabetic principle but had to make some adjustment in the Phoenician alphabet in order that it might adequately represent the Greek language. In the end, the Greeks used 19 of the Phoenician letters to represent Greek consonantal sounds; they used some Phoenician letters that were unsuitable for Greek consonantal sounds to represent Greek vowel sounds. They also added some symbols of their own contriving. Thus, the Greeks wound up with an alphabet of 24 characters. This alphabet was adopted by the city of Athens about 400 B.C. and gradually it spread throughout Greece. The Greek alphabet has undergone very little change since the days of Pericles. Figure 2–1 shows the Phoenician and Greek alphabets. Note that the Greeks reversed some symbols.

Figure 2–1

Phoenician	Athenian	Modern Greek

The Roman alphabet

Although scholars generally agree that the Greeks received the basis of their alphabet from the Phoenicians, they are divided in their opinion on the precursor of the Latin alphabet. It is obviously of Greek origin, but by which route? Some scholars believe that the Romans borrowed their alphabet directly from the Greeks via the Doric-Chalcidian colony of Lower Italy. Other scholars maintain that the Roman alphabet is based on a system brought into Italy by the Etruscans. The latter theory will be recognized here.

The Etruscans, an oriental or semioriental people, migrated from somewhere near Syria to Italy, by way of Greece, and settled in Etruria around 900 B.C. They brought with them commerce, the arts, and an alphabet that was a variant of the early Greek alphabet. The Etruscan alphabet contained 26 letters, as evidenced by an alphabet found on an ivory tablet made in the 7th or 8th century B.C. These 26 letters were reduced to 20 in the 5th century B.C. The Romans originally adopted only 21 letters from the Etruscan alphabet to represent their phonemes. Toward the beginning of the Roman Empire, *y* and *z* were added to take care of sounds in certain loan words borrowed from the Greeks, making a total of 23 characters. A thousand years later, *u* and *w* were added, and 500 years later *j* finally completed the 26 letters that compose our contemporary Greco-Roman alphabet used throughout the English-language community.

Figure 2–2 is a chart showing examples of some of the probable changes that occurred during the process of development and transition of the alphabet from Phoenician to Latin.

Figure 2–2

Phoenician	Early Greek	Later Greek	Roman

Letter formations

An interesting sidelight on the subject of alphabet letters has to do with form. The Greeks for a long time had no fixed form for their letters and, with a fine disregard for consistency, added to the confusion by sometimes writing from right to left, sometimes from left to right, and often both ways. The latter system was called *boustrophedon* which, translated, means "ox-turning." An ox, pulling a plow, went down the field, turned and went back. Using this writing convention today, one would have something like this to cope with:

WEARRIVEDATTHEAIRPORT

ƎИA⅃ꟼƎHTƎʞAMOTƎTA⅃OOT

SOWEHADTORETURNHOME

By the 6th century B.C., uniformity won out and from then on, all Western writing proceeded from left to right.

With the dissolution of the Roman Empire, the freedom to experiment with different styles of letters resulted in a spate of letter patterns known variously as Insular (English), Visigoth (Spanish), Germanica, and Italian. Each of these styles of letter formation contributed to what eventually became the unified and dominant style in England, Europe, and finally the world: the Carolingian (Caroline) style, named for Charlemagne, king of the Franks and Emperor of the Holy Roman Empire. Originally, both Greek and Roman alphabet letters were only in the form of capitals. The Caroline was the first true small-letter alphabet; it very closely resembles our style of writing today.

Movable type: its effect on handwriting

The invention of movable type, about A.D. 1450, for a time encouraged some effort to produce letter molds of distinction. There emerged around 1520 the profession of the *writing master,* a man who produced manuals of letter style that helped keep alive the desirability of beauty in writing. If one wished to send a letter written "in a fine hand," he would employ a writing master to transform his own poor efforts into a manuscript beautiful to behold. The monks in the monasteries, as well as students, learned men, artists, and refugees from life, devoted themselves to creating some of the most beautiful hand-written manuscripts in the world. An examination of some of the old illuminated manuscripts may help pupils to understand and appreciate the monumental efforts of man to perfect a writing system that has facilitated communication over time and space.

Contemporary alphabets

We have discussed the alphabetic principle and reviewed the discovery or invention of the alphabet letters and their refinement of execution. We have concentrated on the Greek and Roman alphabets, for they are the precursors of the alphabet used in most of the Indo-European languages. But there are in existence today probably as many as 100 different alphabets. Certain of these are confined to the geographic area of their origins. For example, the Greek alphabet is used only by the Greeks. The Cyrillic, an augmented Greek alphabet of 33 letters, is used by the Russians, Serbs, Bulgars, and other Slavic peoples. The Arabs have their own alphabet of 28 letters.

Figure 2–3

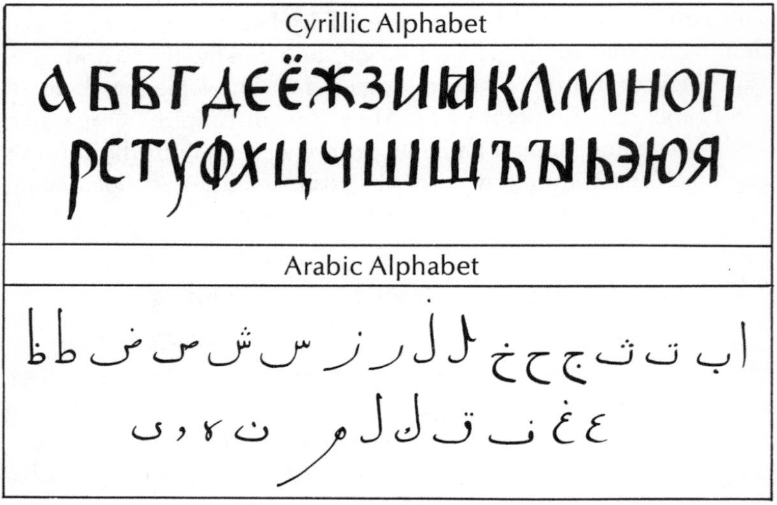

Cyrillic Alphabet

Arabic Alphabet

Oral versus graphic communication

Although there are probably as many as 100 alphabets in use today, there are almost 3,000 languages spoken in the world. The discrepancy in figures can be explained by the fact that while man has been a speaking animal from his earliest times, he has only comparatively recently possessed the ability to encode his language. Indeed, even today man is by no means universally literate.

While no cultural group is without an oral means of communication, there are literally hundreds of small language communities whose communication is confined to the voice and ear, or whose attempts to record it are, at best, crudely pictographic.

There has been much speculation as to why certain peoples in the world developed an alphabetic means of visual communication while others never got beyond the pictographic stage. Why did a creative and artistic people like those of the Inca Empire fail to develop a writing system while their distant cousins, the Aztec and the Mayan Indians, were able to produce pictorial writing? The Aztecs did not progress to the alphabet stage, but did make good use of *rebus* writing (combining one pictured object with another to produce a third meaning). For example, in Modern English, the following represents a rebus:

+ + = **penmanship**

The Mayans used hieroglyphs that stood partly for sounds and partly for ideas, a system somewhere between the ideographic stage of the Aztecs and the fully developed word–syllable system of the Sumerians and Egyptians. Most Indians of North America used both pictographs and primitive ideographs.

There is no definitive answer to the question of why some peoples were able to develop an alphabetic language while others, though equally advanced in many other ways, neglected to do so.

Application of the alphabetic principle

The alphabetic principle, it will be recalled, requires that each phoneme in a language shall have its own unique graphic counterpart. In the languages in which there is nearly a one-to-one correspondence between a sound and its letter representation ($/f/$ = f; $/k/ = k$) the task of learning to spell is quite simple.[2] One

---

[2] The slash marks, / /, used throughout this book, indicate that a phoneme (sound) is the referent rather than an alphabetical letter. Thus, /k/ refers to the first phoneme in *cat* or *kite*. See page 27 for a sound-spelling key. Phonemic systems used by linguists are more precise, but the sound-spelling key used in this book is quite practical for the teacher's use.

would need only 1) to determine which sounds are contained in a word and their order, 2) to know what grapheme represents each sound, and 3) to write the graphemes in the same order in which the sounds occur in the word.

Let us examine the way in which the alphabetic principle forms the basis of American-English orthography. The American-English language contains over 40 phonemes (24 consonant phonemes and a set of vowel phonemes) whose number varies according to the linguistic system used in analyzing our speech. The phonemes /k/, /a/, /t/, for example, produce the word we spell *c a t: cat.* Each of these phonemes is used in numerous other syllables and words of our language. If we refer again to the alphabetic principle and assume strict adherence to the principle, we see that each of the three phonemes in *cat* or *kite,* and each of the other phonemes in our language as well, would always be spelled only one way; we would then have exactly as many different graphemes or graphic characters as there are different phonemes in spoken American English. In other words, theoretically the graphemes of the orthography would be in *one-to-one correspondence* with the phonemes of the language. It is obvious that this is not true and that American English is more complex and departs from the pure alphabetic principle to a greater degree than do some other languages, such as the Hawaiian. Observe the contrast between the two languages in Figure 2–4.

Figure 2–4

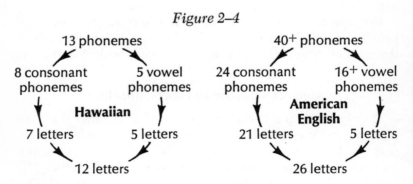

Note the large discrepancy in English between the number of phonemes and the number of alphabet letters — in contrast with the apparently negligible discrepancy in the Hawaiian language. This Hawaiian discrepancy is accounted for by the fact that the early missionaries who encoded the language did not provide a graphic symbol for one of the consonant phonemes — the glottal stop — which appears only under certain circumstances in spoken Hawaiian.

At first glance, this chart suggests that American-English orthography is deficient in the number of alphabetic symbols used to represent phonemes (26 letters, but 40-plus sounds). In one sense, this is true; but as we shall see in the next section of this chapter, the basic cause for our orthography's departure from the alphabetic principle is that it has far too *many* graphemes to represent the phonemes.

The brilliance of an alphabetic orthography stems from its economical use of a limited number of graphic characters to represent the same number of phonemes in speech, thus permitting any spoken word of a language to be represented visually with relatively few graphic symbols, once the system of graphemes has been mastered. The economy and flexibility of the alphabetic principle is the major reason why most contemporary orthographies are based upon this principle rather than upon logographic (a character or combination of characters used to represent a word) or upon syllabic (a character or characters used to represent a syllable) principles.

Encoding speech and decoding writing

We have seen that all writing systems are the vehicles by which man is able to transform language into visual forms (to encode it). We have seen, too, that written communication systems help to overcome the spatial and temporal limitations inherent in communication. But like language (speech), writing systems have as their ulitmate purpose the transmission of information from one person to others, a process that requires an ability on the part of the recipients to *decode* (read).

The use of all writing systems — logographic, syllabic, and alphabetic — therefore necessitates the user's acquiring two closely related processes: 1) the mastery of the graphic symbols needed to set forth speech in writing (encoding or spelling), and 2) the ability to translate written or printed graphemes into the oral forms they represent (decoding or reading). But in American-English orthography, owing to the lack of a precise one-to-one correspondence between phoneme and grapheme, the encoding and decoding processes are sometimes disparate, and confusing to the beginner.

The American-English writing system suffers from a surfeit of optional graphic symbols to represent the phonemes of the language; many phonemes can be spelled several ways; for example, the /s/ may be spelled *c* (*city*); *s* (*sit*); *sc* (*scene*); *ss* (*toss*); etc. Consequently, the correct spelling of American-English words is made more difficult because the speller must choose the correct graphemic option for a phoneme from among the several possible graphemic options for that particular sound.

On the other hand, the decoder suffers from a different plight because many of the graphemes used in American-English orthography can also represent more than one phoneme: the *o* in *go* may also represent different vowel sounds, as in *not* or in *women*. Thus, a decoder of American English must determine which of several possible speech sounds is represented by a grapheme in the word he is seeking to decipher. Note the dictionary sound-spelling key, or pronunciation key, in Figure 2–5.

The different processes involved in encoding and decoding American English can be illustrated by the following example: The branch of a tree is often called a *bough*, a word that is composed of the two phonemes /b/ and /ou/. (See the sound-spelling key.) The /b/ is commonly spelled *b* in our orthography, but the /ou/ can be spelled in several ways, including: *ou* as in *out*, *ow* as in *now*, and *ough* as in *bough*. The encoder must determine which of these possible spellings of the /ou/ is used correctly in spelling *bough*. The grapheme *ough* also can represent different phonemes, as illustrated in the spellings of the /ō/ in *although* and the /ü/ in *through*. A further complication is the combining of *ou* and *gh* for such different vowel–consonant combinations as /of/ and /uf/ as in *trough* and *rough*. The digraph *ou* is used to spell a greater variety of sounds than any other digraph in the language. Here are some of them:

/u/ as in *double*	/u̇/ as in *would*
/è/ as in *journey*	/ȯ/ as in *court*
/ü/ as in *group*	/ō/ as in *shoulder*
/ə/ as in *famous*	

The preceding examples might lead one to believe that the alphabetic principle has been so disregarded in American-English

Figure 2–5

COMPLETE PRONUNCIATION KEY

The pronunciation of each word is shown just after the word, in this way: **ab bre vi ate** (ə brē′vē āt). The letters and signs used are pronounced as in the words below. The mark ′ is placed after·a syllable with primary or strong accent, as in the example above. The mark ′ after a syllable shows a secondary or lighter accent, as in **ab bre vi a tion** (ə brē′vē ā′shən).

Some words, taken from foreign languages, are spoken with sounds that otherwise do not occur in English. Symbols for these sounds are given at the end of the table as "Foreign Sounds."

a	hat, cap	j	jam, enjoy	u	cup, butter
ā	age, face	k	kind, seek	u̇	full, put
ã	care, air	l	land, coal	ü	rule, move
ä	father, far	m	me, am	ū	use, music
		n	no, in		
		ng	long, bring		
b	bad, rob			v	very, save
ch	child, much			w	will, woman
d	did, red	o	hot, rock	y	young, yet
		ō	open, go	z	zero, breeze
		ô	order, all	zh	measure, seizure
e	let, best	oi	oil, voice		
ē	equal, see	ou	house, out		
ėr	term, learn				
		p	paper, cup	ə represents:	
f	fat, if	r	run, try	a in about	
g	go, bag	s	say, yes	e in taken	
h	he, how	sh	she, rush	i in April	
		t	tell, it	o in lemon	
i	it, pin	th	thin, both	u in circus	
ī	ice, five	ŦH	then, smooth		

foreign sounds

Y as in French *du*. Pronounce ē with the lips rounded as for English ü in **rule**.

œ as in French *peu*. Pronounce ā with the lips rounded as for ō.

N as in French *bon*. The N is not pronounced, but shows that the vowel before it is nasal.

H as in German *ach*. Pronounce k without closing the breath passage.

Source: *Thorndike-Barnhart High School Dictionary.* Copyright © 1968 by Scott, Foresman and Company, Glenview, Ill. Reproduced with permission.

orthography that one might as well cease to look for consistency and revert to rote memorization of each word to be spelled. However, if one examines the findings of a study[3] of the spellings

[3] *Phoneme–Grapheme Correspondences as Cues to Spelling Improvement.* Hanna, Hanna, Hodges, and Rudorf. U.S. Office of Education. Project 1991, OE-32008. 1966. (See Chapter Seven for a review of this project.)

of the /ou/ in words, he will find the following informative statistics:

The /ou/ as in *out* occurs a total of 406 times in a 17,000-plus word vocabulary. This sound is spelled *ou* 227 times, or in 56 percent of the occurrences. The major word with this spelling is the word *out* which is responsible for 64 compounds, such as: *outcome, without, outlast, outboard*. Note that in all of these words the /ou/ occùrs in the initial position of a word or syllable.

The /ou/ spelled *ou* also occurs in medial position, as in *cloud, count, doubt, found, mouth, mount, pound, round*, and *ground*. This *ou* spelling of the /ou/ appears a total of 153 times in medial position, or 38 percent of all occurrences. In final word or syllable position, it is found in only five words: *thou, thou' sand, thou'-sandth, tou' sle*, and *trou' sers*.

A second spelling of the /ou/ is *ow*, as in *cow*. This spelling occurs 119 times in the same 17,000-plus word vocabulary. It generally appears in final word or syllable position, as in *how, flow' er, pow' er*, or *vow' el*. Seventy-two of the occurrences of this spelling are found in this final position. The second most frequent position (45 occurrences) is the medial, as in *brown, down, fowl, scowl*, and *howl*. Note that this spelling occurs typically in medial position before the /n/ or the /l/ phonemes.

Only in one word, *owl*, does the *ow* spelling of the /ou/ occur in initial position. Thus, the consequences of these restrictions on the spelling of /ou/ result in the following general principles: When the /ou/ is heard in final position, spell it *ow*; when in medial position, spell it *ow* if it is followed by an /n/ or an /l/; otherwise spell it *ou*.

One may ask, "Of what importance to the teaching of spelling are such statistical findings?" The answer is twofold: 1) If a pupil knows that he may expect a certain phoneme to be spelled a certain way because he has observed that pattern in a sizable group of words, he will watch for that occurrence in the words he is learning to spell and 2) he will give his greatest attention to the spelling of the exceptional or maverick correspondences in words.

To build the power to spell an unlimited vocabulary, one needs to know more than that graphemes are used to spell sounds in words (the alphabetic principle). One must be able to recognize patterns of spellings in order to make correct choices among the possible optional spellings.

Further, both teacher and pupil can profit from knowing something about the development of their language and its writing system — where it came from and what factors influenced its growth and produced some of its curious spellings. Chapters Three and Four provide a highly condensed review of the story of the development of languages in general and of the English language in particular.

CHAPTER THREE

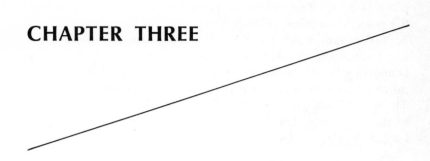

Origins of
the English Language

Chapter One reviewed the steps in man's progress in communication in permanent form, the form of visual symbols that represent various elements of speech. Chapter Two reviewed the emergence of the alphabetic principle and its importance as an economical and practical means of encoding language; it also briefly sketched the use of the alphabetic principle in American English and hinted at some of the maverick spellings in our American-English orthography. This chapter will present a telescopic view of the historical development of languages and in so doing will provide a background for examination of the American-English orthography.

Language families

Today there are approximately 3,000 distinct languages spoken throughout the world. Although there has been much speculation over the centuries with many myths arising to explain the actual beginnings of human communication, an ultimate determination of that beginning is probably unlikely. Linguistic research one day may shed more light on the subject. One proposed supposition, for example, is that *homo sapiens,* as distinguished from the lower forms of animal life, developed the ability to communicate orally by noticing that repetition of certain vocalizations brought satisfactory responses from those to whom they were uttered.

Whether this oral communication facility developed in one particular area of the world and spread abroad or whether it developed independently in many areas is a moot question. Such speculations are not of major concern to us in considering a program designed to teach children to spell. We are interested in presenting background information on the general development of languages which will help explain to pupils some of the reasons for the spellings in American English and will help explain some of the changes in phonology (sounds), and morphology (interrelationships of morphemes in words) that have led, over the centuries, to changes in orthography.

Of the some 3,000 languages on today's communication map, the two largest and most important "families" are the Indo-European, with about one and a half billion speakers, and the Sino-Tibetan, with over eight hundred million speakers. Of course these figures can be only approximations, for even as you read them, untold numbers of individuals are being added to the speaking population. The lack of accurate census figures in many nations or territories further confuses the estimates.

The Indo-European languages are spoken by peoples whose respective languages have evolved from the same ancient language source. Figure 3–1 shows roughly the distribution of the world's chief language families, language families that are classified on the basis of common linguistic features or by descent from a common language ancestor. Note that approximately half of the world's language speakers are members of the Indo-European family; about 22 percent are members of the Sino-Tibetan family.

Among the leading languages spoken throughout the world today are: Chinese, English, Russian, Hindi-Urdu, Italian, Bengali, Arabic, Spanish, German, Japanese, French, and Portuguese. Figure 3–2 shows that approximately twice as many people are native speakers of Chinese as of English. Although more people are native speakers of Chinese than of English, it is a fact that English is spoken and understood by more people around the world than is Chinese or any other language. Four hundred years ago, almost all English-speaking people lived in the area now

Figure 3–1

Chief Language Families

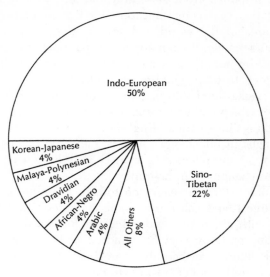

called Great Britain. Then only about one out of a hundred persons in the world used the English language. Today English is used in most parts of the world as the primary means of transcending language barriers to communication.

Figure 3–2

Native Speakers of English and Chinese

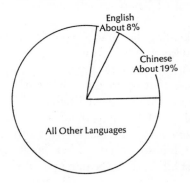

The spread of Indo-European languages

Figure 3–3 diagrams the branching of the Indo-European language tree and helps to illustrate the directions of language distribution. Refer to this diagram and to Map 3–1 as you read the next few paragraphs. Because of the absence of written records, scholars can only hypothesize about the beginnings of the Indo-European family of languages. One such hypothesis follows.

Figure 3–3

Branches of the Indo-European Language Family

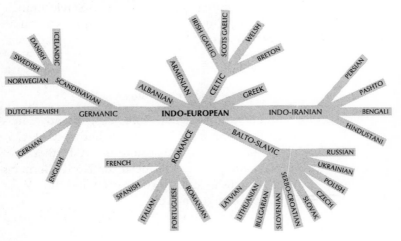

Source: *The World Book Encyclopedia.* Copyright © 1969 by Field Enterprises Educational Corporation, Chicago. Reproduced with permission.

Most of the languages of Europe and many of Asia probably descended from a common parent language called *Proto-Indo-European,* which existed perhaps as long as 5,000 years ago. The speakers of this language lived in north-central Europe, possibly in an area near the Baltic Sea, and likely were nomadic. From samples of cuneiform writing found in Asia Minor, and known to be in use around 1500 B.C., it is thought that one group of these early peoples, called Hittites, migrated southward around 3000 B.C.

About 2,000 B.C. the remaining Indo-Europeans migrated in all directions. Those who went southeast (Indo-Iranian branch) settled in India and evolved a language called *Sanskrit* of which the modern offspring are the Hindi of India, and the Urdu of Pakistan and of the Indian Moslems.

Other peoples travelled southward to Greece and Italy and produced the *Hellenic* language, the mother of modern Greek, and the *Italic* from which came Latin and the Romance languages. Still another group travelled as far as Britain and produced the *Celtic* tongues, of which we shall have more to say later.

Those who stayed closer to home constitute the Eastern branch of the Indo-European migration, called the Balto-Slavic branch. This group is represented today by the languages spoken in Russia, Poland, Czechoslovakia, Bulgaria, Yugoslavia, and some other neighboring nations.

The Germanic peoples

The group of migrators in which we are most directly interested, the Germans (or Teutons), went north and settled Germany, Holland, and the Scandinavian countries. A further subdivision of these Germanic peoples produced the North Germans (Icelandic, Danish, Swedish, and Norwegians) and the West Germans (Dutch, German, and English).

Map 3–1 shows the branching off of the Indo-European peoples.

The peregrinating life of the Germanic peoples was one of the major causes of dialectal changes in their language.[1] There was undoubtedly a cross-fertilization of language patterns as people moved from one community to another and from one culture to another.

---

[1] Language may be defined as a systematized communications code whose usage is accepted by a certain people over a certain time. Since language is ever changing, it is reasonable to expect that different forms of a language (changes in pronunciation, grammar, and vocabulary) will emerge. When the phonological, grammatical, and lexical differences are small, such that speakers can still understand each other despite these differences, such differences are *dialectal*. When these differences are so great as to cause a breakdown in communication, the divergent communication systems are called *languages*.

Map 3–1

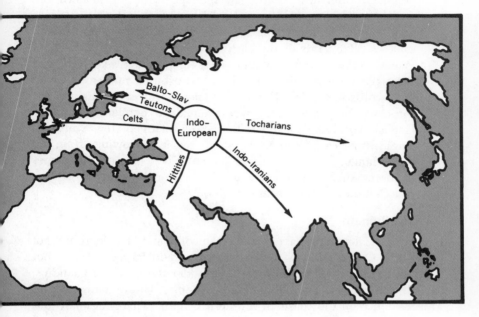

The Germanic language evidently split into several dialects. One of these dialects, the North Germanic, produced the Scandinavian tongues. As we shall see, the criss-crossing, tribal wanderings of these Germanic descendants of the early Indo-European speakers produced inevitable adjustments in language. But before we consider these changes, we should first set the stage for their eventual arrival and adoption in Britain.

A language develops in Britain

English is included as a language in the West German branch of the German languages, but its emergence as the language of Britain was preceded by many events and years of development.

The Celts

The earliest invaders of Britain were the earlier-mentioned Celts. These warlike, sturdy people crossed to Britain from the continent about 600 B.C. and for hundreds of years continued their invasions. They drove the natives back into the wild areas of the North and East in Britain and themselves split up into three language branches: *Gallic*, a language with no modern descendant; *Gaelic*, including the Irish and the Highland Scots' dialects; and *Brythonic*, including the Welsh, Cornish, and Breton dialects. Remnants of the early languages still exist in parts of Wales, Ireland, and Scotland. One might have expected that these powerful people would have contributed numerous Celtic loan words to the Old English language. However, this was not the case. Very few Celtic words remained permanently in the English vocabulary. Today there are relatively few words in English that can definitely be attributed to borrowings from the Celtic language. Among those known to be Celtic are the names of places, such as London, Kent, York, Thames. The river Ouse is a Celtic word that means "water."

The Romans

The Celts might have remained in command of Britain had not Julius Caesar's forces invaded the island in 55 B.C. It was not until a century later, however, that under the Emperor Claudius, Britain was successfully annexed to Rome. The Romans took up residence on the coasts of southern Britain. There they laid out towns in Roman fashion, built Roman roads and camps, and generally turned Britain into a Roman province. The Britons gradually resigned themselves to the domination of the Romans and, in addition to absorbing many of their conquerors' habits and attitudes, accepted the Roman (Latin) language and came to regard themselves as Roman Britons. Many language reminders of this occupancy still exist. For example, the Latin word for *camp* is *castra*. And it is from this old Latin root that such city names as Doncaster, Gloucester, and Leicester sprang.

Although the Romans ruled Britain for nearly 400 years, many of the Britons refused to become Romanized. They zealously guarded their native dialects and customs and waited for the opportune time to rid Britain of its invaders and aggressors.

The Angles, Saxons, and Jutes

Toward the end of the 4th century A.D., Rome was obliged to withdraw its legions from Britain because they were needed for service nearer to home. The withdrawal left the Roman Britons largely at the mercy of bands of northern raiders, the Picts and the Scots. Some scholars believe that the Roman Britons appealed to certain tribes, inhabitants of the North Sea coast from Jutland to the Rhine, to come to their rescue against these northern raiders. Whether truth or fancy, the fact remains that these tribes — the Jutes, the Angles, and the Saxons — arrived and harassed Britain for 200 years. They were successful in driving the Picts and Scots back into the hinterland and in turn settled down to make the land their own. By the end of the 7th century, Britain was largely controlled by the Angles, Saxons, and Jutes who each spoke a different Germanic dialect but were able to understand one another. As Map 3–2 shows, the Jutes settled in the southeast area of Britain, the valley of the Thames, and on the Isle of Wight (1). The Saxons, who came from the North Sea shore, settled in the southwest area (2). The Angles, who had lived south of the Jutes on the continent, migrated to the area in Britain that lies north of the Thames (3).

It is remarkable that the dialects of these three peoples were able to exist side by side, to tolerate and borrow from each other's individuality. But that is the way of languages. In spite of jockeying for leadership from time to time, these Anglo-Saxon tongues were able to keep from destroying or submerging each other and slowly began to build the base for what was to become the national language of Britain and eventually a language used throughout the world.

The Danes

Even after Britain settled on the Anglo-Saxon language, much time and many events intervened before Britain became England with English the official language of the land.

In the early part of the 9th century, the Vikings, Danish raiders, arrived in Britain and harassed the Britons until defeated in battle by King Alfred (A.D. 878). This battle was important, for it decided that Britain was to remain Germanic rather than become a Scandinavian colony.

The Danes again attacked Britain in 1013, this time successfully, and for almost 100 years Britain remained a part of the great Scandinavian Empire; nonetheless, the Anglo-Saxon language continued in its dominant role. There was a great similarity between Old Norse and Old English words (for example, O.E. *blōma* [a kind of iron]; O.N. *blom* [a blossom]). The similarity

Map 3–2

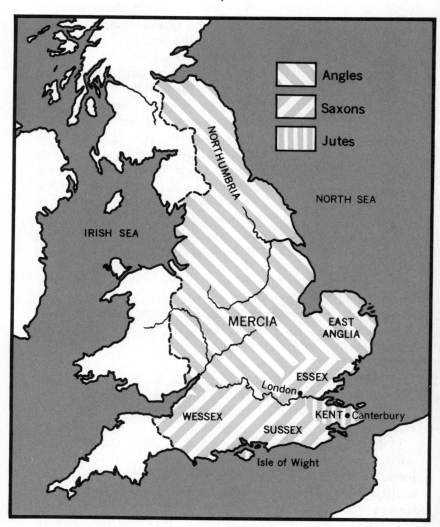

is such that it is very difficult to determine whether an English word is derived from the old Danish or Norwegian, or from the Anglo-Saxon. However, the greatest impact of Scandinavian words came in a later period.

The writing of the Anglo-Saxon language

Thus far, we have discussed only the development of languages in oral forms. What about the written representations of the Anglo-Saxon language? Of the Celtic, the Danish, and the Roman languages?

The Romans, of course, used Latin, and since the Celtic language was much like the Latin, it was readily translated by the missionaries into Latin writing.

The Angles and Saxons had no true written representation of their language. They, as well as other Germanic and Scandinavian peoples, used an alphabet composed of *runes*. The word *rune* comes from a Gothic word meaning "secret." The runes were used mainly for inscriptions and for magic signs. The oldest runic alphabet contained 24 characters, but this number fluctuated from time to time. Just as the name *alphabet* was derived from the first two letters, *alpha* and *beta,* the name for the runic alphabet, *futhark*[2], came from combining the first six runic letters:

f u th a r k

ᚠ ᚾ ᚦ ᚠ ᚱ ᚲ

The runes were not an adequate means for writing the ever-expanding Anglo-Saxon vocabulary and, further, may well have been unacceptable to Christians, who felt the runic script represented a heathen faith. In any case, the Christian missionaries introduced a Latin-based alphabet for the purpose of encoding Anglo-Saxon speech into writing. This script used a somewhat rounded letter style, called *uncial,* and in lower case, or *minuscule* form. The Anglo-Saxon alphabet differed from the Latin in a few letters: the *yogh* (ᠵ), which represented a sound similar to /g/; the *wynn* (ᚹ), which represented a sound similar to /w/; and the *thorn* (þ), which was taken from the runic and which, with the *edh* (ð), variously encoded the sounds now represented by *th* in *thin* and *there.* The following illustration of the Anglo-Saxon alphabet employs, for the most part, modern Roman type because

---

[2] Variant spellings are given this word, including *futhorc, futhork, futharc.*

of the difficulty that unpracticed readers would have in decoding many of the Anglo-Saxon letter forms.

a	æ	b	c	d	e	f	ʒ	h	i	l	m
n	o	p	r	s	t	u	ρ	þ	ð		

Notice the absence of *k* and *z*, two rarely used graphemes, as well as *j*, *q*, and *v*, which are later adoptions.

CHAPTER FOUR

Development of
the English Language

Chapter Three reviewed the origins of languages, with particular emphasis on the Indo-European languages, and sketched some of the historical events that led to the emergence of the English language. In this chapter we shall trace the changes that took place in the English language and its orthography as Old English gave way to Middle English, then to Modern English.

Old English period (449–1066)

The earliest written records of Old English date back to the 7th and 8th centuries A.D. The chief extant relics of such writings are those of the early Christian poets. The most famous of these was the epic poem *Beowulf,* written in the West Saxon dialect during the 8th century. Here are a few lines with a modern transcription:

Hwæt we Gar-Dena
In ʒear-daʒum
Ðeod cyninʒa
Ðrym ʒefrunon,
Hu ða Æðelinʒas
Ellen fremodon.[1]

How we glory in remembrance
Of the Danes in days of old,
Their splendor and their
    acts of valor.

[1] From J. Josias Conybeare, *Illustrations of Anglo-Saxon Poetry* (London: Harding and Lepard, 1826).

41

At first glance, one might think that this poem had been written in a foreign tongue, but closer inspection reveals that some of the words have a slightly familiar appearance. Old English spellings corresponded, in the main, to the sounds of the spoken language. In the poem, for example, the *æ* roughly represents our /a/, the "long" vowels have a macron (‾) over them, *ρ* represents our /th/, *a* our /ä/, and *ð* our /th/.

Old English had a large lexicon; here are a few words and their modern equivalents:

strǣt	(street)	*bāt*	(boat)
tūn	(town)	*bōc*	(book)
hwā	(who)	*lagu*	(law)
hring	(ring)	*ġēar*	(year)
pund	(pound)	*cnēo*	(knee)

Although the English lexicon was quite adequate for written communication, the monks and scribes generally preferred to write in Latin. Late in the 9th century, Alfred the Great (849–899), King of the West Saxons, did much to encourage the writing of Old English. He sponsored the translation from Latin to English of many important works, such as *The Ecclesiastical History of the English Nation* by Bede, and *The Anglo-Saxon Chronicle*, a yearly history of England written by monks.

Middle English period (1066–1500)

It will be recalled that Britain, early in the 11th century, was conquered by Scandinavian invaders. The Anglo-Saxons had scarcely settled down to living in some degree of harmony with their Scandinavian conquerers when once again Britain was invaded and conquered.

William, Duke of Normandy (1027–1087), had long had his eye on the English throne. In 1066 he invaded Britain, defeated the English at the Battle of Hastings, and on Christmas Day was crowned King of England.

The accession of William of Normandy to the throne of England not only affected the subsequent history of England but also profoundly influenced its language. The understandable lack of enthusiasm of the English people for adopting the language of their conquerors resulted in William's peopling his court, army, and clergy with Normans. The Anglo-Saxon language was banished from these important groups and Norman French became the official language and indeed the medium of instruction in the schools. That the Anglo-Saxon language did not disappear during the Norman occupation of England was probably due to the fact that the English were unwilling to abandon their own language. Thus, the French found it useful to acquire some command of English in order to communicate. Both languages profited by a certain amount of interchange. English gradually became more "respectable" but was not restored as the official language of Britain until, after a hundred years of fighting for supremacy, the English defeated the French.

Late in the 14th century, English again became the national language of England. But Norman French had left its imprint on English. Many French words were retained by the English, particularly those having to do with religion, food, society, law, military, and business. Some of those words in their common forms in today's lexicon are: *preach, beef, baron, crime, army, salary.*

Norman scribes were responsible for a number of spellings in our orthography. For example, the digraph *ou* was introduced, replacing the Middle English *ū* as in *hūs–house, lūs–louse.* The digraph *ou* also appeared in such words as *double, touch,* and *young.* Another instance of Norman influence on present-day spelling was the replacement of Old English *cw* with *qu* for the cluster /kw/ as in *queen, quake,* and *quick.*

Further, scribes dropped from the English alphabet certain letters that were not in the French alphabet. For example, the letters *ð* and *þ* that appear in the *Beowulf* quotation on page 41 and in *The Owl and the Nightingale* quotation on page 45, were both gradually replaced with the digraph *th* by the end of the Middle English period.

The contemporary spelling of *bridge* illustrates an interesting example of orthographic change. In Old English, this word was spelled *brycg* (*y* and *i* were interchangeable spellings of /i/ toward the end of the Old English period, while a final /j/ was spelled *cg*), but during the Middle English period the *cg* was replaced by *gge*, producing *brigge.* Ultimately, the *gge* representation of final /j/ after a "short" vowel was changed to *dge*, resulting in *bridge*. Other common words whose final /j/ made the same transition include *lodge, hedge,* and *pledge.*

Another example of an orthographic change that took place during the Middle English period is illustrated in the word *night.* In Old English, this word was spelled *niht*, the letter *h* representing a consonant sound /x/ not articulated in English today. In Middle English, this sound was represented by *gh* and the *niht* spelling became *night.* But by the end of the period the sound dropped out, though its spelling was retained. Today we say /nīt/ but continue to write the word *night.*

To indicate vowel length, Middle English writing often employed doubled letters, such as *ee* for the "long" vowel /ē/, as in **weed** and **tree**. Many of these double-letter spellings have survived to the present. The letters *a, u,* and *i* were not doubled. The letter *y*, which represented a distinct vowel sound in Old English came to represent some occurrences of the /ī/, as in *cry*, and some cases of the final weakly stressed /ē/, as in *jury*. In many words borrowed from the Greek, the *y* was retained to spell the /i/ sound (as in *system*).

Another spelling change that occurred during this period is illustrated by the word *wonder.* Notice that the first vowel sound, /u/, is spelled *o* rather than *u*, its more common spelling. During the Middle English period, a certain type of angular writing was in vogue which resulted in some ambiguity for the reader when *u* was followed by an *m, n,* or *u* (sometimes written *v* or *w*). Consequently, scribes replaced the *u* with *o* and that spelling is retained in some words used today, e.g. *come, monk, love, tongue, some, honey, son.* In the case of *sun*, however, the vowel spelling was not changed, possibly in order to distinguish that word from *son.*

Middle English writing

The small amount of writing done in English during the early Middle English period was largely religious in nature. However, during the peak of the Anglo-Norman period, two important secular poems were written in English. The first, which established the debate style, was called *The Owl and the Nightingale* (c. 1200), author unknown. This poem, written in Old English alliterative line and rhyming couplets, is probably the first example of English *belles-lettres* and provides a vivid example of the contrast between the orthography of Middle English and that of today.

The poem relates an argument between an owl and a nightingale over which bird is more important. Here is a sample of the poem, with a modern translation:

> [Þ]e niȝtingale hi iseȝ,
> ꝥ hi bihold ꝥ ouerseȝ,
> ꝥ þuȝte wel [vu]l of þare hule,
> for me hi halt lodlich ꝥ fule.
> "Vnwiȝt," ho sede, "awei þu flo!
> me is þe w[u]rs þat ich þe so.
> Iwis for þine [vu]le lete,
> wel [oft ich] mine song forlete; [2]

> The nightingale the Owl saw well,
> Scornful her glances on her fell
> She thought right evil of that Owl,
> (Men deem it loathsome and foul).
> "Monster," she cried, "hence must
>   you flee,
> I swear your evil cry, and strong,
> Forces me often to cease my song."

Compare this Middle English work with the Old English *Beowulf* on page 41. Note that many more words in this poem are recognizable than is true of the Old English poem.

Another poem, written about 1250, was called *The Cuckoo*. Notice how much more readable this lyric is. It needs little or no translation.

> Sing cuccu! Sing cuccu nu!
> Sumer is icumen in,
>   Lhude sing cuccu;
>
> Groweþ sed and bloweþ med,
>
> And springþ the wde nu.

[2] From *The Owl and the Nightingale*, edited by J. W. H. Atkins. Copyright © 1922, the University Press, Cambridge. Reproduced with permission.

The most important English writer of the Middle English period was Geoffrey Chaucer (1340?–1400). He was the first great poet to write in English. We do not know the exact date of his *Canterbury Tales;* they were written between 1387 and 1400. Chaucer was well versed in both English and French. By writing his *Tales* in English, he demonstrated the fallacy of the Norman French belief that their language was the only one delicate and refined enough to bè a proper vehicle for poetry.

In the following excerpt from the *General Prologue* to the *Canterbury Tales,* notice these phoneme–grapheme correspondences:

y for /i/ (qu*y*k)
e for /ə/ (heed*e*, lern*e*)

Notice the number of words that end in *e*.

> Of studie took he moost cure and moost heede,
> Nought o word spak he moore than was neede,
> And that was seyd in forme and reverence,
> And short and quyk and ful of hy sentence;
> Sownynge in moral vertu was his speche,
> And gladly wolde he lerne and gladly teche.

(*Cure* = care; *sentence* = significance; *sownynge in* = making for.)

We can see that the language between the 10th and 14th centuries changed quite radically. Notice how much closer to Modern English is Chaucer's work than is the Old English passage.

Observe that in the Middle English quotation, there are only two words that would be likely to cause any hesitancy in translation: *floyting* (flute playing) and *faire* (well, or excellently, or gracefully). With the Old English quotation, in spite of familiarity with the Modern English version of *The Lord's Prayer,* one who is not an Old English scholar must scrutinize each word.

Old English

Fæder ūre þū þe eart on heofonum sī þīn nama gehālgod. Tō be-cume þīn rīce. Gewurþe ðīn willa on eorðan swā swā on heofonum. Ūrne gedæghwāmlīcan hlāf syle ūs tō dæg. And forgyf ūs ūre gyltas swā swā wē forgyfað ūrum gyltendum. And ne gelæd þū ūs on cost-nunge ac ālȳs ūs of yfele. Sōþlīce.[3]

---

[3] *The Lord's Prayer* in West Saxon, c. 960. From I. D. Hook and E. G. Mathews, *Modern American Grammar and Usage.* Copyright © 1956, Ronald Press Company, New York. Reproduced with permission.

Middle English (Chaucer)

Syngynge he was, or floytynge,
　　all the day;
He was as fressh as is the
　　month of May.
Short was his gowne, with sleeves
　　long and wyde.
Wel koude he sitte on hors
　　and faire ryde.[4]

Modern English;
the Renaissance

No sooner had English been reestablished as a powerful and effective language, than it was once again threatened. A wave of cultural advancement began to spread throughout Europe at the close of the Medieval period. The total period of this rebirth, or Renaissance, was from about 1300 to 1600. During the second half of this span, there arose among the upper classes an appreciation of the value of learning. The freeing of learning from the control of the Church and the resultant interest in mortal as well as immortal problems produced profound changes in literature and in attitudes toward literacy. But English, as the language of scholarship, had a struggle. Latin profited greatly by the revival of learning, and scholars took advantage of the movement to advance Greek and especially Latin as the true purveyors of culture and education. Latin became the core of the school curriculum; it was used by scholars as the basis for improving English texts, and many of the learned forsook English for classical Latin. The Latin vocabulary was felt to be more stable and polished and more capable of conveying both abstract and humanistic ideas than was a fledgling language like English. Further, Latin was something of a *lingua franca* that leaped across geographical and political boundaries.

In spite of the revitalization of Latin, written English began to be used for both translations and original works. English writers began to produce a literature specializing in science and in

---

[4] F. N. Robinson, *The Complete Works of Geoffrey Chaucer,* 2nd ed. Boston: Houghton Mifflin Company, 1961.

political theory as well as in humanistic values. The English vocabulary was augmented by words borrowed not only from French but from half a hundred languages. Following are a few examples of words introduced into English between the 1400's and the 1700's — sometimes directly, sometimes indirectly, through other languages:

Latin:	*index*	*library*	*medicine*	*admit*	*instant*
Greek:	*gymnasium*	*caustic*	*parasite*	*atmosphere*	
Italian:	*carnival*	*cameo*	*stanza*	*violin*	*volcano*
Spanish:	*canyon*	*alligator*	*mosquito*	*cargo*	*potato*

William Shakespeare (1564–1616)

The man who probably did as much as any one man to influence the spread and general acceptability of the English language was William Shakespeare, playwright and poet. Shakespeare demonstrated the richness of the English language as an instrument for writing. His ability to combine, to compound, to "turn a phrase," enabled him to use his language to reveal man's complex nature; to speak both to those "in the pit" and to those whose intellect reveled in poetry and philosophy. Shakespeare did a great deal to make the English people proud of their language.

The following passage from *Romeo and Juliet* provides a clear example of the way in which the orthography of the period resembled present-day spelling. Note, however, that some older influences still held sway, such as the grapheme ʃ used for the /s/ and the *v* for the /u/. Also note the number of words that end in *e*.

> She ʃpeakes, Oh ʃpeake againe bright Angell:
> For thou art as glorious to this night
> Being ouer my head,
> As is a winged meʃʃenger of heaven,
> Vnto the white vpturned woondring eyes,
> Of mortals that fall backe to gaze upon him,
> When he beʃtrides the laʃie pacing cloudes,
> And ʃailes vpon the boʃome of the aire.[5]

---

[5] *Romeo and Juliet,* First Quarto: 1597.

The English language matures

Partly as a result of the infusion of the classics and partly because of the continuous improvement of printing equipment, the English were prodded into establishing some order in their orthography. London was the center of the book publishing business and this fact contributed to the rapid adoption of London English as the standard. Even so, printers continued to adapt the spelling of a word to their printer's length of type line, while writers like Shakespeare were at times quite impartial in their selection of graphemic representations for the phonemes in some words.

Further, during the years between 1642 and 1652, England was absorbed in civil wars. The necessity for getting out quantities of political documents allowed the printers little time to dally over various spellings of a word; conformity was the result.

The Great Vowel Shift

Just at the time printers had settled down to a more or less uniform orthography, with established spelling conventions, the English language underwent a change in pronunciation of vowels. The result was that the printer's somewhat stable orthography no longer matched the altered vowel sounds.

Over the centuries between Old English and contemporary American speech, the pronunciation of consonant sounds has remained fairly stable; vowel sounds, on the other hand, have changed over time. During the 15th and 16th centuries, "The Great Vowel Shift" occurred, a slow process which resulted in certain vowel sounds being articulated in new positions. For example, *name*, which earlier had a vowel pronunciation much like that in the first syllable of *father*, acquired its present /ā/ vowel sound. The consequences of The Great Vowel Shift for orthography were equally dramatic because stabilized spellings now came to represent different sounds.

Lost sounds and vestigial letters

Consonant clusters such as *hl*, *hr*, and *hw* were frequent in Old English words, as illustrated in *hlēapan*, *hlūd*, *hwæt*, and *hræfn* (*leap*, *loud*, *what*, and *raven*). During the Middle English period, the beginning /h/ was dropped from some of these words, so they more closely resembled their present form. In words that began *hw*, a different change took place: the /h/ remained, but the spelling was reversed so that *hwæt* became *what*.

In most Old English words, the /k/ was spelled *c*, and only rarely *k*. But, in Middle English times the *c* came also to represent the /s/ before *e* and *i* in words taken from French, while still representing /k/ before *a*, *o*, *u* and consonant letters. Because *c* was now an ambiguous spelling, *k* began to be used to represent /k/ before *e* and *i* and consonants. Thus, the /k/ in such Old English words as *cnēo* (*knee*) and *cnīf* (*knife*) came to be spelled with *k*. Also, over time, the initial /k/ dropped out of the /kn/ cluster in these words, so that today we pronounce only the /n/ as in /nīf/ and /nē/, though the letter *k* remains to remind us of the history of these words.

Similarly the *w* in *two* and in *sword* at one time represented a semivowel /w/. Further, we continue to write *lamb* and *tomb*, even though the final /b/ has long ceased to be pronounced.

After /a/, /ä/, /ȯ/, and /ō/, and before /k/, /m/, /f/, and /v/, the /l/ has generally disappeared, as in *half*, *salve*, *folk*, *calm*, and *walk*. However, after /i/ and /u/, the /l/ continues to be enunciated, as in *milk* and *bulk*.

The use of the letter *e* has varied from period to period. In Chaucer's time, it often represented a final "schwa" sound (/ə/), as in *sofa*, when it occurred at the end of words: (*make* — *makə*; *tyme* — *timə*). The use by printers of *e* in final position sometimes was quite whimsical. They often added *e* to words as a "filler" to lengthen their printer's lines. Today the diacritic *e* is used in word-final position to help spell an internal "long" vowel sound (as in *make* or *like*). The *e* also is used as part of the spelling of a final /v/ (*love*) as well as to indicate final /s/ (*price*), and final /z/ (*cheese*).

The preceding examples are mentioned only to indicate the types of extensive orthographic changes that took place during the evolution of the English language in Britain. As of the middle of the 18th century, more rigid standards of correctness developed. Dr. Samuel Johnson headed the list of dictionary-makers who were concerned with the necessity of establishing a fixed orthography. Dr. Johnson had some rather firm notions of what should be the relation between the spoken word and its written form.

He might have been talking to spelling teachers when he said:

> A double pronunciation, one cursory and colloquial and the other regular and solemn, [has its advantages]. The cursory pronunciation is always vague and uncertain, being made different in different mouths by negligence and unskilfulness and affectation. The solemn pronunciation, though by no means immutable and permanent, is yet always less remote from the orthography and less liable to capricious innovation.[6]

In this chapter we have attempted to give some of the highlights in the evolution of the English language from the Old English period to the Modern and to describe how the orthography reflected or resisted these changes.

[6] Dr. Samuel Johnson, *A Dictionary of the English Language,* 1755.

CHAPTER FIVE

Orthography
of American English

We have seen, in Chapter Four, how several Germanic dialects were carried to Britain and became — after centuries of strife, threats of extinction, enrichment by borrowings, and gradual maturation — the proud and distinguished language of the English people.

English invades the New World

With the wars of Reformation and the accompanying persecutions, many people left their British homes to seek freedom in the new lands of North America. Emigrants from particular regions of England usually settled together in their new homeland, with the result that the English dialects they spoke were transplanted to particular regions along the Atlantic coast. Those who settled in New England brought with them the dialect of southern England with its broad /a/ and softened terminal /r/ as in *father*, and its softened or abandoned /r/ before consonants as in *lard*. Those who came from northern England settled mainly in Pennsylvania, but moved west in great numbers and established their North British pronunciation in the North Central states. The third dialect area extended from Chesapeake Bay south and reflected the dialect of southeastern England.

But the very fact that pioneer society in the New World was in constant flux guaranteed that the American language would evolve rather than remain static. As people moved about, seeking new land on which to settle, they contacted and mingled with others whose speech patterns were different. This cross-fertilization of dialects eventually produced an American language that, despite some variations in pronunciation, can be understood from Alaska to Florida and from Hawaii to Maine. When we consider that the American people represent a great amalgam of immigrants from almost every nation in the world — nearly every nation with its own language — it is even more remarkable that we have managed to establish not only one language, but a language very little different from British English, its parent tongue.

American English seeks standardization in spelling

The first English-speaking settlers in North America were bound by few absolute rules of orthography. The spelling of the language was often dictated by whimsy. There were few dictionaries in those days that could serve as authoritative lexicons, and people tended to spell words as they pronounced them. Although the first printing press in North America (set up in Cambridge, Massachusetts, in 1638) helped to initiate a movement toward some kind of uniformity in spelling, printers in the New World, like those in Europe, were notoriously independent when it came to deciding how a word should be spelled. For example, the word *mosquito* was spelled *mosquito* or *musquito*; *both* was spelled *both* or *bothe*.

However, the publication in England of Dr. Samuel Johnson's *A Dictionary of the English Language* (1755) was a monumental accomplishment which contributed to the stabilization of the English orthography both in England and in America. By the end of the 18th century, spelling was virtually standardized.

American dictionaries and their influence

By this time, about 20 percent of the English-speaking people of the world lived in the United States, and they were determined to establish a system of education that would prepare a literate citizenry. The need for a school dictionary became evident. In 1798, Samuel Johnson, Jr. (an American clergyman and educator, and not related to Dr. Johnson) published *A School Dictionary,* the first English-language dictionary compiled by an American.

Johnson continued his efforts by collaborating with John Elliott to produce *A Selected and Pronouncing and Accented Dictionary* (1800), an expanded and revised edition of his earlier dictionary, which contained about 10,000 words, including many that were borrowed from American Indian languages and were therefore peculiar to America (*tomahawk, tepee, wampum,* etc.).

The Columbian Dictionary by Caleb Alexander of Massachusetts, containing about 32,000 entries, was also published in 1800 and also included a few American-usage words. Some of them were *Yankee, dime, Congress, Congressional, minute-man, dollar, elector,* and *lengthy.* Alexander employed such American spellings as *honor* (for British *honour*), *troop* (for *troup*), *color* (for *colour*), and *favor* (for *favour*); but he did allow a choice between *screen* and British *skreen, sponge* and *spunge, checker* and *chequer,* and *calendar* and *kalendar.*

Noah Webster (1758–1843)

Noah Webster did as much as any one man to advance the cause of literacy in America. He had a great many interests (law, education, politics), but his great passion was language, and particularly the American language. He worked mightily to overcome what he felt to be an unwarranted and slavish bowing to the dictates of British English. He was influenced in this attitude by Benjamin Franklin, who, in 1768, published *A Scheme for a New Alphabet and a Reformed Mode of Spelling.*

Although Franklin's plan of adding six new characters to the alphabet to simplify spelling was too extreme a proposal even for Webster, Webster did propose an overhaul of the English language to make its orthography completely consistent. Had he been given the support he needed, we might today be spelling the word *head* as *hed, friend* as *frend, give* as *giv, thumb* as *thum, bought* as *bot,* and *calf* as *kaf.*

In 1806, Webster published a small school dictionary called *A Compendious Dictionary of the English Language.* This was a dictionary of the American-English language for Americans, and as such it omitted many British-English words that Webster considered useless or inappropriate for American life. It also included words not found in Dr. Johnson's British dictionary, and even new meanings for old words.

New American words arose because the struggle to make a living in an undeveloped country produced new tools and new experiences. These words were not usually included in British dictionaries for two reasons: they were unacceptably crude by British standards, and they held meaning only for former colonists. For example, the colonists added many Indian words to their vocabularies, and these words were adapted to American-English pronunciation and standardized in terms of English orthography: the Algonquin words *segongw* and *moos* became *skunk* and *moose;* from Cree, *otchock* became *woodchuck.* Nevertheless, these words, like others having to do with frontier life in America, were foreign to people in England. Such words as *hominy, possum,* and *spinning-bee* would eventually find their way into the great English dictionaries, but in the meantime they needed to be included in a recognized American authority.

Webster's school dictionary gave a great boost to the development of literacy in the United States. And his revised and enlarged two-volume edition called *An American Dictionary of the English Language,* which he completed in his seventy-first year, was considered superior to Dr. Johnson's British dictionary in the following respects:

1. Dr. Johnson's definitions were gleaned primarily from literary sources; Webster's were based on current usage.
2. As compared with Dr. Johnson, Webster included many more scientific and technical terms.
3. Webster's etymological entries were more extensive and more accurate than Dr. Johnson's.

American versus British usage

Although some Englishmen continue to deride the American language, most of them acknowledge that while certain expressions may not conform to British Standard English, they are both colorful and representative of the life of the American people. Many such expressions have, in fact, been accepted in England. Oscar Wilde's famous witticism, "We have really everything in common with America except, of course, the language" becomes increasingly out of date. Today there are relatively few English words that are not in common use in both Britain and America.

There are, however, a few British-English terms that are not in general use in American speech. Here is a list of a few of these terms with their American counterparts:

British	American
porridge	oatmeal
lift	elevator
waistcoat	vest
vest	undershirt
sweets	candy
biscuits	crackers
mackintosh	raincoat
hood [auto]	top
bonnet [auto]	hood
braces	suspenders
pram	baby carriage
torch	flashlight
chemist	druggist
petrol	gasoline
accumulator	battery
reel [thread]	spool
dustbin	garbage can
draughts [game]	checkers
catmint	catnip
bobby	policeman
rubber	eraser
aluminium	aluminum
goods waggon	freight car
creche	day nursery
walking-stick	cane
bent biscuit	pretzel

When we move on from vocabulary to spelling, we see that although travel and modern communication have helped to level out some of the differences between British and American usage, there are still a few words which Englishmen tend to spell differently from Americans. Nevertheless, usage is by no means standard within each country, as can be seen from the following list; some Americans, for example, would write **grey** rather than **gray**.

Preferred British English	*Preferred American English*
honour	honor
traveller	traveler
programme	program
verandah	veranda
mould	mold
storey [of a house]	story
plough	plow
catalogue	catalog
cheque	check
centre	center
jewellery	jewelry
pyjamas	pajamas
tyre	tire
connexion	connection
theatre	theater
waggon	wagon
vigour	vigor
grey	gray
kerb	curb
defence	defense

American English: a living, growing language

The American-English language has never been static. Today an unabridged dictionary contains more than half a million entries. (Noah Webster and Dr. Johnson each listed about 70,000 entries in their dictionaries.) And contemporary unabridged dictionaries do not even list the entire American-English lexicon; certain technical words and words used largely by the professions are listed in highly specialized dictionaries. Were such words included in the standard unabridged dictionary, very likely an additional 100,000 words would be added to the corpus.

Word borrowing

One reason for this growth of the vocabulary is that we have added many words from languages with which we have come in contact. Sometimes we have kept the original pronunciation and spelling of the foreign word (*parfait*); occasionally, the original pronunciation with altered spelling (*noodle*, from German **Nudel**); frequently, the original spelling but Americanized pronunciation (*sabotage*, which in French is accented on the last syllable). Here are examples of some words we have borrowed from other languages — either directly or through the British — and have treated in one of these three ways.

Spanish	*German*	*Italian*	*French*
tortilla	kindergarten	piano	gopher
vanilla	pretzel	ravioli	sabotage
sombrero	sauerkraut	virtuoso	entourage
adobe	frankfurter	simpatico	parfait

Dutch	*Fr. Canadian*	*Japanese*	*Welsh*
snoop	caribou	kamikaze	cromlech
coleslaw			
waffle			

Scandinavian	*Tibetan*	*East Indian*	*Malay*
skull	yak	bungalow	amuck
skoal		shampoo	bamboo
skirt		cashmere	gingham
		chutney	launch

Hungarian	*Eskimo*	*African*	*Arabic*
coach	igloo	gumbo	lute
paprika		okra	algebra
		yam	

Chinese	*Hebrew*	*Native Australian*	
tea	amen	boomerang	
typhoon	halleluja	kangaroo	
tycoon	behemoth		
chow mein			

Why should we borrow words? Why not simply create new words? One reason is that certain words describe such a subtle idea or situation that it is practically impossible to translate them into another language without losing much of the original flavor. It is often easier to borrow these words than to try to create native equivalents. Two good examples are the Italian word **simpatico** and the French word *élan*. We have no precise English synonyms for these two words; hence, we have simply added them to our American vocabulary unchanged.

And it must be remembered that word borrowing works both

ways. One cannot visit a foreign country without noting the multitude of American-English words and expressions that have been introduced. The ubiquitous "hot dog and Coke" stand has even now given way to Wimpy bars (from a comic strip). And probably the most entirely international word (precise origin unknown) is the native American *OK*, variously spelled *okey*, *O.K.*, or *okay*.

Word formation

The other major reason for the growth of the vocabulary is the invention of new words. For example, two or more known words have frequently been combined to form new compounds, often with metaphorical meanings: *brainwash, dustpan, hangdog, shipyard, countdown, spaceship, skyscraper, upstage.* Sometimes these words are hyphenated, e.g. *round-the-clock*, and sometimes they are completely split into their components, e.g. *foot brake*, but most of them are written solid. Since the spelling conventions that dictate whether such words are to be hyphenated, separated, or completely joined are constantly changing, one ought to keep abreast by referring to the latest standard dictionaries.

Sometimes, only *parts* of words are combined to produce a new formation. Here is a list of such *portmanteau words* (also called *blends*), together with the two words from which each was probably formed. Some of these portmanteau words originated in England (e.g. *smog, brunch, chortle*), but the others are pure Americana.

chortle	chuckle and snort
guestimate	guess and estimate
smog	smoke and fog
brunch	breakfast and lunch
motel	motor and hotel
twirl	twist and whirl
tangelo	tangerine and pamelo (grapefruit)
splatter	splash and spatter
flurry	flutter and hurry
telecast	television and broadcast
Medicare	medical and care
Comsat	communication and satellite

Another kind of new formation, an *acronym*, is created by taking the initial letter from each word in a phrase referring to something — usually an organization or a device — and combining these letters to produce a pronounceable word. Inasmuch as syllables of American-English words must contain a vowel phoneme or a vowellike sound, some acronyms must take more than the initial letter from a word in order to be pronounceable. For example, *radar* was compounded from "*ra*dio *d*etecting *a*nd *r*anging."

Our advanced technological society has produced a great many acronyms. After they have been in use for some time, and have been accepted in formal communication, they are not considered abbreviations and therefore do not require a period after each letter or at the end. Here is a group of acronyms together with the words from which they originated:

EVA	Extra-Vehicular Activity
snafu	situation normal; all fouled up
TIROS	Television and Infrared Observation Satellite
NATO	North Atlantic Treaty Organization
LEM	Lunar Excursion Module
AID	Agency for International Development
sonar	sound navigation ranging
scuba	self-contained underwater breathing apparatus
CARE	Committee for American Relief in Europe
laser	light amplification by stimulated emission of radiation
ANNA	Army, Navy, NASA [itself an acronym], **Air Force**

To describe technological innovations, we often combine root words from the Latin and Greek or add prefixes or suffixes to them. For example, *graph*, from the Greek word *graphos*, means "writing." *Graph* has been combined with other forms of Greek origin (*tele*, *mono*, *photo*, and *auto*) to produce **telegraph**, **monograph**, **photograph**, and **autograph**. Other relatively recent formations of this type are **astronaut**, **stereophonic**, **microbiology**, **microscope**, **helicopter**, **hydrophobia**, **thermostat**, **barometer**, **hydroplane**, **propellant**, **microphone**, **laundromat**, **nylon**, **cellophane**, and **centrifuge**. Sometimes trade names are formed from a Greek or Latin root (e.g. **Plexiglas**, **Vaseline**, **Pyrex**, **Thermofax**, and **Styrofoam**), and later pass into more general use.

The various means by which words entered our language help to explain some of the seeming vagaries of American-English orthography. Therefore, a knowledge of how words have been borrowed or newly formed not only leads to an appreciation of our linguistic heritage but also contributes to the development of spelling power.

Formal versus informal communication

In Chapter Two, we suggested that spelling has not kept abreast of changes in pronunciation — particularly the pronunciation characteristic of informal speech, which is often far removed from that used in formal situations. In informal speech, words tend to flow together because we telescope some sounds and eliminate others. Sentences that sound as if they would be written "I wanna see ya nex week" and "Whena we gonna eat?" are common. And even relatively precise speakers may occasionally say /plēs/ for *police*, /pu' chər/ for *put your*, /li' ber ē/ for *library*.

Of what significance are such oral departures from fidelity to the written form? How can such informal speech be reconciled with a spelling program? The first thing to be recognized is that there is no possibility of controlling or standardizing American speech. Pronunciation, like all aspects of language, reflects the times and the culture of a people. In informal conversation, people cannot be expected to say, "Aren't you going to get your car fixed?" (pronouncing each word separately and distinctly) when they can more quickly ask something that sounds like, "Arencha gonna gechur car fixed?"

Therefore, the teacher must face facts. He must, first of all, teach pupils that there are two patterns of oral expression, one formal and one informal, and that neither is univerally acceptable — the choice depends on time and place. But he must also make it clear that written expression normally adheres much more strictly to formal than to informal patterns of expression, and that certain advantages are gained by this. Charleton Laird's analogy is pertinent:

> Language must not only have flexibility to live and grow, it must have currency to be understood. Like money, it is no fit medium for exchange unless it has sufficient currency so that he who gives the coin values it in roughly the same terms as he who receives it. And like money, it must have sufficient stability so that what is given today has approximately the same value tomorrow. . . . Language is a living thing. It must survive in

men's minds and on men's tongues if it survives at all. In so doing, it changes with minds, lives, and the use of the vocal apparatus. But at the same time, language can function only if it has stability in time and place. . . .[1]

"Stability in time and place" implies that the school has an obligation to see to it that changes are not so abrupt that we lose ability to communicate with others today and to understand the records of the past. If we are to continue to communicate over time and space, our written expression — and therefore our spelling — needs to be much more conservative than our speech. This apparent dichotomy of freedom to change speech without corresponding freedom to change its written surrogate places an extra burden on the teacher of spelling.

In Chapter Six we will discuss some of the ways in which spelling has been taught from Colonial days to the present, and we will examine some of the newer theories and practices characteristic of modern spelling programs.

[1] Charleton Laird, *The Miracle of Language* (Greenwich, Conn.: Fawcett Publications, Inc., 1960), p. 212.

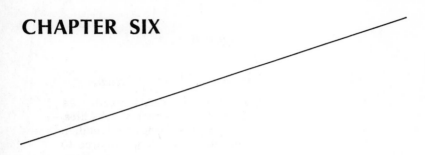

CHAPTER SIX

*Spelling as
a School Subject*

In preceding chapters we reviewed the historical development of the English language and its written code. We now focus on the problem of how to teach spelling of a language which is constantly growing and changing but which resists accommodating its writing system to these changes. It may be profitable to begin by looking back at some early American spellers and observing how spelling programs were conceived in those times.

Some early spelling books

As more and more people received at least some formal education, poor spelling began to be looked down upon. Therefore, numerous spelling books were produced in the early days, some more useful than others. These books generally presented word lists to be memorized followed by short paragraphs to give the pupils practice in reading. Many of these paragraphs were totally unrelated to the spelling lesson and had more to do with the behavior of people than with the behavior of graphemes.

The most popular speller of the early 19th century, written by Noah Webster while he was teaching school in Goshen, New York (1782–1785), was entitled *A Grammatical Institute of the English*

Figure 6–1

88   *An Easy Standard of Pronunciation.*

from which he was unable to extricate himself. As he lay thus exposed to whole swarms of flies, which were galling him and sucking his blood, a Swallow, observing his distress, kindly offered to drive them away. By no means, said the Fox; for if these should be chased away, which are already sufficiently gorged, another more hungry swarm would succeed, and I should be robbed of every remaining drop of blood in my veins.

TABLE XXXV.

In the following words the vowels are short, and the accented syllable must be pronounced as though it ended with the consonant *sh*. Thus, *pre-cious, spe-cial, effi-cient, logi-cian, mili-tia, addi-tion*, are pronounced, *presh-us, spesh-ul, eff-sh-ent, logish-an, milish-a, addish-on.*—These words will serve as examples for the following table.

Prĕ cious	ef fi cient	per di tion
spe cial	es pe cial	per ni cious
vi cious	fla gi tious	pe ti tion
vi tiate	fru i tion	pro fi cient
ad dĭ tion	ju di cial	phy si cian
am bi tion	lo gi cian	po si tion
aus pi cious	ma gi cian	pro pi tious
ca pri cious	ma li cious	se di tion
co mi tial	mi li tia	se di tious
con di tion	mŭ si cian	sol sti tial
cog ni tion	nu tri tion	suf fi cient
con tri tion	no vi ciate	sus pi cious
de fi cient	of fi ciate	trans i tion
de li cious	of fi cial	vo li tion
dis cre tion	of fi cious	ab o lĭ tion*
dis cu tient	pa tri cian	ac qui si tion
e di tion	par ti tion	ad mo n' tion

* The words of four syllables have a half accent on the first except *practitioner. Arithmetician* and *suppositititous* have the half accent on the second, *academician* and *mathematician* on the first.

Figure 6–1—Continued

An Easy Standard of Pronunciation. 89

ad ven ti tious	prej u di cial	co a li tion
am mu ni tion	pol i ti cian	com pe ti tion
ap pa ri tion	prop o si tion	com po si tion
ar ti fi cial	prep o si tion	def i ni tion
ad sci ti tious	pro hi bi tion	dem o li tion
ap po si tion	rhet o ri cian	dep o si tion
eb ul li tion	su per fi cial	dis po si tion
er u di tion	su per sti tion	prac ti tion er
ex hi bi tion	sup po si tion	a rith me ti cian
ex po si tion	sur rep ti tious	ac a de mi cian
im po si tion	av a ri cious	sup pos i ti tious
op po si tion	ben e fi cial	math e ma ti cian

The compounds and derivatives follow the same rule.

—

In the following words, the consonant *q* terminates a syllable ; but perhaps the ease of the learner may render a different division more eligible.

	li quor	an ti qui ty
E qui ty	li que fy	in i qui ty
e qui ta ble	li qui date	in i qui tous
li quid	la quey	ob li qui ty

SELECT SENTENCES.

Never speak of a man's virtues to his face, nor of his faults behind his back ; thus you will equally avoid flattery which is disgusting, and slander which is criminal.

If you are poor, labor will procure you food and clothing—if you are rich it will strengthen the body, invigorate the mind, and keep you from vice—Every man therefore should be busy in some employment.

H 2

Language. This high-sounding title actually belonged to a three-part work: Part 1 was a speller; Part 2, a grammar; and Part 3, a reader. Later the speller came to be known as Webster's Blue-backed Spelling Book. Perhaps as many as 100 million copies were sold. The speller played a powerful role in making people consider correct spelling as important as good manners and therefore as a criterion for social acceptance.

Figure 6–1 is a facsimile of pages 88 and 89 from the second edition of Webster's *The American Spelling Book, An Easy Standard of Pronunciation, Containing the Rudiments of the English Language* (1818). Observe the following:

1. Some help was given on pronunciation and accent.
2. Webster approached spelling from a *decoding* position. Note, for example, "The consonant *q* terminates a syllable."
3. Letters that did not represent a specific sound were printed in italics, thus: "li q*u*or."
4. The reading matter had no apparent relation to the word lists.

A competing speller by A. Picket, written in 1812, explained its *raison d'être* on the title page as follows:

The Juvenile Spelling Book
Being An
Easy Introduction To The
English Language
Containing
Easy and Familiar Lessons
In Spelling
With Appropriate
Reading Lessons
To Advance the Learners by Easy Gradations
and to Teach the Orthography of Johnson[1]
and the Pronunciation of Walker[2]

Figure 6–2 shows that Picket, like Webster, provided gratuitous moral exhortations as a reading lesson, and also that he was apparently as concerned about teaching pronunciation as he was

---

[1] Dr. Samuel Johnson.
[2] John Walker (1732–1807), an actor and lexicographer, published *A Critical Pronouncing Dictionary.*

about teaching spelling. The above lesson on syllabication is interesting, but it does not seem to be especially aimed at producing mastery of phoneme–grapheme correspondences.

A spelling text published in 1825 brings us closer to the texts of the 1930s. The title page reads:

The Orthoepical Guide To The
English Tongue
Being
Perry's Spelling Book
Revised and Corrected, With Walker's
Pronunciations Precisely Applied
On a New Science Containing Also
Moral Lessons, Fables, And Much Useful
Matter For the Instruction of Youth
By
Israel Alger, Jun. A.M.
1825

Figure 6–3 is a facsimile of a page from this speller. Observe the following:

1. All words in the lists were capitalized.
2. The pronunciations were based on those provided by Walker for Dr. Johnson's (British) dictionary.
3. The final sound spelled *y* in words like **Baby** and **Bounty** was /ē/. (In the 1930s and 1940s, many dictionaries presented this sound as /i/. But the 1961 edition of Webster (and others) returned to /ē/.)
4. The initial sound of **Chairman** and **Chalky** is given as /tsh/ in Alger, as /t ʃ/ in the present *Oxford English Dictionary*, and as /ch/ in Webster, 1961.

Thus, we see the importance of consulting the dictionary regularly in order to keep abreast of changes in pronunciation and orthography.

Spelling as a school subject in the early 20th century

One hundred million spelling textbooks ought to have produced orthographically literate pupils, but such was not the case. And we did not improve spelling skill very much in the early 20th century, either. In fact, spelling, which had occupied a position of respect in the school curriculum of our 19th century forebears,

Figure 6–2

116

Reading Lesson.

A habit of idleness is unbecoming in any one.

Idleness and ignorance are the parents of many vices.

True cheerfulness makes a man happy in himself, and promotes the happiness of all around.

The contented mind spreads ease and cheerfulness around itself.

We may escape the censure of others, when we do wrong privately ; but we cannot avoid the reproaches of our own mind.

All the syllables long.

Gla ci ate§	fo li ate	mi cro scope
sa ti ate	o pi ate	vi o late
ra di ate	ra ti o	pro to type
de vi ate	fo li o	zo o phyte¶

The first long, the second short, the last scarcely perceptible.

Ca pa ble	no ta ble	cu ra ble
sale a ble	port a ble	suit a ble
blame a ble	fore cas tle	du ra ble
pay a ble	eat a ble	pli a ble

The two first long.

Fea si ble§	for ci ble	fu si ble

The first short, the second long.

par ti cle†§	fal li ble	pos si ble
ar ti cle	chron i cle*	au di ble‡
fran gi ble	hor ri ble	plau si ble

¶ *ph, gh,* as *f.* * *ch* as *k.*   ‡ *au* as *a* broad.   † *a* mid.

became in the 1920s an unwanted subject — a "poor relation" of reading, and tolerated only as a necessary nuisance.

During this period, children were given lists of words whose spelling was to be memorized by whatever system they found most productive. Whether the system used was largely visual or involved hand learning (acquiring a neuromuscular sense of the

Figure 6–2—Continued

117

cred i ble	ter ri ble	prin ci ple
flex i ble	re gi ble	vin ci ble
le gi ble	fen ci ble	mul ti ple
sen si ble	vis i ble	cur ri cle

The two first short.

Pas sa ble	car bun cle†	rent a ble
pal pa ble	laugh a ble¶	spec ta cle
par a ble	prob a ble	pin na cle
af fa ble	or a cle	mir a cle
trac ta ble	ef fa ble	syl la ble
ar a ble	rec tan gle	cul pa ble

All the syllables short.

Rap tur ous	ban ish er	prot es tant
ran cor ous	mar in er	sol id ness
stam mer er	bar ris ter	pol ish er
flat ter er	mor al ist	gaτн er ing
mar tyr dom†	log a rithms	of fer ing
pas sen ger	laud a num	sat ir ist
man a ger	vol a tile	par ox ism

When *f* precedes *y*, in a final syllable, the *y* is then pronounced as long and open as if the accent were on it; thus, *justify, qualify, &c.* have the last syllable sounded like that in *defy,* or the long *i* as in *pine.*

The first syllable short, the others long.

Grat i fy§	sanc ti fy	ed i fy
rat i fy	scar i fy	tes ti fy
ram i fy	ar e fy	ver i fy
pa ci fy	rar e fy	ver si fy
mag ni fy	am pli fy	spe ci fy

§ *i* 2d syllable as *e*.   † *a* middle.

way it feels to write particular words) or oral repetition of the letters, it was essentially rote memorization of each word. Sometimes a pupil was required to learn to spell as many as 50 words within a week. Friday was test day, and the teacher read the list of words as the pupils sought to recall the letters (in proper

Figure 6–3

TO THE ENGLISH TONGUE. 51

nôr, nŏt—tūbe, tŭb, bûll—ôïl, pôûnd—thin, this.

The plants and the trees are made to give fruit to man ; but man is made to praise God, who made him.

We love to praise him, because he loveth to bless us.

We love God, who hath created all beings ; we love all beings, because they are the creatures of God.

We will think of God when we play, and when we work ; when we sleep, and when we wake. His praise shall be always on our lips.

TABLE II.

More Words of two syllables, accented on the First.

Ab′ject ăb′jĕkt	Bed′lam bĕd′lŭm	Bug′bear bŭg′băre	Chair′man tshăre′măn
Ac′rid ăk′krĭd	Big′ness bĭg′nĕs	Bu′gle bū′gl	Chalk′y tshàwk′kĕ
Ad′verb ăd′vĕrb	Bind′er bīnd′ŭr	Bul′bous bŭl′bŭs	Char′ming tshàr′mĭng
A′gent ā′jĕnt	Blame′less blāme′lĕs	Bush′y bûsh′ĕ	Chast′ly tshāste′lĕ
Am′ber ăm′bŭr	Blem′ish blĕm′ĭsh	Buy′er bī′ŭr	Cheap′ness tshēpe′nĕs
Ba′by bā′bĕ	Blue′ness blū′nĕs	Cab′in kăb′bĭn	Chief′tain tshēēf′tĭn
Bane′ful bāne′fùl	Boun′ty bôûn′tĕ	Ca′ble kā′bl	Civ′et sĭv′ĭt
Bank′rupt bănk′rŭpt	Bra′zen brā′z′n	Cam′brick kăme′brĭk	Clai′mant klā′mănt
Bare′foot bāre′fût	Brigh′ten brĭĭt′n	Cau′tion kâw′shŭn	Clam′our klăm′mŭr
Beard′less bēērd′lĕs	Brief′ness brēēf′nĕs	Cem′ent sĕm′mĕnt	Clean′ly klĕn′lĕ
Beau′ty bū′tĕ	Bri′nish brī′nĭsh	Ce′rate sē′răt	Cli′mate klī′măte

order) used to spell each word. Typical relearning of misspelled
words consisted of an after-school exercise in which children not
blessed with total recall would "learn" the words they had misspelled by writing each over and over until they were supposedly
fixed in memory.

Crosscurrents and confusion

What was not recognized when emphasis was placed on reading vis-à-vis spelling was that the encoding and the decoding
processes are quite different. Spelling is the encoding of speech
or thought into writing; reading is the decoding of writing into
meaningful expression. If one follows logically the development
of language communication, he will note the following order:

1. Thinking of an idea and voicing it in speech
2. Writing what he has thought or said
3. Reading what he has written
4. Reading what others have written

Thus, when items 2 and 3 were reversed in the school program,
crosscurrents and confusion may have been set up.

At any rate, evidence began to accumulate that children who
can read cannot necessarily spell. For example, high school
teachers sometimes complained that certain children had not been
taught to spell in the primary grades. And college professors were
compelled to conduct remedial classes in English composition
and spelling because some students were unable to spell at the
most elementary level. There was also criticism from the business
world. Executives were dismayed by the orthographic illiteracy
of some secretaries. Parents wanted to know why some of their
children were unable to write a literate thank-you note.

Spelling texts of the 1930s

In the 1930s, the general situation began to interest many educators who felt that spelling had received too little emphasis
for too long. Efforts were made to revise the spelling program,
not merely to give it proper status in the school curriculum, but
also to make it a more effective learning tool. Two ideas of the
day stand out as especially innovative: 1) choosing for the basic
study list those words that were most frequently used and there-

fore most likely to be needed by pupils in their writing, and 2) presenting the words for a week's work in an attractive and meaningful package.

Typically, the list of spelling words for levels 2–8 contained about 3,000 words, mainly root words, selected on the basis of frequency-of-usage counts done in the previous decade by such researchers as Thorndike, Gates, and Horn. By consulting newspapers, magazines, personal and business correspondence, etc., these researchers observed millions of words in both handwritten and printed texts, and they published lists of the words which adults wrote (and read) most frequently. When the educators of the 1930s selected such words for spellers, they stressed the assertion that spelling mastery of these 3,000 basic words would give the ordinary individual the ability to write automatically over 96 percent of all the words he might use in his written communication.

In the early 1930s, criticism was levelled against the practice of selecting a spelling vocabulary for pupils on the basis of these frequency-of-usage counts. The critics pointed out the absence of *children's* written work in the corpus examined by Thorndike, Gates, Horn, and others. In a U.S. Government project under WPA contract, Rinsland of the University of Oklahoma examined a great many words contained in children's writing in and out of school and produced a valuable volume showing the grade-by-grade usage of encoding words.[3] As a result of Rinsland's work, the 3,000-word spelling vocabularies were modified to provide a better balance between children's and adults' vocabularies. But the method of teaching and learning still remained unchanged — each word was attacked as an independent unit to be memorized by rote. The alphabetic principle underlying spelling — i.e. the phoneme–grapheme relationship — was almost entirely neglected during this period.

The second innovation of the 1930s consisted primarily of a change in the format of the speller. Instead of being presented only in an unadorned list to be memorized, most of the words were introduced in interesting stories with appealing illustrations and page makeup. In each lesson, the story was followed by a list

[3] Henry D. Rinsland, *A Basic Vocabulary of Elementary School Children* (New York: Macmillan, 1945).

of words to be mastered and by a set of exercises based both on the spelling words and on the content of the story. Comprehensive spelling tests were usually given every six weeks. The spellers of the 1930s represented a decided advance in attractiveness, and this was considered a motivation for the pupils to learn. The pupils' page shown in Figure 6–4 is illustrative of the spelling books of that era. It is from the *Newlon-Hanna Speller* by J. H. Newlon and P. R. Hanna, published in 1933 by Houghton Mifflin Company.

The distribution of the 3,000 words among the several grades was decided primarily on the basis of frequency of usage (the high-frequency words in writing came early in the graded sequence) and the length of the word (the monosyllables preceded the polysyllables). Groups of rhyming words were often used, not to provide pupils with raw material from which they might observe some powerful rule or patterning, but just as a means of selecting the week's list of words to be memorized.

Another feature of spelling texts in the 1930s was *My Own Words,* a plan for providing for individual spelling needs. Pupils were encouraged to keep a notebook in which to record for study any words they needed to learn to spell that were *not* included in the lessons to date, as well as any words they had misspelled in the weekly tests. Thus, a misspelled word was usually not "lost," but was restudied until mastered.

Spelling texts of the 1940s

Although the spelling texts of the 1930s provided *some* relief from the previous dull exercise of memorizing lists of words, ten years later, spelling specialists again attempted to improve the techniques of learning to encode the language. The story idea was continued, with expanded stories. An alteration was made in the previous plan for a week's work. The first test, which had typically been given on the day after the lesson was presented, was postponed one day so that pupils would follow a study–study–test–study–test plan. (The system of two days' initial study before a preliminary test appeared to be more productive and less likely to encourage guesswork.) Educators developed a six-step plan for studying a word by visual learning and hand

Figure 6–4

Alaska

Alaska is a beautiful region of rivers, mountains, and seashore. It is one of America's beauty spots. The natural timber is still standing, and gushing mountain streams are alive with fish. Wild life wanders about freely. We hope to spare Alaska the wasteful destruction that has ruined so much beauty in the United States.

natural	frozen	spare	perhaps
remaining	ruined	guilty	wander
cool	ashamed	solid	region
act	grab	split	timber
largely	selfish	standing	leaving

ACTIVITIES

1. Copy three words from the story which are names of a country or a continent. Notice the capital letters.
2. Write these words without suffixes:
   leaving   ruined   standing   remaining
3. Notice the *self* in *selfish*.
4. Write a Story Word which means the same as:
   to save, s – – – –   to do, a – –
   not warm, c – – –   maybe, p – – – – – –
   spoiled, r – – – – –   snatch, g – – –
5. What is added to *large* to make *largely*?
6. Are you adding words to My Own Words List?

REVIEW WORDS

early	shoes	cottage	quarrel
newspaper	public	copies	anybody

V–27

learning combined — a plan that still has merit, particularly when children must learn to spell words that have maverick phoneme–grapheme correspondences, such as *choir*. The *My Own Words* feature was retained, as well as the six weeks' tests that assured a systematic and spaced review of material previously taught.

Spelling texts of the 1950s

During the next ten years, the number of spelling texts burgeoned, and most of them jumped on the introductory story bandwagon. But uneasiness developed as reports came in that spelling tests revealed a lack of significant improvement in orthographic literacy. And considerable suspicion of the effectiveness of the introductory paragraph was generated as teachers found that the actual business of learning to spell was being sacrificed to lengthy discussions of the subject matter of the stories.

Further, if the window dressing provided by the stories was set aside, we appeared to be teaching, basically, a list of words, without focussing on their construction except to point out that some words had peculiar arrangements of letters. At this point, spelling specialists began to turn to the linguists — and to Leonard Bloomfield in particular — for help. It was learned that a most important fact was being overlooked; namely, that the American-English language, like most languages, employs an alphabetical system of writing in which phonemes (sounds) are represented by graphemes (letters), and that a spelling program ought to begin by teaching phoneme–grapheme correspondences and guide pupils to use them in spelling written words.

The question of regularity in American-English spelling

The idea of studying words with this sound-to-letter approach raised the question of how profitable such an attack could be when our orthography was apparently so inconsistent and irregular. In order to find an answer to this question, Paul and Jean Hanna initiated a research study[4] in which a 3,000-word vocabulary was

[4] James Thomas Moore, *Phonetic Elements Appearing in a Three-Thousand-Word Spelling Vocabulary* (Unpublished dissertation, Stanford University, June, 1951).

analyzed in terms of phoneme–grapheme correspondences. These correspondences were classified as either "regular" or "irregular," and the relative frequency of the correspondences was noted.

This 1951 research study indicated that the American-English language has a surprising amount of consistency in its graphemic representation of speech sounds. Here are some findings:

1. Roughly four-fifths of the phonemes contained in the words comprising the traditional spelling vocabulary of the elementary school child approximate the alphabetic principle in their letter representations.
2. Approximately one-fifth of the phonemes contained in the words comprising that spelling vocabulary deviate substantially from the alphabetic principle in their letter representations.
3. Nearly three-fourths of the vowel phonemes do not represent significant spelling problems, since they have a consistent letter representation from about 57 percent to about 99 percent of the times they occur.
4. About 82 percent of the consonant clusters have only one spelling.
5. Single-consonant phonemes are represented by consistent spellings about nine-tenths of the time they occur.

The results of this study indicated that our written code is not so inconsistent that analysis of phoneme–grapheme correspondences cannot provide the basis for teaching spelling. In short, spelling curriculum specialists had overlooked the most important feature of our written language — that it is alphabetically based — and had failed to recognize the importance of developing the sound-to-letter concept.

New spelling programs were prepared whose aim was to help the child develop spelling power, not by memorizing "X" number of words a week, but by systematically applying the alphabetic principle in the study of the phoneme–grapheme correspondences which were illustrated in the words selected for the week. In these new programs, the correspondences were usually presented in the following order:

1. The most predictably spelled consonant sounds in the language (in order of increasing difficulty)

2. The "short" vowel sounds and the various letters used to represent them
3. The "long" vowel sounds and their major graphic representations

Rules for orthographic behavior were not memorized, but observed. Word groups were examined for patterns of behavior; once the pupil had learned the phoneme–grapheme pattern in a few words, he could spell other words that contained the same pattern.

This approach to the teaching of spelling appeared to be the answer to the pervasive question of how we can teach children to spell. But critics continued to call attention to lack of consistency in the written language and challenged the research findings of the Hanna–Moore study. They asked, "How can we accept findings based on such a small sample as 3,000 words? If the research had encompassed a corpus of 8,000 words, isn't it likely that the results would have been very different?" In short, the critics were inclined to believe that the deeper one delved into the language (i.e. the larger the vocabulary examined and the more complex the words), the *less* consistency would be revealed.

Project 1991

These critics reinforced uneasy doubts already disturbing the complacency of the Hanna–Moore team. If one *were* to analyze the phoneme–grapheme correspondences of 8,000 words, they wondered, what would the findings be? To analyze such a large number of words by hand was impractical. Fortunately, computer technology was available and a massive attack on the problem became possible.

With the financial help of the U.S. Government, a research project — known as Project 1991 — was undertaken on a vocabulary not of 8,000 words, but of 17,000-plus words. The results of this project confirmed the earlier research findings and demonstrated that the deeper one goes into the language, the *greater* the consistency of phoneme–grapheme correspondence. Thus, it became apparent that an effective spelling program could be based on the alphabetic principle that underlies our writing system, and that such a program ought to begin with a study of sounds in words and the letters that represent those sounds.

An assumption fundamental to any such program is that the pupils' analysis of the sound–letter relationships must be based on the phonological (sound), morphological (word-form), and contextual (syntax-meaning) aspects of language. A further important feature is the exposure to data that will help pupils grasp the historical evolution of the American-English language — its beginnings in the Proto-Germanic tongues, its development, and its emergence in America in the 17th century — so that they can take this into account at appropriate times. A knowledge of the evolution of the American-English writing system, in particular, can be of great assistance to pupils who puzzle over such apparent anomalies as *igh* for /ī/, *ph* for /f/, *mb* for final /m/, or *ou* for a whole series of sounds.

Chapter Seven contains a detailed report on USOE Project 1991 and its meaning for a modern philosophy of spelling instruction.

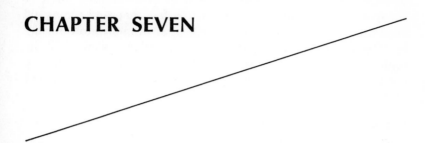

CHAPTER SEVEN

The Alphabetic Base
of Spelling

The preceding chapters have traced the origin and development of writing systems, with particular attention to American-English orthography. We have seen that our writing system is based upon the alphabetic principle that each phoneme should be represented in writing by a unique graphic symbol. We have seen, too, that our orthography departs from this principle for a variety of linguistic and historical reasons.

The result of these departures from the alphabetic principle is an orthography whose efficiency is lessened and whose mastery is made more difficult. However, the extent of these departures was originally overestimated, with the result that spelling was taught in certain traditional ways that were described in Chapter Six. But investigations such as the Hanna–Moore research provided a different picture of the nature of our orthography and suggested important, even basic, changes in the way spelling should be taught.

Project 1991

As noted in Chapter Six, what was needed at that point was a *substantial* study of the alphabetic base of American-English orthography, one whose results could be generalized to most of the words of our language, not just to a few thousand commonly used words. Therefore, in order to determine implications for the teaching of spelling, the authors and their colleagues analyzed the sound–letter relationships of over 17,000 words (a core vocabulary containing most of the words used by educated speakers and writers).

Features of American-English orthography

Before describing this study — which was known as Project 1991 and was conducted at Stanford University — we should first review some of the features of American-English spelling that were considered in carrying out the research. As has been repeatedly pointed out, few of our speech sounds have single spellings representing them in all words of the language. This is, of course, precisely the problem that complicates the mastery of our orthography.

An American-English writer — as opposed to a writer whose language has a highly consistent alphabetic orthography — is required to play odds, to assess the *probability* that a given phoneme is spelled a particular way in the word he proposes to write. Helped by such additional cues as his visual or neuro-muscular memory of the word, or of other words of similar pattern, he usually does achieve a functional mastery of the orthography, although some parts of words present special problems. In short, an ability to spell correctly in our language is largely dependent on the person's knowledge of how closely a given phoneme *approximates* the alphabetic principle of a unique graphic symbol for each phoneme.

Further discussion of sound-letter relationships also must take into account the factors of position and stress. Phonemes are not randomly strung together to form syllables and words. Most have favored positions; and a few, such as /ng/, are not used in certain positions at all. Moreover, the stress patterns of American-English speech sometimes affect the pronunciation of phonemes while the graphemic symbol remains unchanged — and sometimes the reverse occurs. Therefore, in order to determine the productive patterns of American-English spelling, at least three factors must be considered:

1. How phonemes are spelled when position and stress have no effect on them, i.e. when they strictly adhere to the alphabetic principle. For example, the consonant /p/ is almost always spelled *p* (cf. *pit, spot, top*) — regardless of where it occurs in a word and how it is stressed.

2. How the position of a phoneme in a syllable or word affects its spelling. For example, the /f/ sound is normally spelled *f* at the beginning of a syllable or word (*farm*), spelled *ph* when it is the second element in a consonant cluster (*sphere*), and spelled *ff* when it terminates a word (*off*). Moreover, *gh*, another spelling of /f/, represents this phoneme only at the end of syllables and words, as in *cough, rough*, and *laugh' ter*.

3. How syllable or word stress affects phoneme–grapheme correspondences. As noted above, stress may affect the pronunciation but not the spelling. For example, the second vowel sound of *civ' il* occurs in an unaccented syllable and has a pronunciation much like the vowel sound in *rug*, a vowel sound called *schwa* (/ə/). When *civ' il* is changed to *ci vil' ian*, the previously unaccented syllable becomes stressed and the /ə/ changes to /i/, but the *spelling* of the two vowel sounds remains the same. In addition, stress may change the spelling but not the sound, as is seen in the spelling of final /k/ in *at'tic* and *at tack'*.

Phase I: an analysis of phoneme–grapheme relationships

With these three factors in mind, the Stanford researchers employed computer technology to analyze the sound–letter relationships in the 17,000-plus words, with the intention of clarifying the alphabetic nature of American-English spelling. What, then, were some of their major findings?

Simple phoneme–grapheme correspondences

In terms of the first factor, simple phoneme–grapheme correspondences, it was found that the great majority of consonants had single spellings which were used 80 percent or more of the time in the 17,000-plus words investigated. On the other hand, only a handful of vowel sounds had single spellings which

Table 7–1

Samples of Highly Productive Simple
Phoneme–Grapheme Correspondences

Phoneme	No. of Occurrences in 17,000+ Words	Most Common Spelling	No. of Occurrences in 17,000+ Words	% of Use of This Spelling	Examples	
*Consonants**						
/b/	2303	*b*	2239	97.2	*b*ig	ta*b*
/d/	3691	*d*	3611	97.8	*d*ig	ma*d*
/l/	5389	*l*	4894	90.8	*l*ake	he*l*p
/m/	3501	*m*	3302	94.3	*m*an	ha*m*
/n/	7656	*n*	7452	97.3	*n*ow	ca*n*
/p/	3449	*p*	3296	95.6	*p*ill	sto*p*
/r/	9390	*r*	9119	97.1	*r*un	ca*r*
/t/	7793	*t*	7528	96.6	*t*in	po*t*
Vowels						
/a/	4340	*a*	4192	96.6	*a*t	c*a*n
/e/	3646	*e*	3316	90.9	*e*bb	p*e*n
/o/	1662	*o*	1558	93.7	*o*n	t*o*p
/u/	1410	*u*	1212	85.9	*u*s	c*u*p

* Other productive phoneme–grapheme correspondences noticed at this level of analysis included /g/ spelled *g* as in *go*, /h/ spelled *h* as in *him*, /th/ spelled *th* as in *thin*, /t͟h/ spelled *th* as in *then*, /v/ spelled *v* as in *vat*, and /w/ spelled *w* as in *win*.

occurred with such high frequency. Table 7–1 presents a sample of the phonemes which were represented most consistently by one specific grapheme, and examples of words in which they occur.

It can be seen from this table that a person is likely to be able to spell many consonant phonemes and a small number of vowel phonemes (the so-called "short" vowels) correctly if he is aware of the most commonly used graphemic representation of these phonemes. Obviously, however, words are made up of many other phonemes. Are all of the remaining phoneme–grapheme correspondences completely inconsistent with the alphabetic nature of the orthography, or can useful sound–letter patterns be detected?

Positional effects on spelling

In order to resolve this issue, the researchers analyzed the 17,000-plus words in terms of the second factor listed on page 81: the effect of the position of a phoneme in a syllable or word on the spelling of the phoneme. Table 7–2 presents some phonemes, their most common spelling in a specific position, the percentage of times that they were represented by that spelling in that position, and some examples.

The table clearly shows that many phonemes — particularly vowels — have quite predictable spellings in certain positions. For example, although /ā/ is spelled *a* only 45 percent of the time in the 17,000-plus words, it is spelled *a* 81 percent of the time when it ends a syllable that does not end a word. In summary, we can say that the position of phonemes in syllables and words distinctly influences the spelling of many of the phonemes.

The effects of stress on spelling

The results of Project 1991 were not as clear-cut regarding the effect of stress on the spelling of phonemes as the effect of position. However, the factor of stress should not be dismissed as irrelevant, since the form of a word is integrally related to its *total* phonetic characteristics — including its stress pattern. Linguists refer to the study of this relationship as *morphophonemics*. Table 7–3 presents some useful insights about certain phoneme–grapheme correspondences that emerge when stress is taken into account.

The Stanford study we have been summarizing pointed up the basically alphabetic nature of American-English spelling. It showed that, contrary to traditional viewpoints, the orthography is far from erratic. It is based upon relationships between phonemes and graphemes — relationships that are sometimes complex in nature but which, when clarified, demonstrate that American-English orthography, like that of other languages, is largely systematic.

Phase II: a computer programmed to spell

To find out whether these observed phoneme–grapheme relationships could be useful in spelling words, the Stanford group

Table 7-2

Samples of the Effect of Position on Phoneme–Grapheme Correspondences

Phoneme	No. of Occurrences in 17,000+ Words	Position in Syllable and Most Common Spelling	No. of Occurrences of Spelling in That Position	No. of Occurrences of Phoneme in That Position	% of Use of This Spelling	Examples
/ā/	2248	In final position, *a*	860	1062	81.00	f*a* vor
/ē/	2538	In final position, *e*	1740	1921	90.6	l*e* gal
/i/	7815	In medial position, *i*	2772	3346	82.6	b*i*g
/ō/	2587	In final position, *o*	1629	1771	92.00	n*o* tice
/yü/	1188	In final position, *u*	770	870	88.5	c*u* bic
/f/	2019	In initial position, *f*	1381	1630	84.7	*f*an
/k/	4712	In initial position, *c*	2287	2607	87.7	*c*oin
/ng/	615	In medial position, *n*	129	134	96.27	si*n*k
/s/	6326	In medial position, *s*	373	385	96.9	be*s*t

Table 7–3

Samples of the Effect of Stress on
Phoneme–Grapheme Correspondences

Phoneme	Most Common Spelling and % in 17,000+ Words	Conditions for Predicting That Spelling	Example
/ch/	*ch* (97%)	In initial position of primary-stressed syllables	*char'* coal
/j/	*g* (82%)	In initial position of unstressed syllables	co' *g*ent
/sh/	*ti* (84%)	In initial position of unstressed syllables	frac' *ti*on
/y/	*y* (98%)	In initial position of primary-stressed syllables	*y*es' ter day
/y/	*i* (86%)	In initial position of unstressed syllables	on' *i*on

undertook a second investigation in which a computer was programmed to spell the 17,000-plus words by using the orthographic
insights gained from the first phase of the study. Much like a
person who can distinguish American-English phonemes, who
knows the various ways in which these phonemes can be spelled,
and who knows the productive principles that determine how
these phonemes are usually spelled in particular situations, the
computer was to attempt to spell the 17,000-plus words on the
basis of the previously demonstrated sound–letter relationships,
including the factors of position and stress. Table 7–4 lists some
of the relationships that were highly productive in terms of helping the computer spell correctly. Table 7–5 provides examples of
phoneme–grapheme correspondence factors that did not work
as well as might have been expected.

It should be kept in mind, of course, that the spelling principles
used in Phase II of the Stanford project were humanly derived:
the *researchers* selected those sound–letter relationships that appeared to predict most reliably the spellings of the respective
phonemes. Therefore, it is possible that some errors of judgment
were made in the selection of principles, while some principles

Table 7-4

Selected Sample Cases in Which the Algorithm Was Found Highly Productive

Phoneme	Spelled	Condition in Which Phoneme Occurred	Example	No. of Times Phoneme Occurred Under Stated Condition	No. of Times Spelled Correctly	% of Predictability
		Consonants				
/b/	*b*	All other cases[a]	*boy*	2283	2237	98.00
/ch/	*t*	In initial position of unaccented syllable and followed by /ə/	na*'* ture	124	124	100.00
	ch	All other cases	*chart*	284	278	97.9
/d/	*d*	All other cases	*dog*	3681	3620	93.3
/f/	*f*	All other cases	*fish*	1959	1576	80.4
/g/	*g*	All other cases	*go*	1283	1180	92.0
/h/	*h*	All cases[b]	*here*	778	762	97.9
/hw/	*wh*	All cases	*what*	89	89	100.00

Phoneme	Grapheme	Condition	Example			%
/k/	c	All other cases	cow	3881	3342	86.1
/ks/	x	All other cases	mix	233	233	100.00
/kw/	qu	All cases	*queen*	196	191	97.4
/l/	l	All other cases	lamp	5242	4858	92.7
/l/	le	All cases	ta′ble	662	631	95.3
/m/	m	All cases	man	3503	3304	94.3
/′m/	m	All cases	chasm	97	97	100.00
/n/	n	All cases	new	7662	7458	97.3
/ng/	n	In medial position	sink	131	129	98.5
	ng	In word-final position	sing	319	317	99.4
/p/	p	All other cases	push	3443	3299	95.8
/r/	r	All cases	run	9394	9123	97.1
/s/	s	All other cases	say	5354	4337	81.00
/sh/	ti	Initial position of unaccented syllables	fic′tion	851	729	85.7
/sh/	sh	All other cases	ship	448	365	81.5

a "All other cases" indicates that other "rules" were included for spelling the phoneme in question, in addition to the rule shown.

b "All cases" indicates that the "rule" was the only one included in the algorithm for spelling the phoneme in question.

Table 7-4 — Continued

Selected Sample Cases in Which the Algorithm Was Found Highly Productive

Phoneme	Spelled	Condition in Which Phoneme Occurred	Example	No. of Times Phoneme Occurred Under Stated Condition	No. of Times Spelled Correctly	% of Predictability
		Consonants — continued				
/t/	*t*	All other cases	*t*oe	7764	5528	97.0
/th/	*th*	All cases	*th*ing	411	411	100.00
/ŧĥ/	*th*	All cases	*th*is	149	149	100.00
/v/	*ve*	In word-final position	ha*ve*	238	238	100.00
/v/	*v*	All other cases	*v*et	1126	1126	100.00
/w/	*w*	All other cases	*w*et	573	563	98.3
/y/	*i*	In unaccented syllables	jun′ *i*or	73	63	86.3
/zh/	*si*	In all cases when followed by /ə/	fu′ *si*on	50	49	98.00

88

Vowels

/ā/	a	In syllable-final, but not word-final, position	pla′ cate	930	860	92.5
/a/	a	All cases	cat	4340	4328	99.7
/ä/	a	All cases	arm	580	536	92.4
/ē/	e	In syllable-final, but not word-final, position	le′ gal	1832	1715	96.6
/e/	e	In initial position	etch	760	752	98.9
/e/	e	In medial position	bet	2789	2565	92.0
/e(r)/	e	All other cases	but′ ter	2132	1667	78.2
/ī/	i—e	In medial position when next phoneme is word-final	dime	439	398	90.7
/i/	i	All other cases	tip	5845	5506	94.2
/ō/	o	All other cases	told	1710	1615	94.4
/oi/	oy	In word-final position	toy	22	22	100.00
/ou/	ou	In initial position	out	72	70	97.2
/ou/	ow	All other cases	now	80	72	90.0

Table 7-4 — Continued

Selected Sample Cases in Which the Algorithm Was Found Highly Productive

Phoneme	Spelled	Condition in Which Phoneme Occurred	Example	No. of Times Phoneme Occurred Under Stated Condition	No. of Times Spelled Correctly	% of Predictability
		Vowels — continued				
/ò/	*o*	In all cases	b*o*ss	127	123	96.8
/ò (r)/	*o*	In medial position and followed by /r/	c*o*rn	287	280	97.6
/o/	*o*	All other cases	t*o*p	1588	1573	99.1
/u̇/	*u*	All other cases	p*u*ll	182	149	81.9
/yü/	*u*	In syllable-final, but not word-final, position	c*u′* pid	828	777	93.8
	u—e	In medial position	c*u*be	277	225	81.2
/u/	*u*	All other cases	c*u*p	1267	1161	91.6

Table 7-5

Selected Sample Cases in Which the Algorithm Did Not Work as Well as Expected

Phoneme	Spelled	Condition in Which Phoneme Occurred	Example	No. of Times Phoneme Occurred Under Stated Condition	No. of Times Spelled Correctly	% of Predictability
		Consonants				
/j/	*g*	In initial position	gem	456	336	73.7
/k/	*k*	When preceded by /ng/	drink	152	97	63.8
/s/	*c*	In final position of a stressed word-final syllable	lace	129	58	45.0
/z/	*z*	In final position, preceded by /ī/	or′ gan ize	148	97	65.5
/s/	*s*	In all other cases[a]	clos′ et	752	571	75.9
/zh/	*s*	In all other cases	cas′ u al	52	34	65.4

[a] "In all other cases" indicates that other "rules" were included for spelling the phoneme in question, in addition to the rule shown.

91

Table 7-5 — Continued

Selected Sample Cases in Which the Algorithm Did Not Work as Well as Expected

Phoneme	Spelled	Condition in Which Phoneme Occurred	Example	No. of Times Phoneme Occurred Under Stated Condition	No. of Times Spelled Correctly	% of Predictability
		Vowels				
/ā(r)/	*a*	In medial position	ca n*ar*′y	104	65	62.5
/ē/	*ea*	In medial position	r*ea*d	380	167	43.9
	e	In final position of a stressed, non-word-final syllable	h*e*′ro	77	55	71.4
/ē(r)/	*ea*	In medial position in a word-final syllable	f*ear*	49	14	28.6
/ī/	*igh*	In medial position, followed by /t/	f*igh*t	146	78	53.4

Vowels — continued

/ō/	o—e	In medial position of a word-final syllable	dome	150	226	66.4
/o/	o	In medial position of a non-word-final syllable	gol' den	176	271	64.9
/ò/	au	In final position of a non-word-final syllable	fau' cet	79	124	63.7
/ü/	oo	In medial position, all other cases	food	158	218	72.5

were inadvertently overlooked — e.g. the fact that /ou/ is normally spelled *ou* in the medial position of syllables. It should also be understood that the total set of "rules," which is called the *algorithm,* included only phonological information. It did not encompass, as will be seen, important morphological and contextual information needed for a comprehensive mastery of American-English orthography.

But despite these drawbacks, the computer spelled almost 50 percent (49.8%) of the 17,000-plus words correctly — a total of 8,483 words. To be sure, 50 percent accuracy in spelling words is not sufficient for written communication. But what this finding does point to is the generalization that nearly half the words in ordinary usage can be correctly spelled solely on the basis of a functional understanding of the relationships between spoken sound and written symbol. Undoubtedly, with refinement of the algorithm, a second run through the computer would have resulted in an even greater percentage of correctly spelled words. (It should be pointed out, however, that the power of the algorithm lies in its *cumulative ability* to relate phonemes to orthography; the sum of the individual sound–letter principles is considerably more important than are the individual principles viewed unrelated to each other.)

The analysis of computer errors

Equally revealing was the finding that the computer misspelled an additional 37 percent of the words (6,195 words) with but one error, 11.4 percent (1,941 words) with two errors, and only 2.3 percent (390 words) with three errors or more. And when the *kinds* of errors made were examined, some most interesting facts about our writing system emerged. Let us see what the most common causes of misspelling were for the "one-error" words.

The first type of computer error was in spelling compound words; for example, *playground* was misspelled as *plaground.* In this instance, the computer, not yet equipped with a knowledge of compounding, was unable to tell that the two independent words *play* and *ground* were combined to form a single word with a single unit of meaning, and treated *playground* as two *syllables.* In doing so, it followed the sound-to-letter principle that /ā/ at the end of syllables not ending words (as in *va′ cate, na' tion, ba' by*) is usually spelled *a*. Had the computer applied the principle that /ā/ at the end of *words* (as in *day, say, play*) is generally spelled *ay*, this particular misspelling and similar errors in other compound words would not have occurred. In effect, the computer — unprogrammed for such refinements — was unable to detect that compound words are comprised of shorter words, and therefore treated the shorter words as syllables.

A second type of error was made because the researchers did not program the computer to double the spellings of certain phonemes. The word *address*, misspelled by the computer as *adress*, is a good illustration. *Address* is ultimately of Latin origin and is composed of a prefix representing Latin *ad-* and a root representing Latin *directum*. Although when *address* occurs in speech, the final /d/ of *ad-* and the first /d/ of *-dress* are combined so that only one /d/ is pronounced, the spelling of each /d/ remains in the written word. The combining of sounds is quite common in English words that are constructed by combining roots and affixes; but since the programmers did not supply the computer with the "word building" rules of our language, the computer identified only one /d/ in *address* and spelled it accordingly.

Numerous other instances of how a knowledge of *morphology* (how words are formed in a language) would have enabled the computer to spell many of the one-error words correctly were observed in this early phase of the Stanford study. These observations underscored the fact that an orthography represents *language*, and therefore reflects many principles other than phonological that are inherent in the structure of the spoken code.

Another important finding was that many of the computer's misspellings occurred in borrowed words whose original spellings had been kept more or less intact. Although the major "lender" languages — French, Spanish, Italian, Greek, and Latin — possess alphabetically based orthographies, they sometimes use graphemes that differ from ours for their phonemes. For example, the computer misspelled *mosquito* as *mousketo*, failing to take into account the fact that in Spanish, /k/ is often spelled *qu* and /ē/ is often spelled *i*.[1]

---

[1] The unusual spelling *ou* for the /ə/ of *mosquito* resulted because the computer had been programmed to spell /ə/ with *ou* when it was followed by /s/.

Although the bulk of the misspelled words could be accounted for on the basis of the word-building and word-borrowing proclivities of our language, there remained a residue of misspelled words that fell into two categories: 1) a comparatively small number of words in which certain graphemic representations of phonemes are so unpredictable that a knowledge of phonology and morphology is of little help, e.g. *one, acre, iron, forecastle, colonel, victuals, boatswain,* and *of;* and 2) certain words — called *homophones or homonyms* — whose similar pronunciation but different spelling creates special problems, e.g. *bare* and *bear, peer* and *pier,* and *aisle, isle,* and *I'll.* Sound-to-letter principles can be used to spell these words, of course, but the choice of principles depends upon the meaning of the word being used — which the computer was not programmed to know.

The Phase II investigation indicated, then, that about half of the words in ordinary speech can be spelled correctly by the application of principles based on the alphabetic nature of the American-English orthography. And most of the remaining words can be spelled correctly if one couples a knowledge of sound–letter correspondences with a knowledge of the characteristic word-building and word-borrowing patterns of our language. Later research which builds morphological and contextual clues into the computer program will no doubt improve the computer's score.

Implications for spelling programs

The two-phased study we have just described represents the increasing interest of curriculum makers in taking into consideration the *nature* of the subject matter to be taught. In this particular case, linguistic insights into the nature of our orthography provided a fresh point of view regarding how spelling might be taught and, most important, identified *what* should be taught. In Part Two of this book, one modern approach to the teaching of spelling will be explained in detail — an approach that makes use of linguistic information about our written code and of our increasing understanding of the learner and the processes of teaching and learning. But for now, let us recapitulate the major points about American-English orthography which early phases of the Stanford study demonstrated.

The first important fact is that the American-English orthography is an alphabetically based orthography, i.e. it employs graphic symbols to represent the speech sounds, the phonemes, of language. And although our orthography does not perfectly conform to the alphabetic principle that one and only one graphic symbol shall represent each phoneme, there is a more consistent relationship between sounds and letter representations than has traditionally been thought. This consistency is demonstrated by the fact that about half of all the words we would normally use in writing were spelled correctly by a computer that was programmed (somewhat imperfectly) with certain sound–letter principles of our writing system. Such principles, along with further refinements, could become a part of the pupil's spelling repertoire and be applied in spelling words he could pronounce but whose spellings may be unfamiliar. Reinforced by good habits of proofreading, his functional awareness of the alphabetic nature of our writing system could free him from rote memorization of each word.

A second important fact that emerged from the Stanford study is that just as there is pattern and system in the relationships between phonemes and their graphemic representations, there is also pattern and system in the ways words have been created, and continue to be created, in our language. This morphological factor helps to account for many of the seemingly demonic spellings that occur in written American English. A knowledge of morphology contributes importantly to the pupil's development of a power to spell, as well as being inherently interesting.

A third important fact demonstrated by the study is that the number of so-called "spelling demons" scattered throughout our writing system is relatively small (about 3 percent of the core vocabulary fell into this category). Furthermore, such mavericks cause spelling difficulties only because certain *parts* of them depart radically from the basic alphabetic principle. Thus, although the word *women* — for example — may be called a spelling demon, the truly demonic part lies only in the unique spelling of /i/ in the first syllable. The other four phonemes are spelled just as one would expect, so that only one-fifth of this word presents a problem for the speller. In sum, certain words do contain rare, even unique, spellings of phonemes, and such words need to be mastered by whatever means available to the pupil. But these few words hardly constitute a basis for assuming that the entire language is orthographically chaotic, and that most words are spelling problems.

A rational and comprehensive spelling program should begin with the three facts just listed and lead the pupil toward discovering and applying useful generalizations regarding our writing system. Such a spelling program is the central concern of the second part of this book. But before turning to the programming of spelling instruction, we must examine how spelling ability is probably acquired. This topic is treated in Chapter Eight.

CHAPTER EIGHT

A Psychology
of Spelling

An effective spelling program is built upon three important factors: 1) *the subject matter of spelling,* the American-English orthography; 2) *the nature of the learner,* how children learn to spell; and 3) *instructional strategies,* the programming and methods of spelling instruction. The preceding chapters have been concerned with the first of these factors. In this chapter we turn our attention to some contemporary views of the nature of the learner, what he brings to the spelling situation, and how he learns to spell.

The acquisition of language is a truly remarkable and somewhat mysterious event. From birth onward, the child actively pursues the task of learning to speak. If he is immersed in a linguistic environment, the child absorbs from that environment the structure and pattern of language. He learns intuitively that language is composed of sounds and of obligatory rules for combining these sounds into words, which in turn can be combined into meaningful utterances by following other obligatory rules. Thus, mastering a language involves learning what a language *is* — its structural elements — and how its elements in combination constitute oral communication.

Aided by the insights of linguistic scholars, we are now aware

99

that our writing system is *also* structured and patterned, and that an understanding of the orthography develops from an understanding of the structure and pattern of language. Therefore, to the degree that the writing system reflects the oral code, the teaching of spelling should be based upon the study of language itself.

But *how* do we learn to speak? Or, for that matter, how do we *learn?* There are, of course, no simple answers to these important questions. Theories of learning are, after all, man-made constructions, and no single theory has yet been proved to provide an inclusive description of the learning behaviors of complex human beings. And yet, although a detailed examination of these theories is beyond the scope of a book concerned with spelling, the learner and his behavior cannot be overlooked if spelling instruction is to be sequenced for greatest effectiveness. We should bear in mind that learning to spell is an *intellectual* activity and therefore involves the processes that underlie other intellectual pursuits.

Learning as information processing

Many theories have been constructed which attempt to explain how we learn. Each has merits as well as limitations, and each has affected school instruction in some fashion. One particularly convenient way of describing intellectual activity is to view it as a kind of *information processing,* a process that is roughly analogous to the way in which modern electronic computers function.

A computer is a complex problem-solving instrument. When some problem needs resolution, the computer is provided with information necessary to resolve the problem and a *program* is prepared. The program is a plan of action that has been worked out to regulate precisely how the computer will process information in its search for a solution to the problem. Working with awesome speed, the computer retrieves from its "memory" the items of information it has been given and uses this information to solve the problem, following the directions set forth by the program. Finally, the computer transmits its answer to its human users via some medium — usually a "printout," i.e. a written message.

Although obviously more complicated, human problem-solving

may follow somewhat the same pattern in less mechanistic fashion. It is true that each individual learns from his experiences at different rates of development and in different ways. But most human behavior, and certainly all intellectual behavior, originates in the brain, and the brain could be regarded as man's computer. It is the repository of man's experiences in relation to his environment, experiences which are stored as sensory impressions. These impressions arrive in the brain via our senses of vision, hearing, haptics (touch and kinesthetics), taste, and smell, and they are combined to produce the concepts we have of the world about us.

To clarify this process, let us imagine how a young child may develop the simple concept of "apple." Imagine a youngster's first encounter with this fruit. His eyes scan the apple, and some of its physical characteristics — its color, shape, and size — are transmitted to his brain. The child touches and handles the apple, and by means of his tactile and kinesthetic senses, its texture, hardness, weight, and shape are *also* transmitted to his brain. Perhaps his mother then says to him, "That's an apple." Again, more sensory information is provided him, in this case a set of patterned phonemes which form the name of the object he sees and feels, and which label that object as something different from all other objects he knows.

With time, and with recurring encounters with apples, he develops a rather sophisticated concept of "apple," a concept that enables him to distinguish apples from other kinds of fruit and to recognize different kinds of apples. Through his ability to receive sense impressions from the environment and to combine these impressions into categories of experience, he has built a "program" for dealing with one aspect of the world around him.

Although this illustration obviously obscures the complexity of the process by which concepts are formed, it does serve to underscore some important points which have possible consequences for teaching generally and for the teaching of spelling in particular.

First, learning is a multisensory–multimotor process. The sensory impressions resulting from an individual's encounter with his environment are transmitted to the brain, and repose there as increments for the development of concepts. The individual's motor responses to these inputs become an integral part of his concept development.

Second, with recurring experience and responses, the original sensory information and motor behavior are reinforced, fleshed out, and reshaped. There emerges an awareness that the objects and events of the world about us fall into recognizable categories; these categories of information we may call *concepts.*

Third, groups of concepts become associated and form a kind of "cognitive map," a "structure" reflecting our awareness that there is relatedness among some concepts. For example, the mathematical concepts of "set" and "number" provide a rudimentary mathematical structure that enables us to perform simple mathematical operations.

Fourth, ever broader and more complex concepts emerge as new information is added to present knowledge. In other words, our concepts of the world about us develop *hierarchically*, from the simple to the complex.

Fifth, the information we have stored away is made retrievable (and therefore functional) by the development of "programs," or plans of action for approaching the solution of problems.

What has been described is, of course, largely hypothetical, and may at first glance scarcely seem to be related to the teaching of spelling. The foregoing points do, however, have important consequences for spelling, and it is to these that we now turn.

How we learn to spell: sensorimotor mechanisms

As we have seen, American-English orthography is based upon the alphabetic principle — the principle that speech sounds (phonemes) have graphic counterparts in writing. In contrast to orthographies that employ graphic symbols to represent larger units of language, such as syllables or morphemes, an alphabetically based orthography entails the encoding of *phonemes* into graphemes, a task that is compounded in American English because of its surfeit of graphemic options. And since the complexities of our written code obscure this basic alphabetical system, it is extremely important that pupils be helped to understand the system before they examine more complex features of the orthography. But how is this understanding — and a sophisticated mastery of spelling — developed?

Like human learning in general, spelling ability is acquired through the senses. In other words, learning to spell is a multi-sensory–multimotor process involving speech, audition, vision, and haptics. To clarify this point, let us examine the role that each of these senses plays in the act of spelling, bearing in mind, of course, that different learners will employ them in varying degrees, in varying ways, and in different combinations.

Speech and audition

After hearing a language over a period of time, the child develops an ability to speak it. He acquires a functional but largely intuitive knowledge of its structural properties — its sounds, its grammar, its lexicon. He learns that certain phonemes are used in constructing American-English words, even though he may be unable to indicate which specific phonemes are contained in the words he speaks or hears. In short, he is able to speak when he can select appropriate phonemes for the construction of words and can supply the motor responses necessary for pronunciation.

The importance of audition and speech cannot be lightly dismissed when the spelling processes are considered. It is true, of course, that one can learn to spell without being able to hear or speak — perhaps by gaining a visual memory of the word as a whole and its separate graphemes, and transcribing this visual image into writing. But if a person relies solely on visual processes, he fails to capitalize on the premise on which American-English spelling is based: that *in an alphabetic orthography, the act of spelling is basically one of encoding the phonemes of speech into the graphemes of the writing system.*

Vision

Encoding speech into writing necessitates the formation of graphic symbols that can be read by the writer and by others. And when graphemes are introduced, in addition to hearing and speaking, a third sensory mechanism, vision, is called into play.

Visual memory of the spellings of phonemes and of whole words is an important ingredient in learning to spell, an ingredient that reinforces the aural–oral processes. Having spelled a word through his knowledge of phoneme–grapheme correspondences, an individual can check the success of his encoding effort by comparing it with a visual recollection of the word as he has seen it in writing elsewhere or by checking it against a correctly spelled model, as in a dictionary. Since many of the words that we use in writing are introduced to us through the medium of print, we are likely to have abundant visual memories to help us encode phonemes into their written counterparts. And for some learners, the visual process is the primary means by which spelling is mastered.

Haptics

The fourth sensorimotor mechanism involved in learning to spell is that of touch and kinesthetics, i.e. haptics. In writing a word, we call into play, in addition to aural–oral and visual cues, the sense of touch and the motor mechanisms (the muscles of the hand and arm that guide the act of writing). Haptical memory is fundamental to the mastery of activities such as typing and the reading of Braille. And although spelling ability normally is not so expressly dependent upon haptical experiences, sensorimotor impressions created by the writing of graphemes are relayed to our brain as a third kind of memory, a haptical record that — *in combination* with oral and auditory and visual recollections of words — aids in the multisensory–multimotor act of spelling.

What has been described here may be characterized as the development of a "cognitive map" of spelling, a map that in its construction involves the use of sense impressions stored in the brain: memories of sounds, visual forms, and the "feel" of words as they are written. In combination with the motor activities of speaking and writing, these multisensory–multimotor experiences form for most learners the basis of the act of spelling, although their relative importance varies with the individual.

How we learn to spell: concept acquisition

But spelling involves more than sensory memories and motor responses. The ability to spell is also related to the development of concepts about the orthography — i.e. how the writing system reflects, or fails to reflect, speech — so that phoneme–grapheme relationships can be grasped. The acquisition of these concepts can come about primarily in two major ways: deductively or inductively. We shall examine each of these two methods in turn.

The deductive method

To acquire a concept deductively is first to be told the concept and then to seek verifying examples of it. For example, a child might be told that in American English the phonemes /b/, /d/, and /g/ are almost always spelled *b*, *d*, and *g*, respectively. Then, having these concepts available, he would attempt to verify them by searching for words in which such spellings actually occurred.

Much formal learning is, of course, transmitted to pupils in this way in our schools. The deductive approach is presumed to expedite the learning process since the pupil does not have to devise the concept for himself; he needs only to verify it. And in many instances, this is indeed the case. There are, however, dangers involved in excessive reliance upon this mode of learning. One such danger is that a child's ability to verbalize a concept does not necessarily mean that he can apply the concept in practical settings. For example, a pupil who can recite the traditional spelling rule, "*I* before *e*, except after *c*," is not necessarily able to spell *believe* and *receive* correctly.

A second possible danger stemming from undue reliance on the deductive method is that the teacher may not recognize that many concepts are made up of a series of related simple concepts which must be understood before the larger, more complex concepts can be functionally acquired by the pupil. In short, deductive learning, an important intellectual process in and of itself, is necessary but insufficient. It is a significant component of spelling instruction when placed in perspective with other learning processes.

The inductive method

In inductive learning, the learner himself develops a concept by noticing that certain common features exist in his environment. All concepts are essentially nonverbal in nature; they are experimental categories produced as a result of interaction with one's environment. They are said to be acquired inductively if the individual infers from his experiences that there is a common property about certain objects or events which is useful in helping him to organize his view of the world around him; such inferred properties are concepts. Inductive concept formation, then, is inverse to deductive concept formation in that it begins with the observation of raw data (experiences) and ends with the individual extracting and constructing a concept from these data.

The inductive process is an extremely important method of learning, particularly in the early stages of concept development. Speech itself is learned largely through inductive means. A child learning to speak seldom is told what phonemes to use, how to order these phonemes to form words, and how to order words to form intelligible sentences. Rather the ability to speak intelligibly comes about primarily because the child notes relevant elements of the speech of others and induces, over a period of time, concepts regarding the structure and use of language.

The strength of inductively derived concepts lies in the individual's ability to *use* these concepts in his interactions with his environment, rather than merely to verbalize them. Therefore, although deductive learning has an important place in modern spelling programs, much of an individual's spelling power rests in his ability to induce important spelling concepts and then to apply them.

Inductive approaches to learning have sometimes been called "discovery" approaches. But although the terms used are less important than the recognition that these processes underlie a great amount of learning, the word "discovery" does suffer the limitation of suggesting that concept development is a sudden event. What needs to be emphasized is that concept development is an *ongoing process,* a process whereby the individual discovers order out of seeming chaos *over a period of time,* as he recurrently experiences some event. In American-English orthography, much of this order is in the relationship between the phonemes of speech and the graphemes of writing — a relationship which, although imperfect, does in large part govern our writing system.

It has been said that discovery favors the well-prepared mind; that recognizing that regularities and order *are* discoverable helps prepare the individual to seek out these regularities, to search for the patterns that organize one's concepts. Therefore, a pupil is helped to acquire an orderly view of the orthography via modern spelling programs if his sensory perceptions are initially guided toward the search for productive relationships between phonemes and graphemes. For example, he will be more likely to induce such relationships if he is presented with selected words in which functional phoneme–grapheme relationships occur. Over time, if he is properly guided in his search for discovery of spelling principles, he will arrive at many important orthographic insights which can be made a part of his spelling repertoire.

The world is not random, nor is the orthography. The essence of language is pattern and structure, and this is true also for orthography. But for a person to search out and find regularities and relationships, he must be armed with the expectancy that there *is* something to find. And if he then actively participates in the searching (learning) process, his grasp of the relationships he finds is likely to be both firm and lasting.

Individual differences and spelling

In the preceding discussion of the psychological bases of spelling, we may have seemed to assume that all pupils bring to the spelling situation common experiences and a commonality in the way in which their senses and motor mechanisms contribute to concept development. We are all too well aware, however, that human behavior cannot be so universally described. Individuals differ in many ways, including learning rate and learning style, and these differences can have dramatic influences upon the acquisition of spelling ability. Two such influences on learning which can directly affect spelling ability as we have outlined it here are *sensorimotor* and *environmental*.

Sensorimotor differences

Most of us are endowed with a capacity to utilize all of our senses and motor mechanisms in approximately equal measure in the process of learning. For most of us, the sounds, the sights, and the "feel" of words to be spelled are stored in our brains and integrated to give us a cognitive impression of them. But such is not always the case. For some individuals the ability to discriminate speech sounds suffers such deficits that they are in large part unable to isolate these sounds for the purpose of determining how they are to be spelled. For others the visual or the oral memory of words to be spelled is an elusive thing.

Interestingly, much work in the area of psychology expressly concerned with the functions of the human brain helps us to understand that for various reasons (genetic and physiological) some individuals are deficient in developing or recalling auditory sensory impressions, while others are deficient in developing or recalling visual impressions or in employing the appropriate motor responses in speaking or writing.

Not a great deal is known at present about the causes of sensorimotor deficits nor how these deficits may best be identified, compensated for, or ameliorated in the classroom. For the teacher, we suggest that the most equitable approach is to provide a learning situation in which all of the pertinent sensory and muscular modes are brought into play in the course of spelling instruction. Then each pupil will be able to draw upon those sensorimotor behaviors which are dominantly operant for him. If a pupil has marked handicaps, the wise teacher will refer him to a specialist for diagnosis and treatment.

Environmental differences

The effects of a second negative influence on learning to spell, however, can be rectified. Some sensorimotor deficits stem from the nature of the child's early environment, an environment that may have failed to contribute to the natural development of several or all of the sensory modalities. The importance of early sensorimotor stimulation in the development of intellectual abilities is only now beginning to be understood. It is known, however, that in many home and neighborhood settings the opportunity to develop auditory discrimination skills is limited.

Children who come from such limiting environments do not necessarily suffer physiological deficiencies of a sensorimotor nature as do the individuals described in the preceding section. Rather, they have simply lacked the opportunity to develop the sensorimotor mechanisms that are crucial for spelling. With such children, the problem for the teacher is not so much finding ways to compensate for these deficits as helping the children *eliminate* such deficiencies so that they can bring to the spelling situation a balance of multisensory–multimotor skills, so important in developing a functional cognitive map of the orthography.

What we are saying, in essence, is that the schoolteacher should try to help all pupils develop to their maximum possible level of achievement in speech, audition, vision, and haptics, so that they can build spelling power. And in order to do this, he should be aware of the need to differentiate his instruction according to the types and levels of capability of individual children.

Summary

In this chapter, we have reviewed some modern insights into the learning processes generally and into the spelling act particularly. We have seen that learning begins with experiences in the environment and that the association of these experiences within the central nervous system over a period of time leads to the development of concepts. We have also seen that much learning occurs through inductive processes, whereby recurring sensorimotor experiences are organized into patterned views of the world around us.

The acquisition of spelling ability follows these same principles because spelling ability is a *learned behavior.* Ideally, what is learned is the structure of the writing system and how this system, with its alphabetic base, reflects the spoken language. This learning is accomplished through the multisensory–multimotor mechanisms that are involved in the act of spelling — audition, speech, vision, and haptics — and the utilization of the resulting sensory impressions in developing a cognitive map of the orthography. Much spelling instruction has handicapped pupils by failing to help them use all of their ear, voice, eye, and hand capabilities in developing this map. Mapping the terrain — the structure — of the orthography involves the effective use of *all* our sensorimotor equipment.

It should be reiterated, however, that individuals do differ in rates and styles of learning, as well as in the kinds of experiences they bring to the spelling situation, and that a person who is planning instructional strategies should keep this in mind. In addition, not all aspects of learning to spell are necessarily inductive, as for example the process of mastering words with maverick spellings. Spelling instruction can be effective if it combines modern insight into American-English orthography with knowledge of the learner's individual abilities and needs. Only after these vital sources of information are taken into account can educators confidently establish the content of spelling programs and instructional strategies for presenting that content to learners. These important and practical matters are the substance of Part Two of this text.

PART TWO

Strategies for a
Spelling Program

THE AUTHORS of this volume realize that the material contained herein is not sufficiently complete to be used to construct a detailed spelling program for either a particular level or an entire K–8 spelling curriculum. Rather, it is their intention to suggest basic principles and general strategies.

The apparent emphasis in this volume on a program that is sequential throughout the school years may produce some uneasiness in the minds of imaginative teachers who may prefer to design a strategy suited to the needs of their particular class. The authors acknowledge that a degree of structured learning is evident in their presentation, but defend their position as relevant so long as a spelling program must serve an across-the-board clientele, must be productive for those pupils (the majority) who need to follow a sequentially structured program, and must challenge those pupils who readily grasp a linguistic approach to spelling. Further, the authors recognize that any new approach to a discipline (mathematics, science, language arts) is likely to cause some difficulty. A teacher may not be sufficiently knowledgeable about linguistics to be able to design a program for his own grade or level, let alone for an entire elementary school system. A carefully structured program provides a foundation upon which the creative teacher may build.

As indicated in various chapters of this volume, the spelling skill has not received the kind of research attention necessary to assure scientific validation of any one teaching approach. There is certainly a need for controlled studies that will provide statistical data on the results of various types of programming. For example, we need to establish the relative effectiveness of the inductive and deductive methods (so that we can present an optimum mix of teaching–learning strategies); the end results of systematic instruction in phonological and morphological matters; the degree to which the newer linguistic approach, added to the visual (eye) and haptical (hand-learning) approaches, does help bring about the desired end result of building the power to spell; and the possible effectiveness of reversing the standard procedure of teaching the decoding process before the encoding (careful examination of the results of such a reversal might point up a need to reprogram the language-arts strands of the curriculum in order to introduce encoding of the pupil's aural–oral vocabulary first).

Until such research has been conducted and the results have been evaluated, schools and teachers will select those strategies that seem most reasonable and promising in helping all pupils, at all levels, build the power to spell.

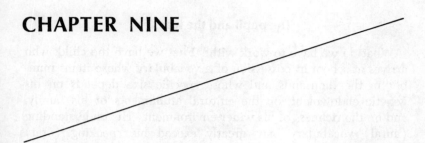

CHAPTER NINE

*Developing a
Spelling Program: A Preview*

The invention of writing and of a convenient system of keeping records on paper has had a greater influence in uplifting the human race than any other intellectual achievement in the career of man.[1]

If this dictum is kept in mind, one approaches the building of a school spelling program with a mixture of awe and of challenge. To develop a spelling program that will satisfy the needs of all the children in a class and yet make allowances for individual differences presents a challenge of major proportions. To meet such a challenge, the authors of this text have attempted to be both general and specific — to recognize that while differences in the capabilities of individual pupils necessitate a degree of flexibility in any program, an effective spelling program must rest on a spirally conceived, carefully planned sequence, and that the individual teacher must bear considerable responsibility for adjusting this basic program to the various levels of maturity present in the individuals in his class.

[1] James H. Breasted, *The Conquest of Civilization* (New York: Harper and Brothers, 1926), pp. 53–54.

113

The pupil and the teacher

What do we have to work with? First we have the child, who arrives at school in possession of a vocabulary whose items number in the thousands and whose specific size depends on his genetic endowment, on the cultural attainments of his family, and on the richness of his wider environment. His understanding (aural) vocabulary may greatly exceed his speaking (oral) vocabulary. But with even a minimal degree of aural–oral capability, he can understand and can be understood at home, in school, and at play.

Then we have the teacher — the person who, out of his own wisdom and training, is able to guide and direct learning in such a way that the pupil is able to develop his language capacities and build his own power to spell. The authors of this book believe that a spelling program should be constructed so that the teacher is a constant participant rather than a mere "examiner," as he often is in the traditional program. To help the child make the most of the great tool of writing, the teacher should use the best programmed spelling materials available and work with the pupil so that the child can learn to spell an ever-increasing number of words.

The child arrives at school, as we said, with an understanding and speaking vocabulary of considerable size — a vocabulary that he has acquired by interacting with his parents, his peers, and others. And he can communicate fairly satisfactorily by means of his ears and voice. But this is not enough. He needs to extend his communication capabilities, and for this he must learn to encode (write) his speech and ideas. Equally important, he must also learn to decode (read) that which he and others have written.

Basic characteristics of an effective spelling program

An effective spelling program, essential if the pupil is to accomplish such communication capability, has seven basic characteristics:

1. The program will be carefully thought out and structured in a logical progression from level 1 (or kindergarten) through level 8.
2. The program will be linguistically based, with the aim of helping the pupil develop a cognitive map of the powerful patterns and principles (phonological, morphological, and contextual) by which we encode language. (See Chapter Seven for a full discussion.)
3. The program will take into account new insights into the importance of the multisensory–multimotor processes: the ear, voice, eye, and hand inputs into the central nervous system and their subsequent retrieval in haptical behavior (handwriting or typewriter-keyboard manipulation). (See Chapter Eight for further discussion.)
4. The program will teach the pupil how to record (encode) his aural–oral vocabulary with alphabetic letters and will encourage him to extend his vocabulary by teaching him how to spell additional useful root words and derivatives.
5. The program will recognize the importance of the dictionary as an aid to spelling mastery.
6. The program will, at appropriate levels, present background information on the language and its evolution. (See Chapters Three and Four for a discussion of this.)
7. The program will be related to other areas of the language-arts curriculum and will seek to coordinate spelling with handwriting and reading.

Planning a K–8 spelling program: an overview

If the above seven characteristics are kept in mind, it can be seen that a first-level to eighth-level (K–8) spelling program should be patterned along the lines suggested below.

1. The teacher begins by training the hearing acuity of the pupil and by pacing his maturing articulatory mechanisms, since these are the means which enable him to hear and say all the words that are necessary for communication in his language community.
2. After his speech skills have been systematically refined

and improved in this way, the pupil is helped to identify
and say phonemes (speech sounds) as they occur in initial, medial, and final position in monosyllabic words,
and later in polysyllabic words.

3. After he has been taught to identify phonemes in position, the pupil next learns how phonemes can be written
or typed (encoded). He is shown what alphabetic letters
are most frequently used to represent certain phonemes
whose spellings are highly predictable (most of the consonant phonemes and several short-vowel phonemes).

4. When he has a rudimentary knowledge of how to encode
his speech into a more permanent written form, the pupil
is led to observe simple but powerful principles that govern the most consistent phoneme–grapheme correspondences. This process takes up most of levels 1 and 2.
(Although the initial emphasis is on such phonological
matters, the visual and haptical aspects of learning are not
to be neglected.)

5. Beginning with level 2, the pupil is led in a spiral fashion
(i.e. by means of developing concepts through recurring
and increasingly sophisticated teaching–learning experiences) to observe and formulate the principles which
govern the less predictably spelled short-vowel phonemes
and the long-vowel phonemes. The pupil also develops
his word-building ability by a) compounding new words
out of known words, e.g. *football* from *foot* + *ball*; and
b) adding prefixes and suffixes to known words, e.g. *re-* +
do + *-ing* = *redoing.*

6. In the upper primary levels, the pupil may be introduced
to contextual (syntactic and meaning) cues that will help
him to spell homonyms. (See Chapter Seven.) He also
continues his study of phonological and morphological
factors related to spelling; and through a systematic spi-
raling program involving these three components — phonological, morphological, and contextual — he develops
a cognitive map that helps him master the spelling of the
great preponderance of words in his aural–oral vocabulary, leaving only a fraction that must be learned by rote.

7. In the middle levels, the pupil learns something of the
history of American-English orthography and also extends

his knowledge of uses of the dictionary to reinforce and extend his cognitive map of our writing system.

The need for review

In a spelling program, each level beyond the first ought to begin with a comprehensive review of the materials covered in each preceding level. This is to ensure that any pupil who enters such a program without prior experience in it — or who has forgotten some of what he has learned — will have exposure to the fundamental principles previously taught. Each teacher should assess his pupils' knowledge and competence and decide how much time should be spent on these review lessons. For some pupils, the review can be completed in a week or so; for other pupils, the review may take considerably longer. And even when new phonological material is later presented, the introduction of complicated phoneme–grapheme correspondences should be accompanied by continuous referral to and review of the more regular correspondences that have been learned previously.

Since most schools in the nation divide the school program into six blocks of six weeks each, most spelling programs are organized to allow for a review every sixth week of material covered in the preceding five weeks. This review lesson gives pupils an opportunity to assess (through written examination) the progress they have made in learning to spell.

In devising such a six weeks' review examination, a programmer should bear in mind that spelling is writing, that most writing is done in sentences, that words ultimately derive their meaning from the context in which they occur, and that testing will therefore be most effective if the words to be spelled are presented *in sentences.* It is conceivable that in a class with a wide range of individual capabilities, the teacher might allow the less mature pupils to write just the test word in the sentence, while requiring more advanced pupils to write the entire sentence, preferably a simple sentence of from four to six words. (See Chapter Twelve for suggestions.)

The need for scope and sequence charts

In the past — as noted in Chapter Six — spelling instruction has been largely a matter of rote memorization, with each word calling for an independent act of learning. Pupils have been expected to master the spelling of a list of words with little or no direction from the teacher and with little or no conscious analysis of the patterns by which the phonemes in each word are spelled. But if used exclusively, rote memorization (via eye and/or hand learning) not only is a tedious exercise in busywork, but also leads to rapid forgetting.

A truly effective program of spelling is based neither on a sequence of unrelated acts of memorization nor on a whimsical plan that a teacher hopes will somehow cover all contingencies at a particular level. Rather, an effective spelling program should be based on a carefully laid out *scope and sequence chart* showing how the most important phoneme–grapheme correspondences, word-building generalizations, and contextual cues can be introduced and then repeated at higher levels with words that have more complex spelling patterns. The chart can also be used to plan the systematic teaching of such matters as the use of a dictionary, writing conventions, proofreading, handwriting skills, and the historical background of our language — all of which are related to spelling. The scope of the pupil's learning takes the form of an ever-widening spiral as he progresses from level to level.

Illustration 9-1 shows how a scope and sequence chart might be laid out if one wanted to develop a program for the teaching of spelling. It has been greatly reduced in size to emphasize the two sets of coordinates:

1. The *rows* presenting the eight levels (commonly, grade 1 through grade 8). By starting with a particular level marker at the left and moving to the right across the columns, one can get a condensed notion of what kinds of materials are presented at that level.

2. The *columns* presenting seven categories of material having to do with spelling (e.g. generalizations, principles, and skills). By starting with the heading of a column and moving downward, one can see the sequential assignment of content from level to level.

Illustration 9-2 is a facsimile of the column on word building for level 6.

Illustration 9–1
Scope and Sequence Chart

	SOUND-TO-LETTER CORRESPONDENCES	WORD BUILDING	MEANING	HISTORY OF WORDS	THE STUDY OF LANGUAGE	DICTIONARY USAGE	WRITING CONVENTIONS
1							
2							
3							
4							
5							
6							
7							
8							

Illustration 9–2
Level 6 Word-Building Column from Chart

Plurals
  forming by adding -s and -es
  forming by changing the root word, such as **children, men, women**
  changing **f** to **ve** and adding **-s**
  dropping the final e before adding -es
  Latin form, such as alumni
  of nouns ending with ay and ey, such as delays, valleys
  of nouns ending with o, regular (ex. ratios) and irregular (ex. buffaloes)
  of nouns ending with s, such as actresses
  of nouns ending with y, such as allies
  of pronouns, such as themselves
  same as singular, such as **prey** and **aircraft**
  sounds of endings
  without plural (used only as singular nouns), such as mathematics, news
  without singular, such as **goods**
Prefixes
  a-, ad-, com-, con-, de-, dis-, ex-, in-, ob-, pre-, post-, re-, sub-, trans-, un-
  adding to change the meaning of a root word
  adding to strengthen the meaning of a word, such as in invaluable
  antonym-forming (**dis-, im-, in-, un-**)
  assimilation (why and how the spelling of certain prefixes changes when preceding
    particular phonemes, such as ad + claim = acclaim)
  identifying
  meanings of
Roots
  cede, fac, fec, fic, fer, gener, graph, ject, micro, miss, mit(t), pet, phon, port,
  pos, script, serve, tain, tele, tract, verse
  changing the spelling and/or sound of a root when adding certain suffixes, as in
    intrusion, musician
  effect of prefixes and suffixes on roots
  identifying
  meanings of
Suffixes
  added to adjectives (**-er**)
  adjective-forming (**-able, -ate, -en, -ful, -ial, -ible, -ic, -less, -ly, -ous**)
  adverb-forming (**-ly**)
  antonym-forming (**-less**)
  noun-forming (**-ance, -ary, -ate, -ence, -er, -ful, -ian, -ion, -ity, -ment, -ology,**
    -or, -orium, -ory, -sion, -tion)
  plural-forming (**-es, -s**)
  tense-changing (**-ed, -en, -ing**)
  verb-forming (**-ate, -en, -ify, -ize**)
  identifying
  meanings of
  rules for adding suffixes, such as:
    *using the **ible** spelling of /əbəl/ when added to a Latin root that cannot stand*
      *alone (ex. **possible**), and using the **able** spelling of /əbəl/ when added to a*
      *root word that can stand alone (ex. **agreeable**)*

Illustration 9–2 — Continued

synthesis (a new sound resulting from a combination of sounds, such as /sh/ resulting from the joining of **manse** and **ion** to form **mansion**)
Syllables
  accented (primary and secondary), unaccented
  as prefixes and suffixes
  closed, (ending with a consonant)
  identifying
  open (ending with a vowel)
  relationship between vowel sounds and syllables
  structure of syllables, their consonant-vowel patterns, such as the CVC (ex. **thing**),
    and more complex patterns, such as CV'· CVC (ex. **ma'ker**)
  syllabication, rules for (based upon the analysis of closed and open syllables, of
    unaccented syllables, and of doubled consonants)

The nature of a linguistically based program

What is meant by a spelling program based on linguistic principles, and how does such a program differ from any other?
Chapter Seven presents some of the prevailing views about American-English orthography which have been set forth by linguists,
and suggests that such information can aid the mastery of spelling
if it is worked into a program of carefully graded phonological, morphological, and contextual (syntax-meaning) analysis.
However, one should be cautious about assigning the term *linguistically based* to a spelling program in which the pupils are
merely directed to observe "what looks different about that word."
Although such observations may be helpful, one should not equate
a superficial knowledge that graphemic representations of phonemes may vary from word to word (e.g. in *lake* the /l/ is spelled
l; in *hill* it is spelled *ll*) with an inductively arrived at conclusion
(e.g. when the /l/ occurs at the beginning or in the middle of a
word it is almost always spelled just *l*; but when it occurs in word-
final position it is usually spelled *ll*). Only when phoneme–
grapheme analyses result in such generalizations can a spelling
program be considered linguistically based.

The use of the inductive approach

Learning to spell is a process that lends itself admirably to the
inductive approach. In the inductive method, as defined in Chapter Eight, a pupil observes certain facts as the basis for develop-

ing a concept or a general conclusion. The odds are good that he will remember the specific options for spelling certain sounds if *he* has discovered, through observation of a set of words, that (for example) *ay* is the spelling of final /ā/ in most words, /f/ is never spelled *gh* when it appears in initial position, and stress sometimes influences the spelling of final consonant sounds (/k/ is spelled *c* in /at′ ik/ but is spelled *ck* in / ə tak′/).

In contrast, the memorization of rules given by the teacher or read in a text is an exercise in recall that cannot be expected to have a general and permanent effect on spelling competence, though memorization may help the pupil to master words containing maverick spellings. Therefore, an effective spelling program is aimed primarily at teaching pupils to induce their own rules and generalizations, although it also relies on deductive modes of learning when necessary. (Refer to Chapter Eight for a fuller treatment of how the inductive method can be used in a modern spelling program.)

The use of the multisensory–multimotor approach

Even if linguistic analysis and the inductive approach are used, they will not be completely effective unless sensory modalities and motor mechanisms are also brought into play to help fix the spelling of words in the pupil's central nervous system. These modalities and mechanisms include ear, voice, eye, and hand learning. In this chapter, we have already discussed the importance of the learning that takes place by means of the ears and voice (i.e. by means of the pupil's hearing and saying the sounds in words) in learning to spell. Yet visual and haptical learning are also important in acquiring mastery of spelling.

Some children are predominantly visual-minded (i.e. they store a visual image of a word in their brains). Such children learn to spell primarily by looking at the graphemes which form the written word. Other children are predominantly hand-minded in learning. They learn to spell primarily through the physical act of writing, an act which involves the muscles and nerve endings in the fingers and arm so that a network of neurons is created in the central nervous system. Such children are likely to rely upon writing a word to be sure they have spelled it correctly.

A modern spelling program encourages pupils to use *all* of their available sensorimotor equipment when they are learning their spelling words. It places particular emphasis on the sensorimotor processes of hearing and speaking, the foundations upon which can be developed a power to spell correctly a very extensive American-English vocabulary. In combination with eye and hand learning, ear and voice learning play the major role in a modern approach to spelling.

Mastering maverick spellings

Some spelling programs include lists of "demons" (words commonly believed to be excessively difficult to learn to spell) that must be mastered. Only lately have we realized that spelling demons, like all demons, can be exorcised if we have the wit to analyze their composition. It is true that there are a few words in our language, such as *of*, whose spelling defies aural–oral analysis and cannot be explained by either morphological or contextual principle. Since these words make up a relatively small fraction of our vocabulary (probably less than 3 percent), it seems best to simply learn them by rote memory — visual and/or haptical.

However, most of the so-called demons are not completely irregular in their orthography. If a word has six phonemes, for example, only one may be spelled in an unpredictable way. In the word *laughter*, which at first glance looks quite irregular, only one phoneme actually has an unexpected spelling: the /a/ of the first syllable. It would be unwise to label such a word a demon. Rather, the teacher should help the pupil observe that only part of the word needs intensive study. In this particular case, the pupil should concentrate on fixing in his mind the *au* spelling of the /a/. And whenever possible, words that have similar orthographic eccentricities should be studied simultaneously (e.g. *aunt*).

As pupils reach the upper levels and become acquainted with the history of the language, they will learn that there are often historical reasons for some of our curious spellings (e.g. *of*), and they will become more comfortable with words whose spelling behavior appears to be unorthodox.

Other word-study techniques

In addition to multisensory–multimotor techniques of teaching spelling, there are others that are useful, particularly in helping children master the spelling of mavericks. Most spelling programs include specific plans for the study of individual words. Over the years, such "Study Steps" have changed to include much more stress on hearing and saying the sounds as an initial step, as it became recognized that our encoding system is alphabetically based, i.e. that phonemes are represented in writing by graphemes. Today, typical Study Steps might read as follows:

1. *Saying the word.* Have the pupil say the word and listen to the sounds in it.
2. *Looking at the word.* Guide the pupil to notice what letters are used to stand for the sounds in the word. Have him pay particular attention to any spellings that differ from what might have been expected.
3. *Writing the word.* Have the pupil write the word without looking at the copy and say the word to himself as he writes it.
4. *Proofing the word.* Have the pupil look to see whether he spelled the word correctly.
5. *Identifying the error.* Have the pupil determine what part of the word he misspelled (if any).
6. *Restudying the word.* Have the pupil study again any word he misspelled, repeating the steps over again from the beginning.

As mentioned previously, study plans such as this can be particularly useful in teaching pupils to spell the few words whose orthography deviates greatly from the alphabetic principle. They should not, however, be used to the exclusion of a phonological, morphological, and contextual analysis of the phoneme–grapheme correspondences that form the foundation of a modern spelling program.

Background knowledge of language

An effective spelling program ought to include, at a level appropriate to the maturity of the pupils, a highly condensed but informative review of the historical development of language in general and of the English language and its orthography in particular. Not only is this a fascinating tale in itself, it also provides a background that puts spelling in perspective and helps the pupil understand the reasons for the spelling of many words in our language. (See Chapters Three, Four, and Five for a brief historical review of this type.)

Acquiring the "dictionary habit"

A well-developed spelling program also recognizes the importance of the dictionary as an aid to spelling mastery. In a good standard dictionary, one can find not only the spelling of a word, but also its pronunciation, oral and written syllabication, meaning or meanings, part of speech, and usually the language or languages of origin. However, many classrooms cannot provide a dictionary for each pupil, and much time can be wasted and much discouragement can result if pupils have to take turns using the single classroom dictionary. Therefore, because the establishment of the dictionary habit is considered so crucial, most modern spelling books include, in the back of the text, what is typically called a "speller dictionary." Such a dictionary usually contains the words in all the weekly study lists plus any additional words that might be called for in the lesson exercises.

Speller dictionaries are patterned after standard dictionaries, but they are necessarily sharply abridged. They cannot possibly compare with a larger dictionary in terms of providing pronunciation variants, or a large number of facts of origin, definitions, acceptable spellings, illustrations, etc. Therefore, the pupil should be checked frequently to make sure that he is using whatever standard classroom dictionary is available as well as his speller dictionary.

The system of indicating pronunciation in the speller dictionaries should be as similar as possible to the systems used by most standard dictionaries, a pronunciation that is commonly based upon an *assumed American standard*. Pupils should be told, of course, that pronunciation of words in ordinary rapid speech often is not as precise as the pronunciation presented in dictionaries, because the natural language of a speaker is a composite of dialect (regional and social variations in pronunciation) as well as idiolect (the totality of speech patterns of an individual at a particular period of his life). But pupils should also be told that dictionary pronunciations provide helpful clues to spelling; their very preciseness makes individual phonemes easy to identify and thereby furnishes important cues to graphemic representation.

Therefore, pupils should be encouraged to check their informal pronunciation against that given in the dictionary when they are trying to figure out phoneme-grapheme correspondences.

Teachers should be attentive to and objective about the variety of dialectal pronunciations that some pupils may use. If they help these pupils realize that although dialect is a normal part of a dynamic language system, *for purposes of mastering spelling* a clear, even stilted and pedantic, pronunciation of a word can be useful, they may prevent many spelling problems that arise from dialectal factors. For acquiring sound cues especially, the dictionary habit is an indispensable acquisition.

Summary

In this chapter, we have briefly summarized the requisites of an effective spelling program in terms of scope and sequence. The following chapters will provide detailed suggestions as to how a modern program of spelling might be constructed, and will include examples of specific teaching strategies. One chapter will be devoted to each level, from 1 through 8. Chapter Ten, which will present samples of material that can be used in either the kindergarten or level 1 or both, will be more comprehensive than the other chapters because the ideas introduced in these beginning levels are applicable to all levels.

CHAPTER TEN

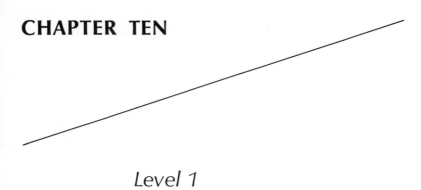

Level 1

In order to help teachers plan a program which builds spelling power, the authors present here some suggestions for developing spelling readiness in kindergarten and level 1 pupils. Throughout the following chapters, reference is made to basic or theoretical materials that have been presented in Part One. The teacher will find it useful and informative to refer back to Part One for background information on the correspondences presented in Part Two.

The authors do not wish to imply that the procedures to be detailed here are the only ones that are productive in developing spelling power. But the strategies suggested do aim at helping teachers provide pupils with a rational means of acquiring spelling ability *that takes into account the nature of our writing system.* Therefore, these strategies focus on ways of familiarizing pupils with the alphabetical nature of the orthography and of teaching them to encode the words they need in their written communication.

In order for pupils to have sufficient background to develop spelling power, they should be helped to understand the following points:

1. Language consists of words spoken in meaningful arrangements.

2. A word is composed of sounds.
3. Sounds in a word occur in a certain order.
4. Alphabetic letters are used to write these sounds.
5. These alphabetic letters are almost always written in the same order in which the sounds occur in the words (*wh* for /hw/ is one exception).

In fact, the whole concept of sound and letter (phoneme and grapheme) is so basic to understanding the alphabetic principle that the teacher should make use of every technique of instruction to help pupils grasp it. If he patiently repeats directions and is continuously involved with pupils in their daily spelling lessons, this task will be easier.

The eight basic purposes of a beginning spelling program

The presentation of a program of spelling to either level 1 or kindergarten children ought to begin with the pupil's own aural–oral vocabulary. In line with the concepts just listed, there are eight basic purposes to be kept in mind when introducing pupils to analysis of the spoken word:

1. To teach pupils that a word is composed of sounds (phonemes). To help them listen to the sounds in a word and note the position and sequence of those sounds. Pupils must have a clear understanding of what is meant by a first or beginning sound in a word; by a second or middle sound; by a last or final sound.
2. To help pupils pronounce the sounds in a word. To teach them that there is order in the arrangement of such sounds and that knowledge of this order is an essential condition of spelling a word. The teacher should make an effort to enunciate clearly in order to provide a model, *for spelling purposes*, that pupils can hear and imitate. (See the comment on dialectal pronunciations in Chapter Nine, p. 126.)
3. To help pupils become aware of the alphabetic nature of written English. This task will be made easier by the fact that many children enter kindergarten or level 1 with an ability to say and to recognize the letters of the alphabet, and some are able to write many of the letters.

Although a few pupils may also have learned to associate a letter with a word, e.g. *b* is for *ball*; *d* is for *dog*, this achievement is not very helpful in developing spelling skill, for it fails to relate the sound — the starting point — to its graphemic symbol. The sound heard at the beginning of *ball* is not /bē/; /bē/ is the *name* of the grapheme while /b/ is the phoneme that *b* represents.

4. To teach pupils how to form the letters of the alphabet and to help them develop habits of neatness and legibility. Whether teachers are using a system prescribed by a particular school district or that provided in a spelling text series, they should encourage pupils to follow a carefully devised system of letter strokes such as is presented in typical handwriting programs.

5. To coordinate the teaching of listening, speaking, spelling, handwriting, and reading.

6. To help children develop automatic encoding responses for the highly predictable phoneme–grapheme correspondences (involving most consonant and short-vowel phonemes) which occur in the monosyllabic words most frequently used by beginners in school.

7. To give pupils a sensible start toward building general spelling power by helping them use these learned sound-to-letter responses to spell a great many words that are already familiar to them in their spoken form.

8. To help pupils make use of as many learning modalities as possible — ear, voice, eye, and hand — in acquiring spelling mastery.

The remainder of this chapter will suggest strategies which are aimed at realizing these eight basic objectives in a beginning spelling program.

Identifying the sounds in a word

The first and crucial task in giving children an understanding of the basic sound-to-letter nature of written American English is to teach them that a word is composed of individual sounds and to help them hear these sounds in words they themselves or others say.

When a child enters school, he thinks of a sound as a self-contained unit that can stand by itself, e.g. a bang, a squeal, a musical note, a clap of thunder, a bark. He is therefore likely to think of a word as representing a single sound rather than (possibly) several sounds blended together. But if a pupil is to build power to spell, he must become aware that a word can be composed of more than one speech sound. He must recognize what these sound components are and how they combine into words; conversely, he must be taught to listen to words and break them down into their components, so that he can later write them.

English consonantal phonemes are not sounded in isolation, but always precede or follow a vowel phoneme (cf. *go*, *me*, *at*, etc.). Therefore, the pupil must learn to listen for and hear in words a great many phonemes that he never hears separately outside the context of the spoken word.

The beginning sound

Spelling American-English words consists of writing letters in a left-to-right sequence that corresponds to the sequence in which speech sounds are uttered in a word. Therefore, the pupil must learn to identify the phonemes in a word in the order in which they are spoken. And since, in transcribing a word, he must start with the first phoneme or sound, the first lesson of a spelling program should deal with the first or beginning sound and the letter used to write it.

The word used to illustrate the beginning sound should be introduced either orally or by means of a picture. (To present the pupil, initially, with a visual input of the beginning grapheme prevents the aural–oral mechanism from having a part in the process of encoding.) For example, suppose the teacher wants to introduce pupils to the beginning sound spelled *m*. The pupils should first observe a series of objects whose names begin with this sound, thus:

Then they should be asked —

1. to name the pictures presented (*man, mouse, moon*);
2. to listen as the teacher clearly and distinctly pronounces the word represented by each picture;
3. to listen again to the first or beginning sound in each word;
4. to listen to the beginning sound as they themselves pronounce the word;
5. to decide which sound is the same in all three words;
6. to think of other words that begin with the same sound.

Ordinarily, the child in his writing will be spelling words that he is thinking of rather than words he is hearing someone else say. But if he is going to be able to think of the right sounds for a word, he ought to have an idea of a rather precise *spelling pronunciation* by which he can match letters to sounds accurately. The authors suggest that, in order to help pupils match letters and sounds, the teacher provide as clear an auditory model as possible.

Teachers should provide as many words (orally or via pictures) as are necessary to make sure all pupils understand the concept of the beginning sound and can identify such sounds. Here are some examples of words that might be used to test these skills. (Pupils would be asked to indicate which words in each group begin with the same sound.)

Group 1:	saw	sell	ham	soup	that
Group 2:	turn	horse	time	baby	tank
Group 3:	pack	pencil	ax	best	picnic
Group 4:	horn	hang	kite	bang	help
Group 5:	watch	red	said	wide	went
Group 6:	fan	door	foot	go	find

Most pupils will have little difficulty in *hearing* the same phoneme in initial position in a series of words; more pupils will have trouble *enunciating* the sound as part of a word. For example, many children who can differentiate aurally between the initial sound in *wag* and that in *rag* may be unable to say anything other than /wag/ for both words. Unless there is an acute speech or hearing handicap, however, maturity and practice will usually resolve these difficulties. Those few pupils who have severe speech or hearing handicaps should be referred to the proper school authority for diagnosis and treatment.

Choosing the sounds to be taught first

In a spirally conceived scope and sequence program, one naturally begins with the phonemes that are most easily enunciated by children and those whose letter representation is most regular. And although there is no hard and fast rule for order of presentation, it is probably wise to avoid teaching certain sounds too close together. For example, many children have difficulty distinguishing between the sounds /p/, /t/, and /b/ in words, and between the sounds /m/ and /n/. Therefore, it would seem advisable to follow a sequence similar to the following: /t/, /m/, /d/, /p/, /n/, /b/, /l/, /s/, /g/, etc. Vowel sounds (only short-vowel sounds in level 1) should be interspersed with consonant sounds so that pupils can have the satisfaction, as early as possible, of hearing, saying, thinking of, and writing whole words.

Writing the first sound in a word

Many children enter school able to name the letters of the alphabet, but few are aware that these letters are the magic key to encoding spoken words. As soon as they develop some ability to recognize the beginning sound in a group of words, however, they will understand that the sounds they hear and say in words can be written with letters of the alphabet. For example, having learned to identify the beginning sound in the words for

they will realize that this beginning sound is always written with the letter *t*.

Level 1 pupils should practice forming the alphabet letters while they are learning how to use them to represent sounds in writing. Therefore, most spelling programs provide model alphabet letters (both capital and lower case) and specific directions for forming the letters. In addition, many school systems have their own handwriting programs that may or may not be coordinated with the school's spelling program. Teachers in such schools will probably use the handwriting method adopted by the system as a whole. In any event, the highly specialized handwriting skill should be related to all school subjects involving writing — but particularly to spelling. In short, mastery of the *formation* of graphemes should accompany mastery of the *recognition* of graphemes as appropriate symbols for particular phonemes (sounds) in a word.

Interior sounds

Ordinarily, pupils do not have too much difficulty in hearing and identifying sounds which begin and end words. But interior sounds are more difficult because they must be pulled out of a larger unit of sounds. Pupils need to learn to separate one phoneme from another if they are to make use of phoneme–grapheme correspondences in developing spelling power.

It is important for the pupil to proceed directly from the initial phoneme to the next phoneme in proper sequence, for this is the order in which these phonemes are enunciated in words. Therefore, rather than jump from the first to the last sound in a word, the teacher should proceed to the second sound immediately after the first has been learned.

Like the first, the second sound should be taught either by means of pictures or by means of oral exercises involving monosyllabic words. Sets of words useful in testing the pupil's auditory competence might include:

1	2	3	4	5
sat	pin	box	run	bed
pan	sit	rock	bug	leg
bag	rim	log	duck	pen

(Each set of three words would be presented orally by the teacher, and pupils would be asked to tell which sound — first, second, or last — in each set of words was the same.) The ability to hear and identify second sounds represents a big step forward in the pupils' awareness that a word is made up of sounds and that these sounds are ordered.

The procedure for teaching pupils to write second sounds in words is similar to that suggested for first sounds. Suppose, for example, that the second sound spelled *a* is to be written. The teacher should review, orally, a few words in which /a/ occurs, such as *ran, pat, tag,* and *mad,* asking pupils to listen to the second sound in each word. (With advanced groups it might be advisable to include a few "ringers" such as *big, get,* and *dog* to challenge the pupils' ability to discriminate among sounds.) As soon as the pupils demonstrate an ability to recognize /a/ in sets of words, they ought to practice writing that sound with the letter *a.* At the same time, they should learn that when the /a/ comes first in a word and is used to begin a person's name (*Alice*), the grapheme is capitalized.

The last sound

When pupils have had some experience in hearing and writing the first and second sounds, they should learn to hear and write the last sounds in words. It is advisable to begin this presentation with consonant sounds that pupils have already encountered in initial position in a word. For example, suppose pupils have learned to recognize the first sounds in such words as *pan, duck, net,* and *top* and have learned which letter is used to write each of the beginning sounds. They should have a relatively easy time identifying the correct letter for each final sound in such words as *cap, bed, pin,* and *not.*

If questioned, advanced pupils in the class should be able to produce a dozen words that begin and end with the same sound spelled with the same letter (e.g. *did*), including some proper names (e.g. *Dad*). This exercise should lead into a discussion of optional spellings for final sounds as the children notice that letters are sometimes doubled (e.g. *pass, lull*).

Some variations in the graphemic representation of final consonant sounds

After pupils are able to identify — and write letters for — final consonant sounds, they should be introduced to alternate spellings such as those just mentioned. (For example, /s/ can be spelled *ss* as in *dress;* /l/ can be spelled *ll* as in *hill;* /d/ can be spelled *dd* as in *add.*) Pupils will learn inductively that /s/ is usually written *s* when it comes in first or second position in a word but is usually represented by *ss* when it occurs in last position (*class*). Later they will be helped to discover that words

that end in /s/ immediately preceded by a short-vowel sound almost invariably have the **ss** spelling. (This device is known as
gemination of consonant letters.)

Advanced pupils will no doubt call attention to the fact that
there are some words whose final /s/ is spelled **s**. Such pupils
should be commended for their observation and asked to contribute all the words they can which end in /s/ spelled just **s**.
Should any pupil suggest words like **has** and **his** and **was**, ask
him to listen carefully to the last sound and note that it is not the
same as the sound he hears in **bus** and **gas**. (The difference
between /s/ and /z/ is an important distinction to learn in
spelling.)

Developing a letters-for-sounds chart

To help pupils associate letters with particular sounds, a spelling chart constructed by pupils and teacher cooperatively is often
useful. Such a device might be similar to the one labelled
Chart 10–1. After identifying the picture, pupils should be asked
to listen to the sounds in the word and take turns writing, in the
appropriate column, the letters used to spell the first, second, and
last sounds in each word. Pupils should be encouraged to par-
ticipate in chart construction by contributing pictures.

As soon as the pupils can identify the sounds in simple two-
and three-sound words and can form the letters that are used to
write those sounds, they should have the experience of writing
whole words, since this is a most important step for the beginning
speller to take. Not only will it increase his awareness of the
alphabetic nature of our language, it will also give him a sense
of accomplishment — a feeling that he is doing something productive.

The teacher might set the stage for the pupils' writing of whole
words by reminding them that there are 26 letters in the alphabet
and that these letters are used to write sounds that occur in
different positions. A special kind of letters-for-sounds chart
that requires pupils to identify a phoneme common to two words
and its position in each word may be helpful. Such a position
chart is presented under the heading of Chart 10–2; the *x* indicates where the pupil should write each grapheme. Again, to be
most effective, the chart should be a cooperative teacher–pupil
venture.

Chart 10–1

Letters for Sounds

Pictures of Words	Spelling of First Sound	Spelling of Second Sound	Spelling of Last Sound
	b	e	d
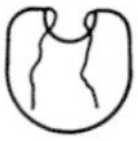	b	i	b
	t	o	p
	f	a	n
	b	u	s
	m	a	n
	p	i	g

Chart 10–2

Spelling of Phoneme in Different Positions

Pictures of Words	First Position	Second Position	Last Position
/e/			
		x	
	x		
/i/			
		x	
	x		
/t/			
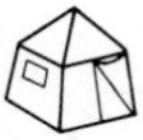	x		x
			x
/g/			
	x		
			x

Consonant clusters

Level 1 is a good time to present consonant clusters, since they begin and/or end many words that pupils need to write. A consonant cluster consists of two or more consonant phonemes which appear sequentially in a word and often appear to blend together (e.g. *stop, strength*). If pupils are familiarized with consonant clusters, they will be able to build many new words by changing a single initial or final consonant in a word they already know to a consonant cluster. Here is a sample lesson which illustrates one strategy for introducing the idea of consonant clusters; since the consonant cluster /st/ is very frequently used and occurs in both initial and final positions, it is a good one to start with.

A sample lesson

Begin the presentation by pronouncing the word *top*. Then write *top* on the chalkboard and ask the pupils to pronounce it. Ask them to name the letter that is used to write the first sound in the word, and underscore that letter on the chalkboard. Repeat these steps for the second and final sounds. Tell the pupils that they are now going to create a different word by adding another sound before *top*. Ask them —

1. to listen to the word *stop* as you pronounce it;
2. to say *stop* and listen to the word as they say it;
3. to tell what sound was added to *top* to make *stop*.

Write *s* before the word *top* on the chalkboard and ask the class to say *top* and *stop* and listen to the difference between the two words. Discuss this difference with the class. Remind the pupils that while the cluster seems to be almost one sound, it is really two separate sounds and must be written with two separate letters. If they have formed the habit of listening to individual sounds in words, they should have little difficulty recognizing the individual sounds that make up a consonant cluster.

The pupils are now ready to construct new words by adding a consonant sound (/s/) to each of the following words: *tub, pin, pot, led*. The words should be presented orally so that pupils will continue to master the sound-to-letter technique, and the class should respond orally. Ask them to say the words in pairs and listen to the difference between them, as follows:

tub/stub   *pin/spin*   *pot/spot*   *led/sled*

Then have the pupils practice writing these pairs of words and underlining the consonant cluster in each pair. (Caution: if advanced pupils suggest that such pairs as *park/spark*, *tool/stool*, and *tar/star* have consonant clusters, accept them as examples but do not require their written form. Pupils should not be required at any time to write words containing phoneme–grapheme correspondences that they have not yet studied.) Pupils can then test their knowledge of consonant clusters by attempting to build on different words such as *lip* and *lap*.

Pupils should have little difficulty in understanding final consonant clusters if the teacher again begins by using the /st/ cluster. Follow the procedures outlined above and present words such as these as examples: *best, left, belt, lamp, desk, wind*. But be alert to the fact that some pupils may fail to say the final consonant sound in the clusters involved. If a pupil does say /bes/, /lef/, /bel/, /lam/, /des/, and /win/, he may not write the final *t*, *p*, *k*, and *d*. While average pupils are studying clusters in these sets of words, advanced pupils can be asked to make lists of less frequently used words that contain either initial or final consonant clusters, or both.

Encoding and decoding

Encoding is the process of recording the words of a language. Decoding is the process of reading what has been written. (For a fuller discussion of these two processes, see Chapter Two.) Teachers who hope to help pupils develop spelling power must be able to distinguish very clearly between encoding and decoding, but they must also understand that while encoding and decoding are reverse processes, they can be mutually supportive. Indeed, they *must* be if pupils are to acquire competence in both of these very important sets of skills.

When a pupil has mastered the skill of encoding, he will find that decoding is a much less mysterious activity. Therefore, pupils at level 1 ought to be given frequent opportunities to decode (read) what they have written, regardless of whether they have had much formal instruction in reading. Again, a spelling chart may help to integrate the processes of hearing, saying, writing, and reading; such a chart is presented under the heading of Chart 10–3.

Chart 10–3

Word-Writing

Pictures of Words	Spelling of First Sound	Spelling of Second Sound	Spelling of Third Sound	Spelling of Last Sound	Complete Word in Encoded Form
	m	a	s	k	mask
	d	e	s	k	desk
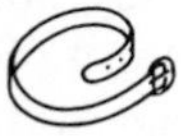	b	e	l	t	belt
	r	a	f	t	raft
	v	e	s	t	vest
	l	a	m	p	lamp

After the pupils have identified the pictures on the chart and have listened to the sounds in each word, they should be asked to write the individual sounds — and, finally, the whole word — in the appropriate column. When this word-writing has been completed, the teacher should write sentences such as the following on the chalkboard and have the pupils find a word in each sentence (aside from articles) that they can read.

1. Harold's Halloween *mask* was frightening.
2. Eight sailors floated on a rubber *raft*.
3. Cousin Laura's new *lamp* is gorgeous.
4. David tried punching holes in his new *belt*.
5. Uncle Wolcott's woolen *vest* shrank horribly.
6. Father's new office *desk* is huge.

These sentences are purposely made difficult for level 1 readers so that pupils will concentrate on decoding the one word in each sentence that they have just encoded on the chart. And if the groundwork has been properly laid, most pupils in the class should be able to recognize the six words. Pupils who are unable to decode any of the words should return to a study of the chart, or of even more elementary charts such as those labelled 10–1 and 10–2 in this chapter. Advanced pupils may want to make their own personal encoding and decoding charts. If so, the teacher might provide small mimeographed chart-sheets for them. Individual pupils can provide their own pictures.

Digraphs

Pupils in level 1 may be given a very elementary idea of the dilemma our language faces if the teacher points out that we have only 26 alphabet letters with which to write more than 40 sounds. If pupils are asked to suggest ways of solving this problem, the more advanced members of the class will probably suggest that a letter could be used to represent more than one sound. This might lead into a discussion of the use of *combinations* of two letters to spell a sound different from that represented by either letter in isolation. Such combinations are called *digraphs*.

The teacher might begin by presenting three of the most useful digraphs for level 1 pupils: *ch*, *sh*, and *th*. All three combinations are used both to begin and to end words (*chest/lunch, ship/dish, thin/bath*). Although pupils may confuse digraphs with consonant clusters at first, aural–oral practice with pairs such as these will help demonstrate the difference: *chair/stair, rush/test, with/mist*.

Variant spellings of the same sound

Level 1 pupils need to learn that many of our speech sounds can be spelled in more than one way. Since they know many words that contain the /k/ sound, its various spellings in these words provide the teacher with an excellent opportunity to use the discovery method. Here is a sample teaching procedure.

A sample lesson

Ask the pupils to listen to the following words and to pay particular attention to the first sound in each: *king, kept, keep, kite*. An advanced pupil might write the words in a single column on the chalkboard. Make sure that the class is aware of the *k* for /k/ that begins each word. Then ask the pupils to listen to the following words: *can, cup, cot, cap*. Have someone write the four words on the chalkboard in a column next to the one already there.

Pupils should then examine the two columns and observe 1) which sound is common to all eight words, 2) what letter is used to spell this sound in the words in column 1, 3) what letter is used to spell this sound in the words in column 2, and 4) what sounds in the words provide a clue to the choice of letter for the beginning /k/. Seek to elicit the observation that *k* is used when the beginning /k/ is followed by the letters *i* or *e*, and that *c* is used when the beginning /k/ is followed by the letters *a, o,* or *u*.[1]

A third spelling of the /k/ sound can then be presented if such words as *pick, rock, pack*, and *truck* are pronounced and written on the chalkboard in a third column. By observation of all three columns, pupils should be able to discover that the /k/ sound 1) may be spelled *k* or *c* in initial position, 2) may be spelled *ck* in final position, and 3) is never spelled *ck* in initial position. (The spelling of final /k/ as *k* in such words as *make* and *bike* should not be presented until level 2, when long-vowel sounds and their spelling are introduced.) Eventually, in a scope-and-sequence program, pupils will round out their knowledge by being introduced to the influence of syllabic stress on spelling (cf. *at′ tic, a tom′ ic, at tack′*).

This exercise will be one of the first tests of the pupils' ability to reason inductively in spelling study — to learn by observation rather than just by rote memorization. Success in this venture will initiate the development of a habit of observation that will be invaluable in helping pupils to build their power to spell.

[1] This requires visual analysis, for the principle works equally with either long- or short-vowel sounds, thus: *king/kind; cap/cape; kept/keep; cot/comb.*

Summary

In this chapter, the authors have presented some detailed suggestions for implementing a program of spelling at level 1. The emphasis has been on a sound-to-symbol approach because this is a relatively new method of helping pupils develop spelling skills. But the teacher will be wise to involve as many modalities of learning as possible — ear, voice, eye, and hand — so that pupils can use all of their sensorimotor equipment rather than just part of it. The teacher should also remember that spelling is *encoding* (writing speech), and that pupils will benefit by reversing the process and *decoding* (reading what they have written).

The succeeding chapters, while presenting strategies in less detail, will give some idea of how a modern spelling program can lead pupils from simple spelling principles to more complex ones.

CHAPTER ELEVEN

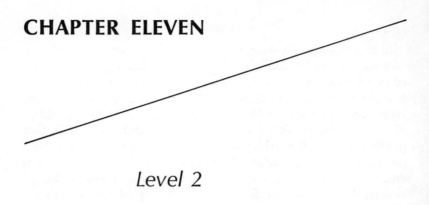

Level 2

Chapter Ten presented some strategies for the teacher to use in initiating a spelling-readiness program for the beginning speller at the kindergarten or first grade level. It was suggested that such a program should supply foundation material by introducing the pupil to the alphabetic principle, to the simplest and most consistent of the phoneme–grapheme correspondences, to a few consonant clusters and their graphemic representations, to some single phonemes that are represented by two letters (digraphs), and to optional spellings for a few sounds.

The content of a level 2 spelling program

Although a modern spelling program is firmly rooted in three aspects of language — the phonological (sound-to-letter correspondences), the morphological (word-building patterns), and the contextual (word-meaning cues in the sentence), the phonological approach should receive primary attention from level 1 through level 3. Therefore, a level 2 spelling program should lead pupils to discover the most consistent graphemic representation of particular phonemes and to observe how position, stress, and surrounding sounds help determine which graphemic option is used in spelling a particular phoneme. Within this phonological area, the level 2 program should be primarily concerned (after a number of review lessons) with enlarging the pupils' aural–oral awareness of the spellings of short-vowel sounds and with introducing the most consistently spelled long-vowel sounds.

After pupils learn that the vowel sounds may be represented by various spellings, they ought to be led to observe that the *position* of a vowel sound in a syllable or word may determine its graphemic representation. They should notice, for example, the *ay* spelling of final /ā/ in words like *day* and *may*. And the spelling of other vowels in other positions should be presented in such a way that pupils are challenged to find the principles governing the phoneme-grapheme correspondences. In other words, pupils should try to determine what factors, such as preceding or following sounds, affect the choice of grapheme in particular situations (e.g. /ī/ is spelled *i* when followed by *ld* or *nd*: *child, kind*). A few of the less common spellings of the short-vowel sounds which occur in high frequency "service" words (e.g. *come, some, said, friend*) should also be introduced in level 2.

Although phonological analysis should receive the major emphasis at level 2, pupils can also profit from an elementary presentation of word-building techniques (morphology). For example, they should be guided in observing how to add the *-ing* suffix to verbs. Morphological matters are taken up in detail at level 3 and thereafter, but an effective spelling program should begin such study before level 3.

Review

A level 2 spelling program also ought to include a very comprehensive review of the spelling-readiness program presented in level 1. As stated previously, there is no fixed national program for any subject in the curriculum. Therefore, it is necessary to make sure that any pupil who transfers from one state or school to another does not become too discouraged when confronted with a comparatively new program that is already familiar to his classmates.

The authors of this volume recommend that teachers have newcomers to a spelling program study the material presented in previous levels and pay close attention to the review lessons which typically open the work of a new school year. But those pupils who came through the readiness and level 1 programs might *also* profit by such a review, especially if it is held during the first weeks of the school year.

The same procedures should be followed in the level 2 review as were followed in the level 1 spelling-readiness program; therefore, many of the techniques described in Chapter Ten may prove useful when review is held. For example, sounds to be reviewed should be introduced through pictures or through oral–aural means rather than through printed graphemes. Furthermore, pupils should thoroughly understand the position of sounds in a word and should be given as much opportunity as possible to practice writing both individual letters and whole monosyllabic words.

Level 2 pupils ought to be familiar with the terms *consonant* and *vowel.* They should be aware that our writing system is alphabetically based and that certain letters of the alphabet are used to write consonant sounds and certain other letters are used to write vowel sounds. If they have been through the first-level program, they should also have had considerable experience in identifying sounds and selecting the alphabetical letters used to write them.

During the review lessons, pupils should be cautioned to pay close attention to neatness and legibility in their handwriting. If a pupil appears to have difficulty writing (or printing) his letters, it may be because he has had little previous practice in developing writing skills. At any rate, all pupils — as in level 1 — should be encouraged to follow a carefully devised system of letter strokes such as that presented in typical handwriting programs.

Some time should also be spent in reviewing the consonant clusters and the letters used to write them. Pupils ought to begin by picking out consonant clusters from words pronounced by the teacher, not from printed texts. It is particularly important for pupils to understand that even though — for example — the first two sounds in **spoon** and the last two in **best** are seldom mutually distinct in ordinary speech, we must *write* letters to stand for both beginning sounds in **spoon** and both ending sounds in **best**. If pupils are entering a spelling program for the first time, they will need extra help on consonant clusters, on digraphs, and on sounds that can be represented by various graphemes — all of which are described in Chapter Ten.

Finally, when pupils are working on review exercises, help them identify the names of any pictures which are used to demonstrate a particular phoneme–grapheme correspondence. Remember that some pupils may not be familiar with such things as turtles, birds' nests, saws, igloos, and foxes. Help them out; if picture identification becomes a guessing game, the whole exercise will be meaningless.

The weekly lesson plan

The main body of a level 2 spelling program ought to be concerned with extending the pupils' knowledge of phoneme–grapheme correspondences, the teaching of which was begun at level 1. The inductive method — in which pupils observe the nature of phoneme–grapheme correspondences in varying circumstances and induce general principles from their observations — should begin to be most effective at level 2.

Each week's lesson in the level 2 program might be divided into five parts, one part for each day of the week. In this plan, Parts A and B (typically given on Monday and Tuesday) would introduce the particular phoneme–grapheme correspondence that is to be taught during the week. Part C (Wednesday) would consist of an inventory test that measures the pupils' grasp of the spelling principle under study and the word list from which it has been induced. Part D (Thursday) would be concerned with extension and elaboration of the week's phoneme–grapheme correspondence, with special challenges for the more advanced pupils. And in Part E (Friday), the pupil would be tested for final mastery of the principle and the word list.

The authors believe that as a general practice, it is important to spend two full class periods on thorough study of the week's topic, so that pupils will have plenty of opportunity to observe, in the list of words to be studied, the phoneme–grapheme correspondence under consideration. However, the teacher is in the best position to determine the length of time to be spent on each part of the weekly lesson. With some classes and with some lessons, it may be advisable to spread Parts A and B over *three* days, and present Parts C and D in one day instead of in two.

In any case, Part D should contain enrichment exercises which allow pupils to build on what they have learned in Parts A and

B, and to extend their comprehension and usage vocabularies. In addition, those pupils who did not do well on the inventory test (Part C) should return to Parts A and B to restudy the week's phoneme–grapheme correspondence. As mentioned previously, Part E should test the pupils' ability to spell the words in the study list and to apply the week's spelling principle or generalization to words which were not previously taught but which illustrate the principle or generalization.

The long-vowel sounds

The first new material presented in a level 2 program could profitably be concerned with the presentation of a long-vowel sound; for example, the /ā/ in final position as in *play*. Such a subject offers an excellent opportunity for pupils to use the inductive method to arrive at a spelling principle. Here are some techniques that could be used in teaching some common spellings of /ā/.

A sample lesson

Have the pupils identify pictures whose names illustrate the /ā/ phoneme in final position. Then pronounce the study words and ask the pupils to tell in what respect they are spelled alike. (If the lesson includes the words *play*, *say*, *may*, and *they*, the answer is that the endings of the words are spelled alike with the single exception of *they*.)

Discuss with the pupils the *ay* spelling of final /ā/ in words, and, while doing so, write the words *play* and *apron* on the chalkboard. After asking volunteers to say each word, draw a line under the graphemic representation of /ā/ in each (*apron*, **play**). Discussion will probably lead the class to the observation that /ā/ is generally spelled *a* when it occurs in first position in a word and *ay* when it occurs in last position.

Should pupils *not* make this observation, help them arrive at it by again asking for suggestions on how to spell the /ā/ sound in the original study words. If the words are those listed above, for example, someone may notice that in all but one (*they*), /ā/ is spelled *ay*. If pupils then remember that *apron* is spelled with *a*, this should lead to the discovery of a rule for writing /ā/, with exceptions such as *they* taken note of. Pupils will learn other spellings of /ā/ later on in the program.[1]

Since any list of monosyllables containing a final long-vowel sound is bound to include several words that begin with consonant clusters, be sure that pupils are able to spell every word correctly *in its entirety.* If a pupil cannot do so, suggest that he turn back to the lesson on consonant clusters and restudy the sounds and their letter representations.

Presenting variant spellings

Various spellings of a particular long-vowel sound ought to be taught in contiguous lessons, i.e. words containing the same long vowel should be studied in "sets" whenever possible. For example, if the lesson is concerned with the spelling of /ī/, pupils should start with words such as *child, find,* and *sight* and write in columns the words that are spelled in like patterns. Thus they will discover that when /ī/ comes between two consonant sounds, it is spelled *igh* in a few common words (cf. *fight, might, light, right*), but when it is followed by *ld* or by *nd*, it is spelled *i.*

Likewise, contiguous lessons on /ō/ and its graphemic representation in different words will help pupils learn, *by contrast,* the variant spellings of this phoneme. But it must be admitted that only a few powerful generalizations are of much help to pupils who are trying to decide how the long-vowel sounds should be spelled in various words. Therefore the use of Study Steps will probably be necessary to provide an input of visual and haptical cues to their correct spellings in words being studied.

A possible set of Study Steps was suggested in Chapter Nine. As mentioned there, such steps are particularly helpful to the pupil who is studying those words, or parts of words, that have unorthodox spellings. But Study Steps should not become a rote-memory crutch used in lieu of applying inductively formed rules, since the majority of the phoneme–grapheme correspondences in a word are likely to be quite predictable. For example, *right* is predictably spelled except for the vowel sound. Therefore, the

---

[1] In a 17,000-plus word list which contained 128 examples of word-final /ā/, this sound was spelled *ay* in 95 words (e.g. *play*), *ey* in 10 words (e.g. *they*), *et* in 9 words (e.g. *bouquet*), *e* in 7 words (e.g. *cafe*), *eigh* in 5 words (e.g. *weigh*), and *ea* and *ei* in one word each (*yea, nisei*).

pupil using Study Steps should center his attention on the *igh* spelling of the vowel sound in the word, and use visual and haptical mechanisms to fix this pattern in his memory. He should also try to associate *right* with a "set" of words that includes *light*, *might*, *bright*, and *fight*.

Helping a class invent an alphabet

Very early in level 2, there ought to be a lesson in which the alphabetic principle and the alphabet as a coding system are discussed. Pupils need to feel at home with the alphabet in order to learn to spell, and they need to master alphabetical order in order to use the dictionary. The authors of this volume suggest that a teacher can greatly stimulate interest in knowing the alphabet and how to use it if he helps the pupils invent an alphabet to encode spoken words.[2]

The teacher should begin by asking the pupils if they have ever tried to invent a secret code that could be understood only by a person who knew the code. Since many TV and radio programs in recent years have introduced children to such notions, there should be little trouble in generating an enthusiastic response from the class.

Then, point out some cutouts or chalkboard drawings depicting objects whose names contain the same phoneme in the same position. For example, here are three pictures representing words in which pupils can identify the same beginning sound:

Say the words represented — *top, table, ten* — but do *not* write the words on the board! Ask the pupils to tell in what position

---

[2] Such an exercise might also be appropriate at levels 3–6.

they hear the same sound in each word, and what new mark (grapheme) they want to use to represent this sound. The suggestions may be quite varied: an animal, a geometric figure, or some object. Suppose the pupils settle on △ to stand for the sound. Write △ on the board along with a large bracket encompassing the three pictures, thus:

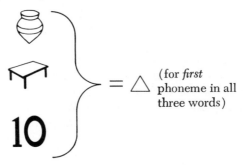

(for *first* phoneme in all three words)

Now show the class pictures of three objects in whose names the *second* sound is identical,[3] e.g.:

Say the words represented by these pictures (*cot, mop, lock*), but again, do *not* write the words on the board. Ask the pupils to tell where in these three words they hear the same sound, and what mark they want to use for this sound. Suppose they settle on □ . Write □ on the board with a large bracket encompassing the three pictures, thus:

[3] The teacher should be aware, however, that the vowel sound in these words is subject to dialectal variation and may not be pronounced in exactly the same way by all pupils.

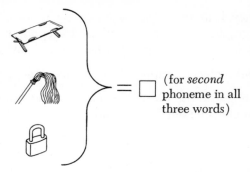

(for *second*
phoneme in all
three words)

Now show the pupils pictures of three objects representing
words in which the *last* sound is identical, e.g.:

Say the names of the objects (*map*, *cup*, *mop*), but do *not* write
these words on the board. Ask the pupils to tell where in all three
words they hear the same sound, and what mark they want to use

to represent this sound. Suppose they decide on   . Write   on
the board with a large bracket encompassing the three pictures,
thus:

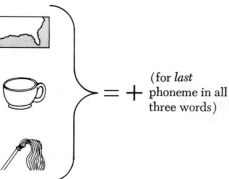

(for *last*
phoneme in all
three words)

Lead the pupils to observe that they now have three new marks to represent three phonemes — a triangle (△), a square (□), and a plus sign (+). To demonstrate that this new secret alphabet can be used to spell words, show the pupils a picture of a top and ask them to say the word represented and listen to the phonemes in it. Ask what new mark they have invented to stand

for the *first* sound in ⊝, and have a pupil write this new "letter" (△) on the board. Then show the pupils the picture again and ask them what new mark they have decided to use for the *second*

sound in ⊝. Have another pupil write the new "letter" on the board after the one previously written, thus: △ □ . Finally, show the picture again and ask the pupils what new "letter" they have

decided to use for the *last* sound in ⊝. Have a third pupil write this new "letter" on the board after the △ and □ previously re-

corded, thus: △ □ + . Ask the pupils to read the word (*top*) that they have written in their new secret alphabet.

Explain to the pupils that the exercise they have just completed may be similar to what our ancestors did when they were searching for a code with which to record their ideas, experiences, and words. (In this connection, teachers may find it helpful to reread those parts of Chapters Three and Four which deal with the development of our writing system.)

Advanced pupils (and pupils at upper levels) may be interested in thinking up symbols for many other phonemes that they hear and say. Remind such pupils that there are over 40 different phonemes in our American-English language, but that there are at present only 26 letters with which to write those phonemes. Perhaps they will want to try to invent an alphabet that has a graphemic symbol for each phoneme in their speech. Although this is obviously a complex exercise, pupils who have the persistence to stick with it and produce a whole new kind of alphabet will have learned a great deal about sound–letter correspondences and the difficulty of inventing a perfect code.

After such coding exercises have been completed, discuss with pupils the reasons why they need to know the correct *order* of the letters of the alphabet. In particular, try to elicit the observation that one must be familiar with alphabetical order in order to find a word in the dictionary. (Some pupils may also suggest that knowing alphabetical order is important when one is looking for a person's telephone number in a directory.) This type of class discussion should lead into a lesson on the dictionary and its use in spelling.

Introducing the speller dictionary

The dictionary is the pupil's ultimate authority when he wants to check the accuracy of his spelling and acquire additional information about words. Because many classrooms do not contain enough copies of standard dictionaries, most commercial spelling programs include a bound-in-text speller dictionary.

This is doubly fortunate for level 2 pupils, since they need a dictionary which is as simple as possible without being inadequate. A standard dictionary, and certainly an unabridged dictionary, would be quite overwhelming for a child of this age. Such a child first needs to learn how to locate a word in a dictionary; how to determine where the syllable divisions fall and which syllables are accented; and how to find useful definitions or examples of the meaning of the word. The speller dictionary should help the pupil master these basic skills. Therefore, when a pupil misspells a word in a test, he should be expected to find the correct spelling in his dictionary or in the study word list and record the word (correctly spelled) in a list of his own words which need further study.

A slight problem is raised by the fact that today, most standard dictionaries are *pronouncing dictionaries*. As such, they are more concerned with recording the way people say words in running speech than with providing a pronunciation guide that gives clues to graphemic representation. For example, modern dictionaries often employ the *schwa* (/ə/) in unaccented syllables because in ordinary rapid speech we tend to obscure vowel sounds in this position. However, we continue to *spell* these vowel sounds with the graphemic symbols which represent them as they were once spoken. Thus, when *Webster's Third International Dictionary* records the pronunciation of **moment** as /mō′ mənt/, this may be considered an adequate guide to general usage but of little help to pupils who are trying to determine the spelling of the vowel sound in the second syllable.

In instances of this sort, and there are many, the authors suggest that the teacher can help pupils remember how to spell the unaccented vowels if he enunciates the word so as to give the vowels their original value (e.g. /mō′ ment/). Unless and until the spelling of such vowel sounds is revised to bring it into line with current pronunciation, there will be the need to use teaching devices such as this to help pupils master certain phoneme–grapheme correspondences. In any case, pupils should be encouraged to use the dictionary (speller or standard) to check the correct spelling of any word that they are uncertain about.

Forming the plurals of nouns

One of the early lessons in a level 2 program should deal with the formation of plural nouns. Pupils should be introduced to the very important fact that such plurals are formed from the singular in one of two ways: 1) by adding a single sound, either /s/ or /z/, spelled with the single letter *s*; or 2) by adding a syllable of two sounds, /əz/, spelled with the two-letter combination *es*.

A sample lesson

Discuss with the class the meaning of the word *syllable*. Help the pupils understand that a syllable can contain either a single vowel or vowellike sound or a vowel sound plus one or more consonant sounds (cf. *a′ pron*). Then say the word *dentist* and write it on the board in syllables (*den′ tist*). Ask the pupils to pronounce each syllable and to name the letter in each syllable which stands for a vowel sound. Suggest that later in the year they will be studying many words that have more than one syllable.

Now turn back to the theme of the lesson — adding sounds to nouns to make them plural. Pronounce the following words: *hat, pet, nest, rock*. Tell the pupils that these words can be made plural if an ending sound is added to each, and ask them what sound should be added (the /s/ spelled *s*). Then ask what sound should be added to *rug* and *frog* to make the plurals of these nouns (the /z/ spelled **s**). Finally, write **lunch** and **branch** on the board and ask the pupils to say these words and then their plural forms (*lunches, branches*). Help the pupils hear that two sounds (/əz/ spelled **es**) must be added for the plural, and ask whether adding these two sounds is the same as adding a syllable.

Suggest that pupils write the following words twice, first as plurals and then as singulars:

hats	lunches	rocks	dishes
pets	buses	nests	dresses
rugs	branches	frogs	foxes
ducks	boxes	toys	watches

Ask the pupils to examine these words and try to discover a rule which tells whether to add an /s/ or /z/ spelled **s** or a syllable spelled **es** to form the plural. Lead the pupils to see that a syllable is used when the singular ends with a phoneme written as **s**, **ss**, **x**, **sh**, or **ch**. (In later levels, pupils will be introduced to other phonemes for which this applies; cf. *judge/judges, freeze/ freezes.*)

Leading pupils to induce such a rule will be worth, in terms of permanent learning, a score of repeated "tellings" by the teacher. But the teacher should also be careful to point out the few exceptions to this rule, i.e. the irregular plurals such as *children, mice, feet*, and *geese*.

The diacritic letter *e*

The diacritic *e* is one of the most useful and busy letters of the alphabet.[4] Pupils will probably have learned, both in level 1 and in the review lessons of level 2, that *e* is quite commonly used to represent the short-vowel sound /e/ in many words. Now they should also observe that *e* can be used to help spell the following:

1. Some long-vowel sounds (cf. *name, ate, cake, home, hide, duke*)
2. The final /v/ in words (cf. *give, have, love, leave*)
3. The final /s/ and /z/ in some words (cf. *nose, chase, house, fence, geese, rise*)

---

[4] Refer to the discussion of diacritic *e* in Chapter Four.

Adding -*ing* to words

A lesson on present participles and gerunds might introduce the word *suffix* to the class, but level 2 pupils should not be expected to use the word *derivative*, just to recognize the principle of suffixation. The more familiar expression, "-*ing* word," is quite acceptable at this level.

A sample lesson

Pupils might begin by listening to the teacher pronounce the words *race*, *trace*, and *face* (or similar words taught during a study of long-vowel sounds and diacritic *e*.) The teacher should then write these words on the board, pronounce each of them again, and ask the pupils to tell what vowel sound appears in all three words (/ā/) and how that sound is spelled (*a–e*). (Some pupils may also observe that the *e* does "double duty" — that it also helps spell final /s/ (*ce*).)

At this point, ask the pupils to write the words, first *without* an -*ing* ending and then *with* an -*ing* ending. If any pupils wrote *racing*, *tracing*, and *facing* correctly, ask them to explain what they did to *race*, *face*, and *trace* when they added the -*ing* (they dropped the *e*). And if some pupils neglected to drop the *e*, write the correct -*ing* forms on the chalkboard and point out the difference between their -*ing* words and those on the board. Finally, ask the pupils whether they see a rule they can follow when adding -*ing* to words like *race*.

Alternately, pupils can begin by observing the -*ing* forms and work backward to discover how the root word is changed when the suffix is added. Either procedure can also be used to analyze the behavior of roots that end in a consonant preceded by a short-vowel sound (cf. *rub*/*rubbing*), or in /v/ spelled *ve*, or in /s/ or /z/ spelled *se*, *ze*, or *ce*. Using the inductive approach in this way is likely to be considerably more effective than simply giving pupils a list of rules to memorize without making them aware of the underlying phonological and morphological principles involved.

Two-syllable words

A few easy and familiar two-syllable words should be presented at level 2. The pupils will already have been introduced to the word *syllable* in the course of the lesson on forming plurals. First review the use of this term as it applies to plurals like *lunches* and *grasses*. Then have the pupils observe in their speller dictionaries the correct written syllabication of some two-syllable words presented in the text. Have them test the rule that each syllable in a word must contain a vowel (or vowellike sound) by dividing such words as *run' ning, lift' ed, main' ly, act' ed*, and *but' ter fly* into syllables.

The vowel and /r/

A combination of sounds that often causes spelling difficulty is that known as *the vowel and r* (/ėr/).[5] The source of the difficulty is that there are several possible spellings of the vowel sound (cf. *her, bird, spur, word*), and the confusion produced by so many options often results in a misspelling. Few spelling principles are useful in dealing with this troublesome combination. (One principle is that stressed /ėr/ is spelled *or* when preceded by *w*, e.g. in *work* and *worst*.) Therefore, pupils should be urged to make use of Study Steps when they are attempting to master the spelling of words containing a vowel followed by /r/.

Maverick spellings and writing conventions

In addition to the study of highly predictable spellings, some attention should be given to the study of frequently used words containing maverick spellings. For example, pupils should be introduced to some of the common words in which the short-vowel sounds are spelled in rare, if not unique, ways, e.g. *friend, build, said, does*. Pupils should be encouraged to use all of their sensorimotor equipment to master the spellings of such maverick words.

Level 2 pupils should also be taught how to spell the number words and the names of the days of the week and the months of the year. Remind the pupils to concentrate their attention on those parts of each word that are unpredictably spelled.

In level 2, as in the other levels of a spelling program, attention should be given to writing conventions: the use of capital and

[5] In some linguistic descriptions, /ėr/ is considered a single phoneme, rather than a combination of two phonemes.

lowercase letters, punctuation, and proper spacing between words. The only reason for learning to spell is to be able to record one's thoughts accurately, legibly, and intelligibly. But in order to do so, one must not only spell correctly but also observe standard writing conventions.

Some general comments

Again, as in Chapter Ten, the authors want to suggest that teachers should make the final decision about the proper pace for individuals in their particular class, and that they should feel free to adapt a program to suit the needs of less capable pupils and provide enrichment for those who are more advanced. Although prolonged departure from a sequential presentation of carefully programmed material is generally inadvisable, since the program has been set up to promote spelling power in the majority of the class members, such a departure may be necessary in order to avoid stifling the creativity of exceptionally mature pupils.

Further, the authors want to emphasize that in every lesson taught in the primary grades, teacher involvement is crucial. If the teacher is truly interested in seeing his class develop spelling ability, he must not rely on haphazard "do it yourself" procedures carried out by the pupils without any guidance.

Chapter Twelve will present teaching strategies aimed at helping pupils extend their knowledge of phoneme–grapheme correspondences and of the morphological and contextual factors that affect the encoding of the language.

CHAPTER TWELVE

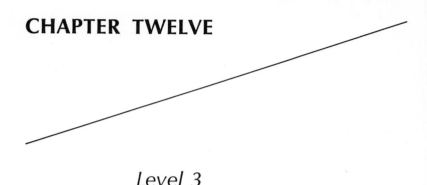

Level 3

A well-organized spelling program should guide pupils to develop a sophisticated understanding of American-English orthography by learning simple, though important, principles. Such a program should extend the pupil's spelling skills and at the same time provide him with opportunities to review and practice those skills he has already acquired. New knowledge of the orthography must grow from, and be buttressed by, previously gained knowledge of our writing system.

As we have seen in Part One of this volume, the three basic sources from which a functional understanding of the structure of orthography emerges are *phonology, morphology,* and *context.* A knowledge of the phonological characteristics of our language is crucial to the acquisition of important sound-to-letter principles and patterns that govern the spellings of thousands of American-English words. A knowledge of the morphological (word-building) principles of American English and how these principles are reflected in writing makes possible the spelling of additional thousands of words. Lastly, a knowledge of the role played by context not only is necessary for meaningful communication, but also has particular relevance in the mastery of the spelling of homonyms.

Chapters Ten and Eleven have described in detail a plan aimed at providing the pupil with a solid knowledge of the phonological basis of our writing system, since this knowledge is the primary foundation on which spelling ability rests. Provided with such a foundation, most level 3 children should be ready to begin more sophisticated study of our written code, a study that will increasingly extend their knowledge of the phonological, morphological, and contextual principles that govern the spelling of words. Let us see how a spelling program can advance the pupils' knowledge in these three areas, as well as contribute in additional ways to their power to spell.

Phonology

Level 3, like every level of a spelling program except the first, should begin with a general review of previously taught sound–letter patterns. Only then should new patterns and principles be introduced.

Review

An intensive examination of the phoneme–grapheme correspondences present in carefully selected sets of words helps pupils refresh their memory of previously encountered spelling principles. It also enables the teacher to determine which of his pupils, for whatever reason, may not have acquired the background information they need for more advanced studies of our writing system, and therefore should review earlier phases of the spelling program.

A sample lesson which would serve as an effective review might be developed from the following list of words:

glad	cot	shut	fox	blush
sick	kid	will	rest	hat
sad	met	still	hug	let
hop	best	lock	lick	hid

These words, or similar ones, can be used to help pupils review some of the simple, though important, concepts about spelling that have been previously presented, including:

1. The distinction between consonant and vowel sounds.
2. The identification of the same vowel sound in different words, e.g. /a/ in *glad, hat, sad*; /e/ in *rest, best, met, let*; /i/ in *kid, hid, still, sick, will, lick*; /o/ in *hop, cot, lock, fox*; /u/ in *shut, hug, blush*.

3. The notion of consonant clusters (as in *glad, blush, still, rest, best* — but not in *shut, sick, lock,* which contain single consonant sounds spelled with two letters).
4. The realization that different words can often be formed by changing a single sound in an old word, e.g. *sad* changed to *bad, rest* changed to *best, will* changed to *fill.*
5. Familiarity with the highly predictable spelling of most consonant sounds, e.g. /b/, /d/, /t/, /m/, /r/, /w/, /h/.
6. Knowledge of the effect of position and environment upon the spelling of some sounds, e.g. /k/ in *kid, cup,* and *lick*; /l/ in *let* and *will.*

New variant spellings

After this initial review period, the pupil's phonological knowledge should be extended in two ways. First, he should be introduced to additional spellings of previously taught consonant and vowel sounds. For instance, consider the consonant phoneme /f/, whose most common spelling — *f* as in *fig* or *fan* — was presented in level 2. The pupil should now be taught that /f/ can also be spelled *ff* as in *off,* *ph* as in *phone,* and *gh* as in *laugh.* At first glance, it would appear that the various graphic representations of /f/ occur haphazardly. A closer examination of words containing /f/ shows, however, that its position in a syllable affects its spelling. By using the following list of words, the teacher can guide the pupils to make this discovery for themselves.

far	flat	sift	draft	graph
photo	telephone	stiff	stuff	puff
laugh	rough	tough	enough	craft
frog	nephew			

Pupils should be able to arrive at these generalizations about the spelling of /f/:

1. /f/ is spelled *f* when it initiates a consonant cluster: *frog, flat, sift, draft, craft.*
2. The *gh* spelling of /f/ (which is rare) occurs only at the end of syllables or monosyllabic words; and the vowels of such syllables and words also have uncommon spellings: *laugh, tough, rough, enough.*

3. The *ff* spelling of /f/ also occurs only at the end of syllables or monosyllabic words: *stiff, stuff, puff.* This reflects the previously learned principle that when a single final consonant sound is preceded by a short-vowel sound, it is often spelled with doubled letters (geminated).

4. The *ph* spelling of /f/ (which occurs about 12 percent of the time /f/ is present in words) can be found in any position: *photo, graph, telephone, nephew.* The teacher and the text should help the pupil use multisensory–multimotor processes to master this relatively uncommon spelling of /f/. (The origin of the word in which /f/ is spelled *ph* helps explain this particular spelling. The history of words can be treated in subsequent levels.)

Lessons of this nature not only help pupils master the spellings of phonemes, they also reinforce the idea that the position of a phoneme in a syllable often has an important effect on spelling. Another phoneme that can profitably be dealt with at this point is the /j/ in final position. Have the class examine the following list of words:

age	change	badge	judge
cage	bridge	hedge	large
dodge	stage	range	edge
huge	strange	fudge	charge

Careful analysis of these words should lead pupils to observe a number of facts concerning the spelling of /j/ in this position:

1. Following a short-vowel sound, /j/ is spelled *dge.*
2. Following a long-vowel sound, /j/ is spelled *ge.* (Note also that the final *e* in these *ge* words does double duty: it helps to spell /j/, and it is part of the spelling of the preceding long-vowel sound.)
3. As the last element in a final consonant cluster beginning with /r/ or /n/, /j/ is also spelled *ge.*

These examples of words containing /f/ and /j/ provide striking evidence that, far from being haphazard, our writing system abounds with useful spelling principles that can be used to develop spelling ability.

Additional phonemes

A second aim of a level 3 spelling program should be to introduce previously untaught phonemes and their principal letter representations. At earlier levels, the focus was on phonemes whose spellings reflect the alphabetic principle — mainly consonants and the short vowels. But beginning at level 3, a linguistically based spelling program should become increasingly concerned with the less predictably spelled phonemes, including the long vowels and diphthongs. It will be seen that even some of these phonemes have quite predictable spellings when the phonological cues provided by position, stress, and environment are taken into account.

For example, the diphthong /oi/ as in *boy* illustrates how position in syllables and monosyllabic words can determine which graphemic option is used. Have the pupils examine the following list of study words and observe how /oi/ is spelled in various positions:

boil	join	point	spoil
broil	joy	voice	oily
noise	toy	enjoy	moist
noisy	coil	choice	soil

Careful analysis will reveal that /oi/ is commonly spelled *oi* when it occurs in initial and medial positions in syllables, and *oy* when it occurs in final position. A level 3 spelling program should increasingly develop the pupils' awareness of positional cues in spelling; /oi/ provides only one illustration of the value of such awareness for mastery of the orthography.

Other phonemes or phoneme combinations that might profitably be introduced at this level include those that occur frequently in words and are frequently the sources of misspellings. Chief among these troublesome sounds is the *schwa* (/ə/), the vowel phoneme typically found in unstressed syllables. /ə/ often occurs in a syllable that has been reduced in stress (for example, the second vowel sound in *present* is /e/ when the verb is intended /pri zent'/, but /ə/ when the noun is meant /prez' ənt/). In the Stanford Study described in Chapter Seven, /ə/ was found to be spelled in 22 different ways.

But even the spelling of /ə/ can sometimes be predicted. The following list demonstrates one useful principle regarding /ə/. The class should determine that principle by examining these words:

ago	across	ahead	alike
alone	along	apart	asleep
awake	aboard	awhile	above
among	alarm	adult	aloud[1]

Syllabication

Because many of the more powerful sound–letter correspondences are governed by the position of the sound in a syllable, the identification of syllables should be one of the first things taught in a spelling program. Although pupils will normally have been introduced to the notion of syllables and syllabication at level 2, it is useful to review these important matters periodically.

Level 3 pupils should know, first, that all American-English syllables contain a vowel phoneme or a phoneme with a vowellike quality. For example, *brittle* has two syllables (/brit′ əl/), the first containing an /i/, the second containing the syllabic consonant /′l/ that is sometimes shown or indicated as /əl/.

Second, they should know that the syllabication of written words does not always correspond to the boundaries beween spoken syllables. For example, *brittle* would be syllabified as *brit′ tle* if written, but as *britt′ le* if spoken. This distinction is useful because it accounts for the fact that in most words such as *brittle* the /t/ is spelled *tt* (since it ends a spoken syllable containing a short vowel).

Subsequent levels of the program should expand the pupil's knowledge of syllabication. But even at level 3, some effort should be made to ensure that each child can identify syllables in both speech and writing. The following word list provides an opportunity for the class to practice identifying syllables in polysyllabic words:

hundred	herself	person	clover
yesterday	number	cartoon	corner
playground	until	potato	because
thunder	belong	also	dentist

---

[1] When /ə/ occurs as an initial unaccented syllable, it is spelled *a*.

In addition, the pupils should be able to discover, by examining the list, two important syllabication principles:

1. Compound words are generally composed of syllables that are independent words (*playground, herself*).
2. Syllables containing a short vowel sound end with consonant sounds, but other than short vowel sounds can occur anywhere in a syllable, even at the end (cf. *hun' dred, per' son, yes' ter day, num' ber, un til', thun' der, den' tist* as contrasted to *clo' ver, car toon', cor' ner, po ta' to, be long', al' so*).

It seems appropriate to conclude this section on the treatment of phonology in a level 3 spelling program by repeating that *American-English orthography is predicated upon principles that govern the spellings of phonemes.* The search for these principles, and their application in spelling, lies at the heart of the development of spelling power. Therefore, a modern spelling program should help the pupil discover such principles, and should then provide him with ample opportunity to apply his discoveries in meaningful spelling situations.

Morphology

One of the most powerful spelling tools is a knowledge of the morphological (word-building) properties of our language. Together with a functional knowledge of the phonological structure of the writing system, it can enable an individual to spell thousands of words he may have occasion to write in his lifetime. Therefore, a linguistically based spelling program will give high priority to the teaching of important morphological principles and how they affect spelling.

It will be recalled that in level 2, the pupil was introduced to the basic principle that most nouns are made plural by adding one of the inflectional suffixes — /s/ or /z/ spelled *s*, or /əz/ spelled *es.* (Sometimes we must alter the spelling of the root word first; e.g. the *y* of *sky* must be changed to *ie* before *s* is added.) Thus, almost from the beginning of the pupil's formal study, he has been exposed to the word-building principles of American English. The aim has been to enable him to spell new words that have been constructed from roots he already knows how to spell without having to learn each new derived word individually. And at level 3, his knowledge of word-building should be developed even further. Let us examine some of the principles that might be studied at this level.

Compounding

One of the most productive word-forming mechanisms in our language is compounding. When *play* and **ground** are combined, for example, the compound word **playground** is formed. The two words form another word with a meaning different from that of its components: "an area where one may play."

Familiarity with compounding is particularly useful for spelling purposes, since if we know that a word is a compound, we can spell it immediately as long as we know how to spell its components. Any set of compounds appropriate for pupils at level 3 can be used to make the class aware of this basic principle. Here is one set that might be used:

anybody	understand	anyway	sometimes
cannot	anyone	everyone	yourself
bedroom	everywhere	whatever	something
anywhere	without	grandmother	somewhere

After examining this list, pupils should be able to perceive the following points:

1. Compound words will not present spelling problems if the component words have already been mastered. (Pupils should be reminded, however, to be alert for unusual spellings in the components, e.g. in *one* and *some*.)
2. Some words appear in numerous compounds (e.g. *any* appears in *anybody, anyone, anyway, anywhere*). Pupils could be asked to select from the list of study words those compounds that have components in common, and then to supply other words they may know that contain these components.
3. Compound words (e.g. *bedroom* and *grandmother*) have their own meanings which may differ from the sum of the meanings of their components.

Affixation

A second basic process by which words are constructed in our language is that of *affixation,* i.e. the adding of prefixes and/or suffixes to roots. For example, most singular nouns are made plural and most verbs are altered in tense by the addition of *inflectional suffixes,* suffixes that alter or extend the use of words without changing their grammatical function. A level 3 spelling program should extend the pupil's knowledge of this important process and its relationship to spelling.

After reviewing previously learned principles having to do with the addition of inflectional suffixes to roots (see pages 155–157) of Chapter Eleven), the child should be introduced to additional nouns that do not form their plurals according to the usual pattern. The following set of words can be used to demonstrate to pupils that not all nouns are made plural by the addition of *s* and *es,* and that pupils should continually be alert for the relatively few exceptions to the principles of pluralization that are present in our language.

| clock | hat | glass | girl | match |
| house | man | flag | mouse | fox |

From this list, or a similar one, pupils will be able to see that although most nouns are made plural by the addition of *s* representing either /s/ or /z/ (*hats, girls, flags*) or *es* representing /əz/ (*matches, houses, glasses, foxes*), a few nouns are made plural by alteration of the sounds and spelling of an internal vowel sound (*men, mice*).

Another kind of affixation that should be introduced at this level involves *derivational affixes,* suffixes and prefixes which not only permit roots to be used in extended ways but which ordinarily also alter their grammatical function. Notice how *tight,* an adjective, can be altered by the use of derivational suffixes:

tight	(an adjective)
tight + *-ness*[2] = *tightness*	(a noun)
tight + *-en* = *tighten*	(a verb)
tight + *-ly* = *tightly*	(an adverb)

---

[2] A hyphen *before* an affix signifies a suffix (e.g. *-ing*).

A knowledge of the process of derivation not only helps the pupil in spelling, but also provides him with a basic technique for unlocking the meanings of unfamiliar words. Level 3 is none too early to acquaint the pupil with this fundamental word-building mechanism.

Pupils might begin with the common derivational suffix *-er*, which in words such as *writer, farmer, driver, camper* provides the meaning "one who . . . [writes, farms, drives, camps, etc.]." They should be helped to see that the *spellings* of such derived words normally should present no particular spelling difficulties if the roots have already been mastered. Certain spelling conventions may have to be followed, however, such as the removal of a final *e* from a root when a suffix that begins with a vowel is added, e.g. *bake* + *-er* = *baker*.

A final type of affixation that can be introduced in simple yet functional fashion at level 3 is that of *prefixation,* i.e. the adding of prefixes to roots to change their meaning but not their grammatical function. A knowledge of the use of prefixes can help the pupil decipher the meaning of unfamiliar words as well as spell them.

For example, the prefix *un-*[3] commonly indicates negation or opposition when added to roots. Therefore, children who know the meaning of words such as *happy, real, cover,* and *even* can be guided to understand that when *un-* is added, words of opposite meaning (*antonyms*) are produced (i.e. *unhappy, unreal, uncover, uneven*). Children of this age are usually able to supply numerous other words they know which contain the prefix *un-*.

Re-, on the other hand, commonly means "to do [something] again," as in *review* ("to view again"). Words such as *recount, reform, review, repaint, revisit, reuse,* and *rewrite* can be used to illustrate this function of *re-*. Through such simple exercises as this, pupils can be helped to understand another important way in which we form words in our language.

The following list of words can be used to underscore for pupils how a knowledge of prefixation can help them both to spell, and to determine the meaning of, unfamiliar words they may encounter.

load	paint	visit	fold	cover
paid	fasten	hook	mark	nail

[3] A hyphen *after* an affix signifies a prefix (e.g. *re-*).

Have the children observe that each word may be used in a different way, if either *re-* or *un-* is added, and that if an inflectional suffix is *also* added, they can be used in still further ways. For example, *load,* the first word in the list above, can become either *reload* or *unload.* Each of these derivatives in turn can be further altered by the addition of inflectional suffixes; cf. *reloading, reloaded, reloads, unloading, unloaded, unloads.*

The treatment of morphology at level 3 is aimed at helping children realize that patterns exist in morphological as well as in phonological features of our language, and that knowledge of these patterns can aid the development of spelling power.

Context

Another important part of a linguistically based spelling program is the element of *context,* i.e. how the structure of a phrase or sentence can clarify the meaning — and therefore the spelling — of an individual word. Context provides particularly important clues to the spelling of a small but troublesome group of words called *homonyms.* Homonyms are words which differ in meaning but not in sound; they create spelling difficulties because their spelling often differs along with meaning. For example:

bear/bare	be/bee	doe/dough	eye/I
fur/fir	for/four	hair/hare	heard/herd
led/lead	maid/made	oar/or	one/won
pair/pear	raise/rays	red/read	seam/seem

Any spelling program should give special attention to homonyms, since many commonly used words have phonological "twins" or even "triplets" (cf. *aisle/isle/I'll*). When confronted with homonyms, we cannot determine the proper spelling from sound clues alone because such clues are not reliable. For example, hearing /bār/ by itself does not tell us whether to spell the word *bare* or *bear.* But a knowledge of the context in which the word appears can help us decide on the appropriate spelling — as long as we already know how each of the possible homonyms is spelled. For example, *his feet were bare* provides clues that are very different from those provided by *the bear growled.*

Once the word intended is identified, however, sound-to-letter cues can often be used to advantage, since at least one word of a set of homonyms usually has a predictable spelling. In the preceding list, for example, notice that *led, made, red,* and *seem* contain the graphemes that one would expect. But even in the homonyms *lead, maid, read,* and *seam,* two-thirds of the phonemes — the first and last in each word — are consistently represented according to the alphabetic principle. The pupil will have to give special attention only to the vowel phoneme, the most common source of spelling difficulty when homonyms are involved.

Word history

In Part One of this volume, the history of the English language and its spelling system was outlined. This information can be of value to the pupil as well as to the teacher. Tracing the histories of words, particularly those containing unpredictable sound-to-letter correspondences (e.g. *once* and *sword*), can sometimes help pupils understand why spellings depart from the alphabetic principle. And such an understanding may also help them remember these unpredictable spellings later on.

Although a rigorous study of the history of words is unreasonable at level 3, the groundwork for later study can be laid. Pupils at this level will find it interesting to observe, for example, that the spellings of *once* and *sword* more nearly represent the way they were pronounced many hundreds of years ago than the way we say them now. (In Middle English, *once* was spelled *ones* and was pronounced something like *"own us"*; *sword* was at one time pronounced with a /w/ included.)

Writing conventions

A level 3 program should also contribute to the child's growing knowledge of the writing conventions: capitalization, abbreviation, hyphenation, and the use of the apostrophe in possessives and contractions. Among the abbreviations that can profitably be studied at this level are the shortened forms of 1) titles (*Mr., Mrs., Dr.*); 2) the days of the week (*Sun., Mon., Tues., Wed., Thurs., Fri., Sat.*); 3) the months of the year (*Jan., Feb., Mar., Apr., Jul., Aug., Sept., Oct., Nov., Dec.*); and 4) other commonly used expressions, e.g. *Ave., St.*

The use of the apostrophe in the writing of contractions can profitably be taught in a level 3 spelling program. Pupils can be led to observe that in the contractions which they themselves commonly use (e.g. *I'll, I'd, didn't, we'll*), an apostrophe replaces the graphemes corresponding to the deleted speech sounds. They should be able to see, for example, that the apostrophe in *we'll* is a conventional representation of the *w* and *i* which stood for /w/ and /i/ and were dropped when *we* and *will* were combined to form *we'll*. Although the use of contractions is limited in formal writing, we do have occasion to use them in informal communication (e.g. in personal letters), and therefore pupils will need to know about this function of the apostrophe at a relatively early age.

The use of the apostrophe in the formation of possessives should also be introduced at this level. Much confusion can be eliminated if pupils are helped to discover, early in their writing careers, that the principles governing the placement of the apostrophe are simple and few:

1. When a *singular* noun is used in possessive form, we add *'s*, as in *dog/dog's* and *church/church's*.
2. When a *plural* noun is used in possessive form, we add only an apostrophe, as in *dogs/dogs'* and *churches/churches'*.
3. When an *irregular plural* noun is used in possessive form, we add *'s*, as in *men/men's* and *sheep/sheep's*. Even though this ending is "singular," we can tell from the form of the noun (*men's*) or from context that the noun is plural.

The dictionary

The dictionary, of course, is the final arbiter in matters of spelling, and therefore its use is of prime importance to those who want to master American-English orthography. At this level, speller dictionaries should minimally provide opportunities for pupils to develop their skills in the following:

1. Using alphabetical order.
2. Using guide words to locate information.
3. Finding the dictionary meanings of words.
4. Using the pronunciation key and sound spellings to deter-

mine how words are pronounced, so that they can then be spelled by the application of sound–letter principles. (The development of this dictionary skill is particularly appropriate at level 3.)

5. Determining the syllables of oral and of written words.
6. Finding the different meanings and spellings of homo-nyms.

A good dictionary not only serves as an important tool for spelling purposes, it is also a rich source of information about our language's structure, heritage, and conventions. A well-planned spelling program should provide pupils with ample opportunity to become acquainted with and to use this invaluable reference work.

Summary

In this chapter, we have outlined some ways in which a linguistically based spelling program can extend the pupils' spelling power by allowing them to practice what they have already learned while they are mastering more advanced knowledge and skills. At level 3 — as at all other levels — an effective spelling program should guide pupils from simple to increasingly complex characteristics of our written code. In the next chapter, we shall see how such a spelling program continues to foster the development of spelling power at level 4.

CHAPTER THIRTEEN

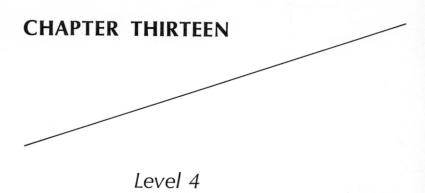

Level 4

A linguistically based spelling program seeks to do more than simply teach children how to spell lists of words. It seeks to guide them toward a functional understanding of their oral code and its visible counterpart, American-English orthography. A modern spelling program is, in brief, a study of language as a whole, with special reference to the written language.

Because such a program is founded upon premises markedly different from those of traditional spelling instruction as described in Chapter Six, its content and organization are distinctive. For example, the words that pupils study are selected on the basis of their utility in demonstrating orthographic principles as well as their utility in writing. And the lessons at each level both strengthen and broaden the pupils' knowledge of the written code.

At the beginning levels, pupils are made aware of the orthography's alphabetic base, and begin to learn fundamental word-building (morphological) principles that can greatly extend their spelling repertoire. Although each level is concerned with all three aspects of language that have special relevance to orthography — phonology, morphology, and context — there is an increasing emphasis on morphology as pupils mature. Let us examine some of the major learning activities suitable for the fourth level of a modern spelling program.

Phonology

The first few weeks of study should be devoted to a review of previously taught spelling principles so that the pupils can refresh their memories and the teacher can assess how well the principles have been mastered. An opening lesson, for example, might contain the following set of words whose respective spellings illustrate a number of important orthographic principles:

sang	blend	wigwam	prompt	cast
fetch	sniff	notch	latch	grasp
thrill	hitch	jot	struck	smack
mess	blunt	sketch	gruff	stunt

Pupils can use this list to review the following matters:

1. The distinction between consonant and vowel phonemes and between long and short vowel sounds.
2. The identification of initial consonant clusters (in *grasp, blend, prompt, blunt, stunt, sketch, smack, sniff, thrill, struck, gruff*), final clusters (in *blend, prompt, cast, grasp, blunt, stunt*), and their spellings.
3. Some previously taught spelling principles. For example: final /ch/ is usually spelled *tch* when preceded by a short vowel (*fetch, notch, latch, hitch, sketch*); final /k/ is usually spelled *ck* (*struck, smack*), but initial /k/ is spelled *c* (*cast*) when followed by a vowel sound spelled *a*; final /f/ after a short vowel is typically spelled *ff* (*sniff, gruff*).

New material

Most of the consonant and vowel phonemes, and their usual graphemic representatives, have been presented by this level. Therefore, as soon as the review of phonology is completed, pupils should become familiar with additional variant spellings of phonemes. In the process, they should use their growing understanding of the effect upon the spelling of phonemes of their position and stress, as well as the effect of adjacent sounds and their letter representation.

For example, a lesson might be developed in which pupils study the variant spellings of two previously taught phonemes,

/n/ as in *now*, and /ng/ as in *ring*. They will have learned that /n/ is usually spelled *n* and that /ng/ is usually spelled *ng*. To gain more sophisticated knowledge, they could consider the following list of words:

wing	single	blank	blanket	drank
shrink	wrinkle	hungry	finger	angry
bang	ceiling	tongue	knit	knob
knock	knot	kneel	knelt	knowledge

With guidance, pupils should be able to determine from such a list the following rules:

1. Although /ng/ is usually spelled *ng* when it ends a word (*wing, bang, ceiling*), it is spelled *n* in other environments. (See principles 2 and 3.)
2. When /ng/ is part of a final consonant cluster (*blank, drank, shrink*), it is spelled *n*.
3. When /ng/ ends a syllable but is followed by a syllable that begins with /g/ or /k/ (*blan′ ket, wrin′ kle, hun′ gry, fin′ ger, an′ gry*), it is spelled *n*.
4. In the word *tongue*, /ng/ is spelled *ngue*, which seems not to fit any principle. This is a most unusual spelling indeed in American English; it occurs only in *tongue, meringue,* and *harangue* (all words of French origin). Its presence in the list can be used to demonstrate to pupils that they should be constantly alert for such maverick spellings, and should make special visual and haptical efforts to master them.

The above list also provides an opportunity (in the form of the *kn* spelling of /n/ as in *knob*) to strengthen the pupils' historical sense of the orthography. Many unusual phoneme–grapheme correspondences, such as this one, have quite rational causes. Therefore, an awareness of *why* some sounds are spelled in unusual ways not only provides pupils with interesting facts about our language, it can also serve as a "memory aid" so that the unpredictable spellings will be remembered. In this particular case, if pupils are told that the *k* in words like *knob* originally represented /k/, they can be made aware of an important linguistic fact: that the sounds of language change with time, but the writing system ordinarily does not change much. Thus, they should be able to understand more clearly how some spellings reflect the way words were pronounced at an earlier stage of our language, and that such vestigial letters persist to this day as graphemic options.

Vowel phonemes, particularly the long vowels, usually present more spelling difficulties than do consonants. Therefore, it is especially important that the principal spellings of vowel phonemes be reviewed throughout a spelling program and that pupils be provided with examples of familiar words that contain these spellings. In mastering such words, pupils should be encouraged to supplement whatever phonological clues are available with visual and haptical clues. As was suggested in Chapter Eight, a multisensory–multimotor approach to spelling is important in any spelling situation, but it becomes particularly so when words containing unusual phoneme–grapheme correspondences are involved.

Morphology

During the early levels of a linguistically based spelling program, the emphasis must necessarily be on the alphabetic nature of the orthography, since the early establishment and constant reinforcement of important phonological principles lies at the heart of the development of spelling power. But by the time pupils reach the fourth level, their awareness of the alphabetic principle underlying written American English should be firmly enough fixed so that they can move on to other areas. In particular, a level 4 spelling program should seek to develop the pupils' understanding of morphological principles and to help them apply these principles in spelling. It is a *combination* of phonological and morphological knowledge that eventually leads to the ability to spell accurately a large vocabulary.

The morphological component of level 4 should begin with a review of the word-building concepts that the pupils have already acquired, especially the concept of inflection: how to make nouns plural and how to change the tense of verbs. Pupils should be reminded that a knowledge of inflectional suffixes greatly expands their word repertoire, since by knowing how to spell and attach a few simple endings, they will be able to use most nouns and verbs in new ways without having to learn each new formation separately.

The concept of derivation, first presented at level 3, should also be reviewed at this time. Pupils should be reminded how to use derivational affixes that alter *both* the meanings and the functions of roots. Useful for this purpose are the suffixes *-er* and *-ly* that were introduced previously. See pages 168–170, Chapter Twelve.

New material

Once these major word-building principles have been reviewed, pupils can be introduced to new morphological material that will help them both in spelling and in extending their vocabularies. For example, a lesson might be built around the following set of words. (The pupils should be reminded to notice phoneme–grapheme correspondences even though the exercise deals mainly with word building.)

disobey	unafraid	inspect	include	increase
appear	install	buckle	approve	infect
inflate	connect	insert	inhale	broken
agree	incline	common	certain	invade

The following sequence might be effective as a teaching procedure:

1. Ask the pupils to examine the first two words in the first row: *disobey* and *unafraid*. Help them to observe that each consists of a prefix plus a root (*dis-* + *obey*), *un-* + *afraid*) and that the prefixes give each derivative a meaning opposite to that of its root.
2. Have the pupils examine the next word, *inspect*. Help them to notice that the second syllable of this word is not itself a word. Point out that *inspect* is made up of a prefix *in-*, meaning "into," and a syllable *spect*, whose origin is a word in another language (Latin) that meant "to look." Thus, the combination of *spect* and the prefix *in-* basically means "to look into."
3. Pupils should be helped to contrast words such as *disobey*, which is comprised of a *prefix and of a root* that is an English word by itself (sometimes called a *free morpheme*), and words such as *inspect*, which is comprised of a *prefix and of a root* that is not an English word by itself (some-

times called a *bound morpheme*). Then they should be
asked to decide which of the words in the study list are
composed of prefixes and roots that are not English words
by themselves (bound morphemes) (*inspect, include,
insult, indulge, infect, inflate, connect, insert, insist,
incline, invade*).[1]

4. Remind the pupils that the prefix **dis-** sometimes provides
   the meaning "not" when attached to a root word, and that
   dis- + *obey* means "not obey." Have the pupils add **dis-**
   to the study words *appear, connect, approve,* and **mount**.
   With guided observation, they should notice that each
   derivative has a meaning opposite to that of the root.
   Pupils might also be asked to use the words they have
   formed in sentences of their own in order to fix the meanings of the new formations in their minds.

5. Next, point out that **un-** can also reverse the meaning of
   a root word — as in **unafraid**. Have pupils add **un-** to
   common, broken, certain, and **buckle,** and ask them to
   notice what happens to the meaning of each root word
   when **un-** is added.

6. Remind the pupils that the **in-** prefix that appears in
   inspect sometimes means "into." Then — after supplying
   the meaning of the roots — ask the pupils to determine
   the meanings of the following study words and to use
   each in a sentence: **inflate** (*flate* = "to blow"), **increase**
   (*crease* = "to grow"), **invade** (*vade* = "to go"), **insert**
   (*sert* = "to put"). For example, *in-* + *flate* = "to blow
   into." Discuss with the pupils the fact that meanings of
   this type are literal meanings, and that they are often
   slightly different in actual usage.

This sample lesson serves to illustrate how the benefits of a
linguistically based spelling program can extend far beyond the
rote mastery of a list of spelling words. The teaching of spelling,
in a modern program, involves the total language — the sounds,
forms, and meanings of words.

---

[1] Although *appear, approve,* and **agree** are also technically of this type,
the introduction of words with assimilated prefixes should be delayed until
later.

At the fourth level, pupils should also extend their familiarity with derivational suffixes as important word-building elements. The noun-forming suffix *-tion* is a good one to begin with. For purposes of linguistic accuracy, it should be noted that *-tion* is a common form of the suffix *-ion,* pronounced /yən/. When *-ion* is added to roots ending with /t/, /s/, or /k/, a new sound found in neither root nor suffix — /sh/ — is created through a process called *synthesis: act + -ion = action, confess + -ion = confession, music + -ion = musician.* Pupils at upper levels can be introduced to this linguistic phenomenon; variants such as the *-cian* of *magician* and the *-sion* of *suspension* are discussed in Chapter Fifteen, pages 204–205. For now, however, it is best to refer to the suffix in its most common form, *-tion.*

To learn how *-tion* functions, pupils might be asked to compare the use of *subtract* and *subtraction* in the following pair of sentences:

1. Can you *subtract* 8 from 11?
2. Yes, that is an easy problem in *subtraction.*

Pupils can be helped to see that in these two sentences, **subtract** functions as a *verb* but **subtraction** functions as a *noun,* and they should be able to conclude that this difference in function is caused by the presence or absence of the suffix *-tion.* (It should also be pointed out to them that /sh/ is spelled *ti* in these words.)

The pupils might then be asked to determine the roots in *action, direction,* and *election* (*act, direct, elect*), and to write pairs of sentences using the root and its derivative (as was done with *subtract* and *subtraction*). They could also reverse the process by practicing adding *-tion* to roots such as *connect, infect, inspect, object, erupt, protect, invent,* and *prevent.*

Numerous other derivational suffixes can be presented at this level once the pupils fully understand the derivational process and its importance in word building. Some suffixes that can profitably be studied at this level are *-able* (e.g. in *enjoyable*), *-ful* (*beautiful*), *-hood* (*brotherhood*), *-ly* (*lonely*), and *-ness* (*stillness*).

Spelling study at the fourth level should also continue to develop the pupils' understanding of compounding. A separate lesson may not be required for this purpose, since it is quite likely that compound words will occur in lessons that have other objectives. But whenever compound words do appear, attention should be called to them and pupils should be reminded that such words present few spelling problems if their components have already been mastered. A useful strategy when working with compounds is to present their separate parts in sentences such as the following: "The cowboy arose at the *break* of *day*." By examining such illustrations, pupils should be able to see how the forms and meanings of compounds develop through the combining of two or more existing words (here, *day* + *break* = *daybreak*).

A thorough understanding of the morphological principles governing our language is of enormous importance when one is attempting to acquire mastery of spelling. Therefore, it is an attentive teacher who seizes every opportunity to encourage the pupils' acquisition and application of these principles. If the pupils also master the spelling conventions that often accompany the word-building process (e.g. the dropping of final *e* before *-ing* is added), they will have taken a major step on the road to spelling power.

Context

The third element of language that should be studied at this level is context, i.e. the functions and meanings of words in English sentences in relation to their surroundings. It will be recalled from earlier chapters that context provides important clues to spelling of *homonyms* (words of like pronunciation but of different meanings and usually different spellings). In general, whenever study words have homonyms, the latter should be presented too. For instance, if *birth* appears in a lesson on /ėr/, *berth* should also be introduced so that pupils are aware of the existence of these homonyms from the very beginning. In addition, if the speller dictionaries provide homonyms for the words listed, this should be pointed out to the pupils.

In relation to the total number of words in the American-English lexicon, the number of homonyms is not particularly great. But many *frequently used* words do have homonyms, so that pupils will encounter them almost as soon as they start school. Consequently, a level 4 program should include a lesson about homonyms and how their spellings can be learned. Here is a list of commonly encountered homonyms that might be used for this purpose.

pour	brake	haul	peek	plain
sale	hour	sail	steel	main
pale	break	male	mane	through
pane	steal	son	meet	peak

1. Pupils should be asked to pair the homonyms contained in the list (*break/brake, peak/peek, sail/sale, steel/steal, mane/main*) and to list the words left over (*pour, hour, male, meet, pale, plain, son, through, haul, pane*) and supply their homonyms, using the speller dictionary if necessary. They should then be directed to study the homonym pairs for appropriate sound–letter clues. For example, in *plane*, the /p/, /l/, and /n/ are regularly spelled; only the /ā/ is a source of difficulty. (Interestingly, it is the spelling of the vowel sound that usually distinguishes one word in a homonym pair from the other.)
2. Pupils should also be directed to contrast the homonyms in sentences so that they will realize that contextual clues can help indicate which word of a homonym pair is meant (e.g. "Jane wore a *plain* white dress for her trip on the *plane*.").

Homonyms need not be a major hurdle in spelling if the pupil is alerted to their existence early in his spelling career and is helped to apply phonological, morphological, and contextual information to master them.

At level 4, the pupil can also engage in vocabulary-enriching activities that would not be possible in traditional spelling programs. Because he can bring to bear upon new words a growing number of phonological and morphological principles, he need not be restricted solely to words of high frequency or words thought to be otherwise appropriate for a child's repertoire. Spelling study can be an activity that extends the pupil's vocabulary and enables him to become a facile user of American English, both in speaking and in writing.

Writing conventions

At least one spelling lesson at this level should be devoted to a review of previously learned writing conventions (e.g. the use of the apostrophe in possessives and contractions) and to the review and extension of the pupil's knowledge of commonly used abbreviations. The study of abbreviations can be especially meaningful at this level, since the pupil is likely to encounter them in reading and to have cause to use them in writing.

A number of commonly used abbreviations suitable for study in a level 4 program are listed below. It is best to have pupils analyze, and demonstrate their ability to spell, both the whole word and its abbreviated form.

year/yr.	second/sec.	quart/qt.	hour/hr.
gallon/gal.	pint/pt.	teaspoon/tsp.	tablespoon/tbsp.
pound/lb.	inch/in.	chapter/chap.	foot or feet/ft.
yard/yd.	railroad/RR.	week/wk.	mile/mi.
mountain/mtn.	Mount/Mt.	ounce/oz.	dozen/doz.

Word history

The authors have continually expressed the opinion that the ability to spell is only one aspect of an individual's understanding of *language* as a whole, and that therefore spelling should be presented within the context of general language study. By the fourth level, then, a pupil should begin to learn something about the origins of the words he commonly uses. In so doing, he will be exposed to a great deal of fascinating material, and he may also acquire considerable (and helpful) insight into the causes of some uncommon spellings. (See Chapter Four.)

The study of word origins can demonstrate to young children that our language is enriched by words from many languages. They will be able to see that some of our seemingly uncommon spellings are caused by our having borrowed words and their spellings from a lender language, and on the other hand, that an original spelling has sometimes been altered to make it more consistent with our spelling system or our pronunciation. A representative list of borrowed words suitable for use at this level follows. When these words are being studied for spelling purposes, pupils should be directed to make use of all available phonological, morphological, and contextual clues.

Word	Origin of Word
noodle	*Nudel* (German)
boss	*baas* (Dutch)
chipmunk	*chitmunk* (American Indian: Algonquin)
coyote	*coyotl* (Mexican: Aztec)
chili	*chilli* (Mexican: Aztec)
alligator	*el lagarto* (Spanish)
chute	*chute* (French)
depot	*depot* (French)
canyon	*cañon* (Spanish)
cigar	*cigarro* (Spanish)
rodeo	*rodeo* (Spanish)
vanilla	*vainilla* (Spanish)
hamburger	*Hamburg* (German)
waffle	*wafel* (Dutch)
piano	*pianoforte* (Italian)
opera	*opera* (Italian)
cookie	*koekje* (Dutch)
Santa Claus	*Sante Klaas* (Dutch)
kangaroo	*kangooroo* (Australian) [origin not confirmed]
bamboo	*bambu* (Malay)

The dictionary

As the child's knowledge of language becomes more and more sophisticated, the dictionary becomes an increasingly valuable tool. At earlier levels, he will have learned how to find in the dictionary the pronunciation, meaning, spelling, and oral and written syllabication of words. At the fourth level, he should be introduced to the use of the dictionary as a source of information about the grammatical functions of words. It is particularly important for the pupil to have access to "part of speech" information at this level, because he is studying derivational affixes and how they can alter the grammatical function of roots.

In any event, it is important that teachers of spelling encourage pupils to use both the speller dictionaries and any available classroom dictionaries. Spelling, after all, is not an activity relegated only to formal spelling study. The ultimate test of spelling ability is whether the individual is able to use correctly spelled words in his daily writing situations. It is here, particularly, that a dictionary becomes a speller's best friend by serving as an authoritative source of spellings that the writer might not yet have mastered. A dictionary is one of the richest language resources available; its use should be fostered.

Summary

By the time the fourth level is reached, modern spelling instruction more nearly resembles the study of language in general than of individual words. The emphasis on general knowledge is intentional. Just as a command of language (the spoken form of communication) develops from familiarity with its phonology, grammar (morphology and syntax), and lexicon, so also a command of orthography (language's written counterpart) develops from the same sources.

A pupil who has conscientiously progressed through the levels thus far described stands on the threshold of functional spelling power. In the next chapter, we shall see how a fifth-level spelling program continues to guide the pupil toward that objective.

CHAPTER FOURTEEN

Level 5

In many ways, the fifth level of a modern spelling program marks a major turning point in the pupil's formal study of spelling. When he completes this level, he will have learned most of the major phonological generalizations that can be made about American-English spelling. He will also have become well acquainted with many of the morphological principles that govern the construction of American-English words. In brief, the pupil who has conscientiously been guided through such a program stands on the threshold of possessing substantial spelling power. Let us see how his fifth-level spelling experiences lead him even further toward this goal.

Review

Here, as at preceding levels, an extensive review period is strongly recommended in order to set the stage for new learnings and to permit an assessment of prior learnings. The opening review lesson should include informal diagnosis of each pupil's general spelling skills so that the teacher can then adapt instruction to individual needs. Previously taught spelling patterns should be tested and reviewed through the presentation of new words that illustrate the major generalizations introduced at earlier levels.

For example, in an opening review lesson, the teacher might help the pupils review some important spelling principles by having them examine the following words:

hobby	catfish	blush	clog	smock
bluff	plastic	drench	bedspread	cucumber
clad	grip	hunch	impress	discuss
indent	contact	bond	shrug	clinch

Some important orthographic factors which are illustrated by this list, and which pupils should review, are:

1. Phoneme–grapheme correspondences that are highly predictable without positional, stress, or environment clues, such as the spellings of the vowel phonemes in *hobby*, *bluff*, and *clad*, and the spellings of the initial consonant phonemes in *bedspread*, *discuss*, and *hunch*.
2. The typical spelling of consonant clusters, as in *blush*, *clog*, *smock*, *bluff*, *plastic*, *drench*, *clad*, *grip*, *shrug*, and *clinch*.
3. How the position of a phoneme in a syllable sometimes affects its spelling; for example, a final consonant spelling is often geminated when preceded by a short vowel phoneme, such as the final /b/ spelled *bb* (*hobby*) and the final /f/ spelled *ff* (*bluff*).
4. How adjacent phonemes and their spellings may affect the orthographic representation of a phoneme; for example, /k/ in consonant clusters is almost always spelled *c* (*clog*, *clad*, *clinch*, *contact*) and initial /k/ followed by vowel sounds spelled *a*, *o*, or *u* is also spelled *c* (*catfish*, *contact*, *cucumber*).
5. How stress can affect the spelling of a phoneme; for example, final /k/ is usually spelled *ck* in a stressed syllable (*smock*), but *c* in an unstressed syllable (*plastic*).
6. Some morphological processes pertinent to spelling and general word study; for example, compounding (*catfish*, *bedspread*) and derivation (*indent*, *contact*, *discuss*, *impress*).
7. The presence of occasional unusual spellings of particular sounds; for example, the *ea* spelling of /e/ in *bedspread*.

In addition, any program of review should stress the fact that the orthography is largely systematic and that a knowledge of the system helps one to develop spelling power. Review lessons should continually reinforce this point so that pupils will be disposed to search for pattern in their spelling studies.

Phonology

In the phonological area, as indicated in the preceding section, the major phoneme–grapheme correspondences and a few unusual spellings should be reviewed. After this is done, the fifth level is commonly concerned with presenting any previously untreated phonemes. An example of such a phoneme is /zh/ (as in *garage*) — perhaps the most infrequently used American-English phoneme, but one whose several spellings are a potential source of difficulty. It is best to delay presentation of this sound until level 5 because an understanding of its principal spellings requires fairly extensive phonological and morphological analysis of words not commonly used by very young children. The phoneme can be studied effectively through a representative word list such as:

confuse	confusion	provide	provision
collide	collision	decide	decision
conclude	conclusion	revise	revision
erode	erosion	equate	equation
pleasure	mirage	treasure	garage

By studying this list, pupils should be able to perceive the following:

1. /zh/ appears when the suffix *-ion* (see Chapter Thirteen, page 180) is added to certain roots; *confuse* + *-ion* = *confusion* — the final /z/ of *confuse* becomes /zh/ spelled *si*; *provide* + *-ion* = *provision* — the final /d/ of *provide* becomes /zh/ spelled *si* (and the vowel of the second syllable also changes).

2. /zh/ is unpredictably spelled. Although its principal spelling is *si*, as part of a suffix it can also be spelled *ti* (*equation*) or *s* (*pleasure, treasure*). It should be explained to pupils that in words such as *garage* and *mirage*, the *ge* spelling of /zh/ is a result of the fact that

when these words were borrowed from French, their original pronunciation and spelling were left unchanged.

Another phoneme whose several graphemic options are best reserved for study at level 5 is /sh/. Early in the child's schooling, he will have learned that /sh/ is typically represented by *sh* in one-syllable words (e.g. *shop, push*). It is now appropriate to introduce him formally to other ways of spelling this sound. The following list can be used to help pupils observe some important facts about the various spellings involved.

shown	shack	radish	publish	fiction
special	shoulder	social	shelter	shone
shaft	correction	sherbet	bashful	machine
schwa	ocean	chef	shrub	appreciate

A careful analysis of this list of words should lead pupils to observe these two points:

1. /sh/ is quite consistently spelled *sh* (as pupils were taught previously) at the beginning or end of a word: *shown, shack, radish, publish, shoulder, shelter, shone, shaft, sherbet, shrub*. (It should be pointed out to pupils that *chef* and *schwa* are notable exceptions — *chef* having been taken from French and *schwa* being ultimately of Hebrew origin, and part or all of the original spelling having been retained in each case.)

2. Except for the borrowed spellings, the unpredictable spellings of /sh/ occur when it initiates a suffix or otherwise appears in an interior part of a word; for example, *ti* occurs in *fiction* and *correction*, *ci* occurs in *special* and *social*, *c* occurs in *appreciate*, *ch* occurs in *machine*, and *ce* occurs in *ocean*.

The many graphemic options of this phoneme demonstrate that some spellings must be mastered by the use of multisensory–multimotor techniques. Pupils should, of course, be reminded that often only one or two phonemes in a word are unpredictably spelled (cf. *special*).

Syllabication should continue to be studied at this level, since the ability to analyze words into syllables becomes more and more crucial as the pupils' vocabularies become increasingly polysyllabic. Only after polysyllabic words have been broken up into their constituent syllables can phonological clues to spelling be used to the fullest degree possible.

Morphology

It has repeatedly been noted that a modern spelling program proceeds in a spiral fashion, constantly adding to pupils' previous knowledge in order to lead them toward the major understandings that explain our writing system. Thus, because simple morphological concepts have been developed with care, the pupils' skills of morphological analysis can be greatly enhanced at the fifth level. They will already be aware of the ways in which roots and affixes serve as building blocks, and how such knowledge can aid both in spelling and in vocabulary enrichment.

At this level, numerous prefixes can be studied effectively, e.g. *sub-* (meaning "under" or "near") as in *submarine* and *suburb*, *per-* (meaning "through" or "thoroughly") as in *permit* and *perfect,* and *ex-* (meaning "from" or "out of") as in *export* and *explode*. A review and extension of the pupils' knowledge of roots is a natural (and necessary) complement to the study of such prefixes. For example, if they already know the roots *sist* and *mit*, they can construct new words simply by adding on certain prefixes.

The use of a diagram form is often effective when such word-building activities are introduced. A typical diagram might look like this:

sist = "to stand"   *mit* = "to send"

in-   *re-*
re- } + *sist* } = _____   *trans-* } + *mit* } = _____
con-   *sub-*

Pupils would be asked to fill in the blanks (*insist*, etc.), and to figure out the approximate meaning of each derivative by combining the meaning of the prefix with the meaning of the root. They might then be asked to use the new words in sentences to fix the meanings in their memories. A classroom dictionary or speller dictionary is a tool that pupils — for reasons previously discussed — should be encouraged to use in exercises of this type.

The study of derivational suffixes should also be continued at this level. As a result of the pupils' growing linguistic sophistication, such suffixes can now be analyzed both in terms of their sounds and in terms of their effect on the grammatical function of a root. Let us examine in some detail a lesson dealing with the noun-forming suffixes *-ure, -ment,* and *-ist* and the adjective-forming suffix *-ous.*

A sample lesson

Using *mixture, equipment, humorist,* and *humorous* as key words, ask the pupils to determine the root word of each (*mix, equip, humor,* and *humor*). Then ask which of the derivatives might be used as nouns (*mixture, equipment,* and *humorist*), and how *humorous* functions in the sentence "He is a *humorous* fellow" (as an adjective).

At this point, direct the pupils to examine the following list of words:

fixture	creature	shipment	druggist	failure
signature	punishment	mysterious	nervous	adventure
attachment	pianist	arrangement	violin	state
govern	motor	harp	marvel	vary

Ask them to pronounce the words and analyze them for noticeable sound–letter relationships. Then have them divide the study words into groups that contain the same suffix, as follows:

-ure:	fixture, creature, adventure, signature, failure
-ment:	shipment, punishment, attachment, arrangement
-ist:	druggist, pianist
-ous:	mysterious, nervous

Guide the pupils to observe that *-ure* has formed nouns from the roots *fix, create, advent, sign,* and *fail.* (They may need special help to discover *advent,* since it will probably be unfamiliar to them, and to discover *create* and *sign* because of the spelling changes that occur.) Help the pupils to notice that when *-ure* is added to words ending with /t/, the /t/ changes to /ch/ (*create* vs. *creature, advent* vs. *adventure*). And point out that the *t* of *fixture* was added to the spelling of *fix* + *-ure* because a /ch/ is pronounced in that word too. Also help the pupils to observe how the second vowel sound of *create,* /ā/, is obscured, even lost, in *creature.*

A similar morphological analysis can then be carried out for each of the three remaining groups of study words. Make sure that the pupils notice that the following spelling changes occur during the derivational process:

1. When a suffix beginning with a vowel is added, final *e* is deleted from the root (*nerve* + *-ous* = *nervous*) and final *y* representing /ē/ is changed to *i* (*mystery* + *-ous* = *mysterious*).
2. When a root ends with a single consonant spelled with a single letter, the letter is doubled before a suffix beginning with a vowel is added (*drug* + *-ist* = *druggist*).

The pupils should then be directed to add to the remaining study words as many of the four suffixes under examination as are appropriate, making the necessary spelling changes as they go. They should end up with a list that includes *violinist, statement, stature, government, motorist, harpist, marvelous,* and *various.*

The foregoing lesson illustrates how a modern spelling program increasingly stretches the pupil's knowledge to encompass ever more complex and more powerful spelling principles. If accompanied by phonological and contextual (syntax-meaning) information, morphological information provides the pupil with a means of developing his spelling and lexical repertoire that he can use during his entire lifetime.

Context

At this level, additional homonyms should be studied as potential spelling problems. A typical list might include *in/inn, loan/lone, scent/sent/cent, taught/taut, hire/higher, serial/cereal, cheep/cheap, waste/waist, pier/peer, bored/board, piece/peace, stake/steak,* and *fare/fair.* Pupils should be reminded that they will need to be attentive *both* to spelling *and* to meaning in order to master homonyms.

The fifth level is also an appropriate time to introduce *homographs,* i.e. words that are alike in spelling but differ in meaning and origin — and, in some cases, in pronunciation as well. Although homographs usually present problems in decoding rather than in encoding (see Chapter Two, page 26), their inclusion in a spelling text is warranted because they *can* be sources of spell-

ing difficulty. In addition, and equally important, their study contributes to the pupil's general knowledge of his language and of
its interesting writing system.

Three kinds of homographs can be effectively introduced at
this level:

1. Homographs whose pronunciations differ because they
   contain graphemes that can represent more than one
   phoneme, e.g. *ow* for either /ou/ or /ō/ (cf. the *bow* of
   a boat and the *bow* of a dress). Point out to pupils that
   such homographs illustrate how some graphemes do
   double duty in our writing system, and should be noted
   carefully as sources of possible spelling difficulty.

2. Homographs whose pronunciations differ primarily in
   terms of syllable stress. Some homographs of this type
   are:

con′ duct/con duct′	*com′ bine/com bine′*
proj′ ect/pro ject′	*sub′ ject/sub ject′*
ref′ use/re fuse′[1]	*per′ mit/per mit′*

   Pupils should pronounce these homograph pairs and
   practice using them in sentences; for example, "You will
   need to obtain a *per′ mit*" vs. "I will not *per mit′* you to
   go."

   By examining such contrasting sentences, pupils should
   be able to observe an interesting phenomenon: when the
   homograph is stressed on the first syllable, it usually
   functions as a *noun*, but when it is stressed on the second
   syllable, it usually functions as a *verb*. This illustrates
   once again that our language is systematic in structure.

3. Homographs that are alike in pronunciation but different
   in meaning and origin. An example of this type of homograph is *scale*, as in the *scale* of a fish and a musical *scale*;
   the first *scale* is of Old French origin (*escale* = "a husk")
   and the second is a Latin borrowing (*scala* = "a ladder").
   Such homographs will be entered separately in dictionaries, and if dictionaries are available that contain information about word origins, most pupils will find it
   fascinating to look up more words of this type, e.g. *pelt*,

---

[1] Pupils should be helped to observe that /z/ occurs in *re fuse′* where /s/
occurs in *ref′ use*.

loaf, host, lean, cape, and *toll,* noting the differences in their meanings as well as in their origins.

Word history

As the preceding discussion indicates, a pupil's familiarity with the history of our language, and particularly with the history of the words that he may have occasion to spell, can contribute greatly to his spelling ability as well as to his general understanding of language. At earlier levels of the program, the origins of some commonly used words were introduced. (See, for example, Chapter Thirteen.) At level 5, word study of this type should be continued, and pupils should be helped to discover other ways by which our lexical stock grows and changes. A useful lesson for this purpose might be based on the following set of words, a set which presents some fascinating examples of various types of word origin.

patio	plaza	mosquito	macaroni	gorilla
waltz	raccoon	cafeteria	banjo	hurricane
radar	astronaut	motel	smog	twirl
flurry	gas	van	broadcast	satellite

In terms of origin, these words fall into six groups:

1. *Borrowings:* words borrowed from other languages. (The fact their original meaning has been altered in some cases can be used to demonstrate to pupils that language is not static.) In this list, borrowings include:

   patio: a Spanish word meaning "a space"
   plaza: a Spanish word meaning "a place"
   mosquito: a Spanish word meaning "a little fly"
   macaroni: an Italian word designating the food
   gorilla: a word of probable African origin designating
     that creature
   waltz: a German word meaning "to roll"
   raccoon: an Algonquin (American-Indian) word designating
     the nocturnal animal
   cafeteria: a word of Mexican-Spanish origin meaning "a
     coffee house"
   banjo: a word of African origin designating the stringed
     instrument

hurricane: a word of Spanish origin designating a violent
   storm
satellite: a word of Latin origin meaning "an attendant"

2. *Acronyms:* coinages constructed from the first letter or
   series of letters in each word of a phrase. In this list,
   radar is an acronym from the phrase "*ra*dio *d*etecting *a*nd
   *r*anging."
3. *Derivatives:* a new formation constructed from roots and
   affixes. In this list, *astronaut* is a word representing a
   combination of the Greek *astron* ("star") and the Greek
   nautēs ("sailor") — a most appropriate term indeed.
4. *Blends:* words made by combining sounds from two or
   more words, thereby creating a new word having a unique
   meaning. In the list above, the blends are *motel* (*motor* +
   hotel), *smog* (*smoke* + *fog*), *twirl* (*twist* + *whirl*), and
   flurry (*flutter* + *hurry*).
5. *Clipped forms:* abbreviated forms of polysyllabic words.
   In the above list, *gas* is a short form of *gasoline* and *van*
   is a short form of *caravan.*
6. *Compounds:* words made by combining two or more
   words in their entirety. In the above list, *broadcast* is an
   example.

Lessons of this type not only serve to make pupils aware of
their fascinating linguistic heritage, they also aid the development of spelling ability by providing explanations for many uncommon spellings.

The dictionary

The development of the dictionary habit should continue to
receive a major emphasis at the fifth level. As pupils mature in
their understanding and use of language and, through their various school subjects, are made aware of the diversity and richness
of the American-English lexicon, the dictionary will become one
of their most valuable allies. Therefore, a lesson or two should
be devoted to a formal review of the ways in which a dictionary
can be used.

At this level, the content of a speller dictionary should approximate that of a good standard abridged dictionary. Without being

too complex, it should contain enough information so that pupils can study spelling words in terms of pronunciation, spelling, oral and written syllabication, major meanings, part of speech represented, homonyms, and origins.

Summary

A pupil who has progressed through the five levels described in the past few chapters will have achieved an understanding of American-English orthography not readily attainable through traditional spelling programs or through chance. Above all, he will have become aware of the existence of pattern within our writing system. He will be able to detect the phonological clues which can aid in mastering the spellings of words. He will be able to construct and dissect words as necessary — both for spelling purposes and for vocabulary enrichment. He will be aware of homonyms and how their spellings should be studied. He will have a growing sense of our linguistic heritage and its richness and diversity. He will know how to use the dictionary as an invaluable ally. In short, by the end of the fifth level, the pupil should be well on the way to being a self-directed user of the writing system.

As will be seen in the next few chapters, subsequent levels will strengthen his growing spelling power even further. But before he proceeds to these levels, the teacher should make sure that he has mastered certain major concepts. Below is a list of words that can be used informally to assess the pupil's knowledge of phonology, morphology, and context as applied to spelling. The reader is invited to try his hand at determining 1) which words can be spelled solely by the use of phonological principles; 2) which words might have morphological information brought to bear on them; and 3) which words cannot be spelled correctly unless their meaning is known, e.g. through contextual clues.

thus	foolish	cause	hew	signal
civil	step	glow	sphere	sleeveless
moonlight	hue	sprang	liberty	bakery
kettle	review	employ	knead	pronoun

CHAPTER FIFTEEN

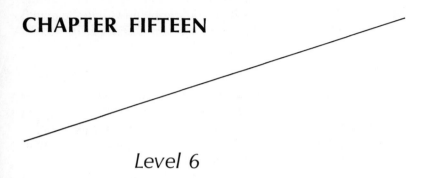

Level 6

A child who has progressed satisfactorily through the first five levels of a modern spelling program should have at his command a substantial set of orthographic generalizations that can be applied in most spelling situations. Rather than having to memorize the spelling of each word, he should be able to determine many spellings through his knowledge of the phonological, morphological, and contextual characteristics of our language.

Since the level 6 pupil will thus have accumulated a great deal of knowledge about his spoken language and its writing system, a sixth-level spelling program can deal with these subjects in a relatively sophisticated manner. In short, principles and processes that have been presented by means of examples and inductive methods can now be explained on linguistic grounds. At the sixth level, then, pupils should not only know *how* our orthography is structured in certain ways, they should also begin to understand *why*.

Spelling study at this level should both recapitulate for youngsters what they have learned about spoken and written communication and provide an analysis of such prior learning, adjusting this study to fit the needs of individual pupils. Since the emphasis will thus be on the review and explanation of important principles and processes, the precise number of words presented in each lesson is not of great consequence; the number should be dictated by what is necessary for the review to be adequate or for the explanation to be understood.

In the main, then, spelling study at this level should contribute to the pupils' developing spelling abilities by providing them with explanatory power as well. Let us see how this might be accomplished.

An introduction to various types of writing systems

A good way to initiate spelling study at this level is to discuss various writing systems and how they differ. Such a discussion sets the stage for subsequent lessons concerning our own alphabetically based orthography, and will help youngsters see that, although our writing system is not as precise as it might be, it is still a quite efficient means of representing spoken language in graphic form. (See Chapters One and Two for background information that may prove useful.)

Pupils should be helped to understand that there are three major types of writing systems — logographic, syllabic, and alphabetic — and that alphabetic systems are the most efficient because in such systems, relatively few graphic symbols are needed to encode speech into writing. This latter point can be demonstrated to pupils through a discussion of Hawaiian orthography, in which adherence to the alphabetic principle — one letter for one sound — is nearly perfect.

An alphabetic writing system

Explain to the class that when early English and American missionaries observed that the Hawaiian language had 13 phonemes, including a glottal stop used in certain phonetic environments, they devised an alphabet with 12 letters, one for each sound except the glottal stop. Hawaiian phonemes and corresponding graphemes, then, are as follows:

Consonants	*Vowels*
h = /h/ as in **hit**[1]	**a** = /ä/ as in **father**
k = /k/ as in **king**	**e** = /ā/ as in **ate**
l = /l/ as in **look**	**i** = /ē/ as in **he**
m = /m/ as in **man**	**o** = /ō/ as in **go**
n = /n/ as in **no**	**u** = /ü/ as in **rule**
p = /p/ as in **push**	
w = /w/ as in **wish**	

[1] Some of the phonetic equivalents shown are slightly inexact, e.g. Hawaiian /k/ is actually pronounced a bit more "softly" than English /k/. However, the equivalents are sufficiently precise for present purposes.

Point out to the pupils that once they know these sounds and their graphic symbols, and once they understand that every Hawaiian syllable ends in a vowel, they will be able to spell correctly almost any Hawaiian word they can pronounce, as well as pronounce any such word they see in print. Any list of Hawaiian words can be used to demonstrate the ease with which this skill may be acquired. Here is one presented in a convenient form: the first-column list can be used to let the pupils practice *pronouncing* Hawaiian words; the second-column list can be read off by the teacher so that pupils can practice *spelling* the same words.

Hawaiian Words	Pronunciation	Meaning
aloha	/ä lō′ hä/	hello; good-bye; greetings
kahuna	/kä hü′ nä/	doctor [in olden days]; witchcraft [now]
pilikia	/pē lē kē′ ä/	trouble; nuisance
kane	/kä′ nä/	man
wahine	/wä hē′ nä/	woman
Pehea oe	/pä hä′ ä/ /ō′ ä/	How are you?
kumukula	/kü′ mü kü′ lä/	schoolteacher
mahalo	/mä hä′ lō/	thank you

The ultimate test of the usefulness of an alphabetic writing system is provided by the following very long word for a very small fish: *humuhumunukunukuapuaa* (/hü′ mü hü′ mü nü′ kü nü′ kü ä′ pü ä′ ä/). If the pupils can spell and pronounce this word correctly, they should be convinced of the values of alphabetic writing.

Lessons such as the foregoing should be accompanied by the observation that American-English orthography is *also* based upon the alphabetic principle. Even though our writing system is complex, it is largely systematic; but the system cannot be understood without a knowledge of the phonological, morphological, and contextual characteristics which govern how we spell. The remaining sections of this chapter will be concerned with some principles that are especially appropriate for review, discussion, and application at the sixth level.

Phonology

American-English orthography is, of course, not as alphabetic as Hawaiian. To determine the correct spelling of many phonemes, we are consequently obliged to rely upon cues provided by position, stress, and/or environment. A review of these factors should be a major element in a sixth-level spelling program.

Positional effects on phoneme–grapheme correspondences can be reviewed, for example, if pupils are asked to state the principle governing the spelling of /oi/ that seems to be operative in the following list of words (/oi/ is usually spelled *oy* when it occurs at the end of a syllable, and *oi* when it occurs elsewhere).

convoy	royal	corduroy	loyal
ointment	joint	pointer	rejoice

The influence of syllabic stress on spelling can be reviewed in a similar manner. Pupils can be directed to examine a list of words containing /k/ in word- or syllable-final position in order to determine the rule governing its spelling (final /k/ is spelled *c* when it occurs in an unstressed syllable, and *ck* when it occurs in a stressed syllable).

attic	magic	pocket	frantic
attack	slick	trick	wick

The influence of neighboring sounds (environment) on the spelling of some phonemes can also be reviewed through the use of a set of words, this time containing /k/ in *initial* position.

catalog	coop	curtain	coastal
carnival	kennel	caper	cowardly
kindergarten	cultivate	cloudburst	crusade
control	coin	keepsake	kindness

By examining such a list, pupils should be able to determine that initial /k/ is spelled *k* when it is followed by /i/, /e/, /ē/, and /ī/, but otherwise it is usually spelled *c*.

Another example of the effect of environment is provided by the numerous spellings of /ȯ/, a vowel whose pronunciation is subject to considerable dialectal variation. Although it might at first seem that the spellings of this sound are completely random (cf. *all*, *or*, and *law*), a close observation of /ȯ/ in certain words brings out a few reasonably reliable spelling principles. The following list might be used:

reward	salt	because	autumn	jaw
quarter	squawk	applause	recall	flaw
falter	clause	outward	authentic	audience

Through careful study of this list, pupils should be able to see that:

1. when /ȯ/ follows /w/, it is usually spelled *a* (e.g. *reward*).
2. when /ȯ/ comes before /l/, it is usually spelled *a* (e.g. *salt*).
3. when /ȯ/ comes before /z/, it is usually spelled *au* (e.g. *clause*).

And if none of the environments just listed is present:

4. when /ȯ/ begins a word, it is usually spelled *au* (e.g. *autumn*).
5. when /ȯ/ ends a word, it is usually spelled *aw* (e.g. *flaw*).

Troublesome sound–letter relationships

Unfortunately, some phonemes do not conform very well to orthographic principles, and pupils need to be alert for these phonemes when they are attempting to spell words that they may not have written or seen in print before. Therefore, at the sixth level, the following potential sources of spelling difficulty should be reviewed: /ā/ before /r/ as in *care*, /ē/ before /r/ as in *here*, /ė/ before /r/ as in *urn*, /ü/ as in *food*, /ə/ as in *circus*, and /'n/ as in *button*.[2]

Morphology

A sixth-level spelling program should provide for extensive review of the word-building characteristics of our language. It should also enable pupils to apply previously learned morphological principles to new roots and affixes, so that spelling skills and vocabularies can be expanded.

Suffixes

For example, a class discussion of derivational suffixes could be initiated with a list of word pairs such as:

familiar/familiarize (contains the verb-forming *-ize*)
popular/popularity (contains the noun-forming *-ity*)
spirit/spiritless (contains the adjective-forming *-less*)
crazy/crazily (contains the adverb-forming *-ly*)

[2] In some dictionaries the vowel in *care* is symbolized as /ā/ or /â/; in *here* as /î/; in *urn* as /ė/ or /û/; in *button* as /ən/.

Ask the class to determine the suffix involved in each case, and the grammatical function it brings to the root word. Then ask the pupils to use the same suffixes to form derivatives of *real* (*realize, reality, really*), *immense* (*immensely, immensity*), *limit* (*limitless*), and *lazy* (*lazily*). (In the last example, remind the pupils of the spelling change required when suffixes are added to a word ending in a vowel sound spelled *y*.)

Similar exercises can be constructed for any number of derivational suffixes. Among the more useful suffixes to work with at this level, because of their wide utility, are *-ful* (*mournful*), *-ence* (*dependence*), and *-ance* (*disturbance*). (The use of *-ence* as opposed to *-ance* does not follow any predictable pattern.)

Prefixes

The use of prefixes should also be reviewed at this time in order to enhance both spelling ability and vocabulary development. The words *defense, decline, defraud, defrost,* and *define,* for example, can be used to illustrate the several meanings *de-* can contribute to a derivative. (In *defense* and *decline* it means "turn away from"; in *defraud* and *define* it means "derived from"; and in *defrost* it means "removed from.") Advanced pupils may find it interesting to locate other words containing the prefix *de-* and to note its meaning in each word; a good standard desk dictionary will be required for such an activity.

De- can also be used to illustrate how familiarity with prefixes aids in spelling. In ordinary rapid speech, *de-* is pronounced in a variety of ways, e.g. /də/, /di/, and /dē/. Therefore, sound-to-letter cues alone will not ordinarily provide the correct spelling; one has to know that the prefix *de-* is invariably spelled *de*. Words such as *deface, denote,* and *delight* can be pronounced for the class to spell in order to illustrate this point, and other prefixes such as *pre-* (*preview, prefix, prefer, precede*) and *re-* (*retract, reentry, replace, research*) can be treated in the same manner.

Roots

A review and extension of the pupil's knowledge of roots (both free and bound morphemes) should be an integral part of morphological study at this level, since roots are the basic building blocks of language. Sixth-level youngsters can be helped to observe that a few "powerful" roots can form a large number of American-

English words. The following list, for example, contains three of these widely used morphemes (*script*, *phon*, and *ject*):

prescription	trajectory	symphony
microphone	description	transcript
subjected	phonograph	phonics
scripture	reject	inject

The class should be asked to examine these words carefully and to group together those that have the same roots (*script* meaning "writing" in *prescription, scripture, description, transcript; phon* meaning "sound" in *microphone, phonograph, symphony, phonics;* and *ject* meaning "throw" in *subjected, trajectory, reject, injection*). If speller dictionaries or classroom dictionaries containing etymological information are available, each of the above words can then be analyzed in terms of the spelling and meaning of its prefix, root, and suffix.

In the process, it should be pointed out to pupils that *prescription*, for example, need not cause spelling difficulty, since they are probably already familiar with the prefix *pre-* and the suffix *-tion,* and they have now been introduced to the root *script*. The pupils should be led to observe, too, that the meaning of *prescription* can be roughly determined since they know that *pre-* commonly means "before," that *-tion* forms a noun, and that *script* means "write"; and the combination of these three elements would give a literal meaning of "something written before."

All of the words on the foregoing list can be analyzed in this way. However, lessons of this type are not intended to be completed in one class period — or at the same rate of progress by all pupils. Since such word study can be extremely profitable, every pupil will need adequate time to do the exercises with care and to assimilate the knowledge gained.

At this level, pupils should also be introduced to certain processes in which morphology and phonology combine to influence the way sounds are spelled. Two such morphophonemic processes are *assimilation* and *synthesis*.

Assimilation

Assimilation is a linguistic phenomenon in which a speech sound *becomes similar* to an adjacent sound. The importance of assimilation for our writing system stems from the fact that the spellings of words formed from prefixes and roots are often influenced by this process, words such as *acclaim, appraise,* and *assign.* Each of these derivatives is composed of the prefix *ad-* (meaning "to") and a root, thus: *ad- claim', ad- praise', ad- sign'.* But if *adclaim* is pronounced rapidly several times, it can be observed that the /d/ of *ad-* becomes muted, if not lost entirely; this is assimilation in action. And for spelling purposes, it is important to realize that even though the pronunciation of the prefix changes, its presence is indicated graphically by a doubling of the letter that represents the speech sound that assimilates the lost sound: thus *adclaim* becomes *acclaim.* This process explains numerous double-consonant spellings in American-English words.

Familiarity with the process of assimilation, coupled with a knowledge of roots and affixes, can be invaluable when it is necessary to spell unfamiliar derivatives. Simply hearing /ə klām'/ and depending solely on sound clues will not produce *acclaim,* but a knowledge of morphology and assimilation can lead one to the correct spelling.

Pupils might be presented with the following prefixes and roots and then asked to write correctly real American-English words, using their new understanding of assimilation in the process.

ad- + cord	*ad- + fair*
ad- + prove	*ad- + sume*
ad- + nex	*ad- + tack*

Synthesis

Synthesis is a linguistic process whereby two adjacent speech sounds combine to form a totally new sound. (See Chapter Fourteen, page 188.) The phoneme /sh/ that occurs in such words as *facial, rejection, partial,* and *mansion* is an excellent example of synthesis. To demonstrate the process of synthesis to pupils, have them identify the root of *facial* (*face*). Then have them say *face -ial* more and more rapidly until the /s/ and /y/ of /fās' yəl/ combine to form /sh/ in /fā' shəl/.

Synthesis is likely to occur whenever the suffixes *-ion, -ial,* and *-ian* are added to roots ending with /s/, /t/, or /k/. Here are some words that can be used to demonstrate both synthesis and some of the major orthographic representations of /sh/.

congressional (*ssi*)   depreciate (*c*)
suspension (*si*)   magician (*ci*)
martial (*ti*)

A knowledge of morphophonemics can even make it easier to deal with the old spelling bugbear /ə/ in certain situations. To be more specific: once youngsters become familiar with the usually quite predictable spelling of most affixes, the many suffixes in which vowels are reduced to /ə/ should not present insuperable spelling problems. For example, the usual spelling of /ə/ in words containing the suffix *-ion* is *o* as in **retraction, discussion, suspicion** (the /sh/ presents a greater spelling problem than the /ə/ in this suffix).

Morphological studies at the sixth level should not only allow for review of previously learned principles, they should also extend the pupil's understanding of such principles and increase his ability to use them in spelling and in word study. Coupled with phonological cues, morphological cues are an extremely important source of spelling power.

The dictionary

As the pupils' ability to analyze words becomes greater and greater, the dictionary will be an increasingly valuable ally. Therefore, a sixth-level spelling program should include extensive use of the dictionary, particularly for the study of roots and affixes; and a lesson or two should be devoted to making sure that all pupils know what kinds of information can be found in a dictionary. The following skills should be at least briefly reviewed:

1. Using alphabetical order
2. Using guide words to locate words
3. Using pronunciation keys to understand sound spellings
4. Determining the meanings and/or the spellings of words
5. Determining part-of-speech information
6. Determining the presence and/or the meanings of roots and affixes
7. Finding out etymological information about words

Speller dictionaries should include enough information for this type of exercise to be carried out, since otherwise a standard desk dictionary will be needed for this purpose.

Word history

A level 6 spelling program should continue to advance the pupil's knowledge of the historical development of the English language, and should provide him with further illustrations of how such knowledge can contribute to spelling and vocabulary improvement. (See Chapters Three and Four.) At this level, pupils might, for example, be introduced to the reason why many of our names for live animals are very different from our names for the foods they provide. (During the Norman occupation of Britain, the Anglo-Saxon words *calf, sheep, cow,* and *pig* were supplemented by the French words *veal, mutton, beef,* and *bacon,* since the ruling French were likely to come into contact with such animals only at table.) Awareness of the French influence on English can also help to explain not only the origins and meanings of some words but also their spellings, e.g. *ballet, courage, cadet,* and *garage.*

Context

At this level, the importance of context should continue to receive emphasis, since it is one of the basic keys to spelling power, especially when homonyms are involved. Some homonyms that can be studied profitably by level 6 pupils are:

team/teem	stationary/stationery	wave/waive
sear/seer/sere	idle/idol/idyll	wrote/rote
flow/floe	roll/role	soul/sole
seed/cede	beach/beech	tide/tied
vain/vane/vein	medal/meddle	

Pupils ought to be reminded once more that most of the phoneme–grapheme correspondences in a homonym are usually quite predictable, and that they should pay particular attention to those correspondences that present possible difficulty. They will be able to observe in the above list, for example, that a vowel phoneme is usually the source of spelling error in homonyms.

Summary

By the time the sixth level is reached, a modern spelling program will have familiarized the learner with the systematic nature of American-English orthography. He will have acquired an understanding of the productive phonological, morphological, and contextual principles that govern American-English spelling. Most importantly, he will have learned how to *use* these principles in all his spelling activities, both in formal exercises and in the process of writing at home or in school.

The sixth level of such a program is, for many children, the culmination of their formal education in spelling. For this reason, this level ought to include activities that synthesize and summarize the many techniques that lead to spelling power. That the pupil's inquiry into our language and its writing system can and should be continued even after level 6 is completed is our contention in the next two chapters.

CHAPTER SIXTEEN

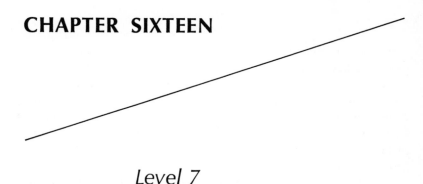

Level 7

Spelling is not a subject that the pupil ceases to study after he completes level 6. Rather, it is a set of skills that requires a lifetime of continuous replenishing if these skills are to keep abreast of the individual's language development, as well as growth and change in the language itself.

Up through the sixth level, the elementary school pupil is led to understand and apply the alphabetic principle through an analysis of phonological, morphological, and contextual aspects of language. But then, too often, he is left without any systematic school instruction that could help him perfect and enlarge his writing vocabulary. Therefore, some teachers at the seventh and eighth level, and many language-arts specialists in the secondary schools, have expressed the belief that spelling should not be considered "finished" when level 6 is completed.

The authors of this volume agree with these teachers and specialists: spelling instruction should be continued through levels 7 and 8, but on a more sophisticated plane than has usually been characteristic of spelling programs of the past. The continued acquisition of knowledge about our writing system and the words that it represents not only can be informative and entertaining, but also can enhance the development of spelling power.

The general plan of a level 7 spelling program

A level 7 spelling program should provide for intensive study of American-English orthography and the ways in which it is related to the oral code. It ought to begin with a general review of the basic facts and principles relevant to written English, with the aim of increasing the pupil's interest in — and understanding of — the place of writing in his life.

Such a program need not be organized, as it often was at previous levels, according to a weekly lesson plan in which subject matter is laid out day by day or session by session. Instead, information, practical applications, and questions may be informally presented so as to encourage pupils to pursue the mastery of spelling in a somewhat independent fashion.

Review

The opening review of a level 7 spelling program should provide enough background for pupils to understand the new material to be presented at level 7. By doing so, it will not only serve as a refresher course for those pupils who have been through a linguistically based spelling program in levels 1–6, it will also give pupils who have *not* been exposed to such a program a comprehensive idea of the alphabetic nature of our written language and of its phonological, morphological, and contextual characteristics. Among the matters that should be reviewed at this level are:

1. The syllabication of words
2. The effect of position, stress, and environment on the choice of grapheme used to represent a particular phoneme
3. The /ə/ of unaccented syllables and its various graphemic representations
4. The use of the diacritic *e* to represent certain long-vowel and certain final-position consonant phonemes
5. The use of two or more graphemes to represent a single phoneme
6. The use of a single grapheme to represent more than one phoneme

7. The effect on pronunciation and spelling of combining certain vowel and consonant phonemes
8. The formation of plurals and other derivatives

The basically alphabetic nature of the orthography

A seventh-level spelling program should stress the fact that while the phoneme–grapheme representations in our language are not always predictable (i.e. they do not exist in a one-to-one relationship), the American-English orthography is nonetheless alphabetically based. Many of its seeming irregularities can be explained if one considers the effect of position, stress, and environment.

Maverick spellings

However, some maverick spellings do exist, so pupils should study words of like pattern in sets and note any departures from the usual spelling in any part of the word. For example, analysis will reveal that in the word *iron*, the unpredictable spellings are represented by *r* and *o*. (The letter *i* is used for initial /ī/ more than 80 percent of the time, and *n* is used for final /n/ about 93 percent of the time in a 17,000-word vocabulary.) And in the word *choir*, the highly irregular spellings are the *ch* for /kw/ and the *o* for /ī/. Words such as *iron* and *choir* are probably best mastered on an individual basis. Their spellings are so dramatically unpredictable that pupils can rather readily acquire a mental image of them by visual and haptical means.

Syllabication

A thorough review also ought to emphasize the importance of syllabication for mastery of spelling. First of all, the position of a phoneme in a syllable often helps determine its spelling. For example, /ch/ is never spelled *tch*, and /k/ is never spelled *ck*, when these sounds occur in initial position; and /oi/ is usually spelled *oi* only at the beginning or in the middle of a syllable (exceptions are *doi′ ly*, *poi′ son*, and *toi′ let*). Second, many pupils find it easier to spell a word if they say and hear it in syllables. Such a procedure should accompany, rather than replace, a careful analysis of phoneme–grapheme relationships.

Environmental influences on spelling

It often happens that the phoneme that appears before or after certain phonemes helps determine the correct spelling. For example, /f/ can be spelled *f*, *ff*, *gh*, or *ph* in various positions, but when it is preceded by an initial /s/, it is invariably spelled *ph* as in *sphere*. Pupils should be led to observe this behavior by examining groups of words in which such a correspondence occurs. They will also notice, if they refer to a dictionary, that words beginning with the consonant cluster /sf/ spelled *sph* have a common origin.

The influence of stress on spelling

The pupils' success in building spelling power will depend, to a large extent, on their ability to carry out a careful, rational, and mature phonological analysis of words. They will need to know the effects of syllabic stress — as well as of position and environment — on the choices one makes among alternative graphemes for certain phonemes.

In particular, they should review the matter of accented and unaccented syllables, and the fact that reduced stress has led to the presence of /ə/ in words like *able* (/ā′ bəl/), *about* (/ə bout′/), and *admirable* (/ad′ mər ə bəl/). Teachers may find it advantageous to pronounce these unstressed vowels with their full original value in order to help pupils remember which letter is used to write them. For example, for spelling purposes only, teachers might pronounce the following words with special emphasis as indicated: *pioneer* as /pī′ ō nēr′/, *worship* as /wėr′ ship/, *effort* as /ef′ ȯrt/.

The diacritic *e*

Many spelling difficulties are the result of the fact that numerous options are available for spelling long-vowel sounds. In particular, pupils should learn to pay particular attention to those long vowels that are spelled with two or more letters. They should be reminded that the diacritic *e* as in *theme* is not a silent letter where spelling (as opposed to decoding) is concerned. There *are* no silent letters in spelling, since no vocalization is involved. They should be reminded that diacritic *e* is *also* not silent in the sense that it helps to represent certain sounds in spelling.

The letter *e* has many uses. It helps to represent the long-vowel sound in words like *make* and *ripe*. It also helps to spell /z/ and /s/ in such words as *rose* and *fence*. In *rose*, the *e* assumes an additional role: it helps to spell the long-vowel sound as well as the /z/.

Lost sounds

Pupils will find it easier to remember the initial *gn* in words like *gnaw* and *gnat* and the final *mb* in words like *lamb* and *climb* if they understand that the *g* and *b* represent sounds that were once pronounced. (See the discussion in Chapter Four, page 50.) Over a period of time, the sounds were dropped, but the letters remained.

Pupils should be encouraged to discover other lost sounds by examining such pairs as *autumn/autumnal, hymn/hymnal*, and *solemn/solemnity*. In this case, if they extract the roots from the derivatives, they will be able to see that the final /m/ is spelled *mn* in each root.

Letter combinations

Ordinarily, consonant clusters do not cause much difficulty as long as pupils remember that although such clusters blend together in speech, they consist of individual sounds with individual spellings. The letter combinations that are most frequently misspelled are, rather, those involving vowels. For example, the combination *ough* can be used to write /ō/ (*though*), /ü/ (*through*), /ou/ (*bough*), and /uf/ (*rough*). Such spellings are best learned via sets of words which are patterned alike and from which generalizations can be induced.

The gemination of consonants should also be studied, as an example of an effort on the part of our forebears to spell sounds in certain consistent ways. The fact that a doubled consonant was already often used to write a final consonant sound preceded by a short-vowel sound (*add, egg*) led to a new rule that such a final consonant should be doubled when a suffix beginning with a short-vowel sound was added (*bat/batting*).

Writing conventions

Spelling cannot become a set of valuable skills unless pupils remember that spelling is writing and that certain conventions must be observed if one's writing is to be considered acceptable. For example, the appropriate use of capital letters and of marks of punctuation such as apostrophes can make the difference between writing that is readable and understandable, and writing that is awkward and confusing.

Exercises such as the following will challenge pupils to be meticulous about their punctuation. Instruct the class to copy the following sentences twice, using a different punctuation each time so as to produce two different meanings for each sentence:

1. The trip ended happily.
2. The baby crumbles his crackers and rolls in his milk.
3. The seeing-eye dog knows its master.
4. Fourteen club members voted secretly all told.

Handwriting

Poor handwriting is not necessarily a spelling problem. However, if it is so poor as to be illegible, and confusion of meaning results, then this is properly the concern of a spelling program. Each school should provide handwriting instruction, either as part of a spelling program or as a separate but related set of skills. Legible handwriting is not only a mark of care and consideration for others, it also guarantees that correct spelling will be recognized as such.

Proofreading

Proofreading skills also play an important part in the development of spelling ability. If pupils not only learn the basic method of proofing their written work, but also acquire the habit of doing so whenever they write, their progress toward mastery of the orthography will be enhanced. Therefore, spelling programs ought to contain proofreading procedures that will help pupils detect various kinds of errors in their written work — whether they be errors in phoneme–grapheme correspondences, in writing conventions, or in word choice. Proofreading skills involve pupils' awareness of their handwriting and their skills in using the dictionary, and if habitually used, they will reduce the number of misspelled and misused words.

New material

The main section of a spelling program for level 7 could ideally be organized into units of study similar to chapters in books. Rather than presenting lists of words for study, each unit might contain its own reservoir of words that would be introduced informally to illustrate a spelling principle or a linguistic fact.

The general intent of such a program would not be to enforce the mastery of a specific number of words per week or per year, but rather to engage pupils in the process of determining why some words are spelled as they are. To this end, level 7 pupils should be exposed not only to the history of our language, but also to advanced morphological analysis. They should learn how to break words down into their simplest elements and how to trace their roots back to their earliest known origin.

The use of the dictionary

Obviously, then, the dictionary habit should be developed as early in the school program as possible. The dictionary is as important for a speller as a compass is for a forest ranger or a navigator. It is the final authority on information about spelling, pronunciation, usage, and etymology, even though dictionary makers are not always in agreement on some matters. The teacher may help pupils understand the dynamic nature of our language by studying slight changes in dictionaries over a period of time.

Therefore, at every level from 2 through 8, pupils should have access to a bound-in-text speller dictionary. Its contents should vary from simple syllabified word entries listing meanings alone (at the lower elementary levels) to entries also listing pronunciation spellings, class forms, singular and plural forms, and derivatives (at the seventh and eighth levels).

For pupils to get the most use from a dictionary, they should be taught, through a series of spelling lessons, how to find a word quickly and how to interpret the information given. Well before they reach the seventh level, they should certainly know that words are entered in the dictionary in alphabetical order and that guide words are provided to indicate what words are likely to be found on a given page.

At level 7, pupils should be asked to examine a dictionary to determine the order in which information is listed in each entry. They should also practice finding words both in their own bound-in-text speller dictionary and in a standard desk dictionary — and in an unabridged dictionary if one is available. It is important that pupils at the upper levels seldom be given the correct spelling of a word by the teacher; they should be expected to go to the dictionary for such information.

The history of dictionary making

Level 7 pupils are intellectually curious, and this natural desire to learn should be encouraged in all areas of a school subject. Pupils' interest in the dictionary can be stimulated by presenting a summary of dictionary history as part of the spelling program: how dictionaries originated; what their precursors (syllabaries, glossaries) were like; how the dictionaries of the Middle Ages differed from Dr. Johnson's and Noah Webster's dictionaries; and how the latter differed from the dictionaries of today. (See Chapter Five.)

Historical information of this kind demonstrates to pupils that the dictionary, like the language, has developed over a long period of time; and that it has greatly influenced the written language by prescribing acceptable spelling and usage. And at this level, pupils should also be made aware of the vast amount of information contained in the various specialized dictionaries. Thus, they will see that dictionaries can function not only as arbiters of correctness but also as treasure troves of synonyms and antonyms for the enrichment of speaking and writing vocabularies.

Vocabulary enrichment

The pupil at this age is usually quite interested in words and their effectiveness in getting results. He tends to try out new words and expressions on his parents and peers. Furthermore, the world of science and technology is likely to be fascinating to him; and he realizes that in order to talk and write intelligently about such matters, he needs an appropriate vocabulary. A level 7 spelling program ought to deal with the subject of vocabulary growth: why we are constantly adding new words and where we get them; why we abandon words; how words acquire new meanings.

Unabridged dictionaries can be used to demonstrate to pupils that many of our words "don't look like American English," and this can lead into a discussion of word borrowing. The pupils should be made aware that American English has added hundreds and hundreds of words from both ancient and contemporary languages. What happened to those words when they were brought into a new linguistic environment is in itself fascinating, and can also help pupils understand why certain words are strangely spelled. (See Chapter Five.) Further, the more pupils are exposed to such information, the more meaningful language and its written form will become for them, and the more likely they are to want to develop their own vocabularies.

The history of our language

Pupils of this age are usually curious about the fact that human beings are the only inhabitants of the earth capable of transcribing past events in permanent fashion for present and future use. They may want to know when, where, and how human beings learned to express themselves orally in such a way that others could interpret their speech. They may wonder how writing began, what its earliest forms were, who initiated the alphabetic encoding system, how our language has changed over the years, and what forces caused the changes. (See Chapter One.) Therefore, a level 7 spelling program can provide additional background information about our language, including 1) theories about how language began; 2) the stages in the development of writing from pictographic through alphabetic; 3) the development of the Greco-Roman alphabet; 4) the Germanic origins of Old English; 5) the characteristics of Old and Middle English; and 6) some of the changes in sound and spelling that have occurred as the English language gradually acquired its present form. (See Chapters Three and Four.)

Such a spelling program would contain a unit on the origins of language, including some speculations about the "first" language and a brief history of early forms of writing: cave drawings, hieroglyphics, syllable writing, and ideography. (See Chapter One.) Another series of lessons would be concerned with the emergence of alphabetic writing — the contributions of the Egyptians, Phoenicians, Greeks, and Romans to our present Greco-Roman alphabet. Pupils will be much interested in the changes that have taken place in the forms of our letters over the centuries, and in the differences and similarities among the nearly 100 different alphabets in use today. (See Chapter Two.)

Level 7 pupils should also be exposed to a historical survey of the development of their own language with special emphasis on its Anglo-Saxon heritage and its struggles to survive both dominance by foreign languages such as French as well as its dialectal divergences. In addition, they might enjoy examining selections from Old English writings such as *Beowulf* and contrasting the graphemic forms with those of Middle and Modern English. Such an exercise can provide pupils with an appreciation of, and a feeling for, their language, and it can also lead to deeper understanding of the architecture of American-English orthography. (See Chapter Three.)

Spelling systems, then and now

Given this historical focus, pupils may be curious to know how boys and girls of other generations studied spelling — especially if they know that many different methods are advocated today. Therefore, a level 7 spelling program might well present some examples of typical spelling books used at various times in the past. (See Chapter Six.) The pupils may be surprised to see what their forebears considered to be acceptable texts; they may determine that we have made some progress since then in equipping them to spell the several thousands of words that they are likely to need in their writing.

Pupils should also review the various methods that have been developed for learning the spelling of individual words. This review should reinforce the value of using all available sensorimotor techniques (visual, haptical, aural–oral), of making an analysis of the phoneme–grapheme relationships in a word, of taking into account such factors as position, environment, stress, and context. Pupils should be given opportunities to find when traditional rote memorization works best for them in situations, and when the application of spelling principles holds the greatest overall promise. They should see the necessity for being phonologically alert (able to hear sounds and judge what graphemes should be used to write them), morphologically adept (able to build words by compounding and affixation), and sensitive to context (able to discriminate among homonyms and homographs so that the intended meaning will be conveyed).

Encoding and decoding

One of the major obstacles to spelling mastery is the confusion between encoding (writing) and decoding (reading) that often exists in pupils' minds. The level 7 pupil should be reminded that in *en*coding, one records words that have been thought of or spoken, and that in *de*coding, one translates written symbols into thought-of or spoken words. If a pupil has a functional knowledge of the encoding process, he should encounter less trouble in decoding than would otherwise be the case.

Throughout, it should be recognized that encoding and decoding are interdependent processes and should be closely linked in any spelling program; but no text or teacher should make the mistake of assuming that if a pupil has learned to read, he will automatically know how to write, i.e. spell. A level 7 spelling program should remind pupils of the many important distinctions between encoding and decoding.

Syllable patterns

As mentioned previously, pupils must be familiar with syllabication in order to be able to allow for the position of a phoneme when they must choose among graphemic options. They will be aided in the process of dividing words into syllables if they know that there are various syllable patterns in American English, some of which are:

1. CVC consonant–vowel–consonant (*cat*)
2. VC vowel–consonant (*am*)
3. CV consonant–vowel (*me*)
4. CCVC consonant–consonant–vowel–consonant (*clap*)
5. CVCC consonant–vowel–consonant–consonant (*last*)
6. CCVCC consonant–consonant–vowel–consonant–consonant (*glance*)
7. etc.

Pupils can learn quickly how syllables are formed by studying the above patterns in monosyllabic words and then finding the same patterns in words of more than one syllable. They should be reminded that a syllable must contain a vowel or vowellike sound, and that it almost always also contains one or more consonant sounds.

Word building

Level 7 pupils should already be familiar with the word-building process. But it may be necessary to review the meanings of the terms *affix, root, prefix, suffix,* and *compounding* (see Glossary) for some members of the class.

In studying affixation, pupils should be given examples of roots and asked to build new words by adding affixes. In the process, they will discover that certain prefixes reverse the original meaning of a root (*valid/invalid*), and that certain suffixes can change nouns to adjectives (*grass/grassy*), or verbs to nouns (*run/runner*). They will also observe that under certain conditions, the spelling of the root word or stem must be changed before the suffix is added.

When the pupils study affixation and compounding, the dictionary should be their constant companion. They should practice building many types of compounds, e.g. noun–noun formations (*horseback*) and noun–gerund phrase words (*sleepwalking*).

Morphemes

Level 7 pupils who have progressed through a modern spelling program will be familiar with the term *phoneme,* and they will understand that it is the smallest distinctive sound unit in a language. They should now become acquainted with the concept of a *morpheme,* a unit of form that can consist of one phoneme or of a combination of phonemes. A morpheme is the smallest linguistic unit that carries meaning; the members of a particular language community determine what that meaning is.

The word *morpheme* is based on the Greek root that means "form": *morph.* Just as a unit of sound is called a phoneme, a unit of form is called a morpheme. *Show* and *pie* are two-phoneme morphemes ($/sh + \bar{o}/$, $/p + \bar{\imath}/$); *ink* and *ax* are three-phoneme morphemes ($/i + ng + k/$, $/a + k + s/$).

Pupils can learn a good deal about their language by performing exercises in which they break words down into their component morphemes. Such experiences will help them understand why the term *morpheme* is more precise than the term *word*. They will learn that morphemes can consist of free morphemes (*catch*), bound morphemes (*-es*), free and bound morphemes (*catches*), or two or more free morphemes (*homework*).

Once pupils grasp what morphemes are, they can practice creating new words by adding different prefixes and suffixes to both free and bound morphemes. They should be cautioned, however, that merely adding any bound morpheme to any free morpheme will not necessarily produce an acceptable word. Although neologisms are often produced in just this fashion, level 7 pupils should probably limit themselves to "creating" words that are already in use in the language. Therefore, they should check their inventions against the dictionary.

A useful morpheme for pupils to start with is the common word *new*. With a little thought, pupils should be able to expand this free morpheme into its ultimate derivative, **unrenewability**. Such exercises can be expanded almost indefinitely for the more advanced pupils in a class.

Although pupils will find it relatively easy to build words by adding affixes to free morphemes like *new*, they should be made aware that there are thousands of words in the language that are built on morphemes that cannot stand by themselves. These bound morphemes usually consist of originally Latin or Greek forms to which prefixes and suffixes have been added to make useful American-English words. Many of our technical words are based on just such bound morphemes.

Pupils who become acquainted with certain roots will be greatly aided in building spelling power. For example, consider the bound morpheme *sist*, from a Latin word meaning "to stand." *Sist* itself has no recognizable meaning in our language, but when we add to it such prefixes as *in-*, *con-*, *de-*, *sub-*, *re*, and *per-*, we have created many words. If we then attach suffixes such as *-ence* or *-er*, to these derivatives, we have added still more *sist* words to our vocabulary. We have taken dozens of such powerful bound morphemes from the classical languages and have combined them with prefixes and suffixes to build many new words.

Allomorphs

Some prefixes, like some roots, have *allomorphs* (different forms of a morpheme carrying the same meaning). As indicated by the discussion of assimilation in Chapter Fifteen, the prefix form often depends on the beginning of the root or stem to which it is attached. For example, observe the word *appear*, made up of the root *pear* from Latin *parere* ("show") and the prefix *ad-* ("to"). The derivative might therefore be expected to be *adpear*. But in pronunciation, the /d/ becomes assimilated to the /p/, so that the *ap-* allomorph of *ad-* is present in the final word *appear*. Another example is provided by the assimilation of the /b/ to /p/ when the prefix *sub-* is added to *press* to produce *suppress*.

Pupils will add greatly to their understanding of the language and its orthography by studying allomorphic variations that are the result of assimilation of a prefix. In the same way, they will find it stimulating to examine allomorphic suffix forms that are caused by synthesis (see Chapter Fifteen) — a process which, like assimilation, is based on ease of pronunciation. An example is provided by the /sh/ sound found in words like *contention*, *suspicion*, and *confession*.

The meanings of derivatives

The original meanings of roots and affixes are often obscure in present-day derivatives, so that pupils may have to concentrate to detect the relationship between the root and the modern form. It is relatively easy, for example, to see how the Latin root *nect* ("to knot") combines with prefixes to produce *connect* and *annex* (*nex* is an allomorph of *nect*), and how the root *mong* ("to mix") combines with prefixes and suffixes to produce *among*, *mongrel*, and *mingle*. But without the benefit of an elementary course in Latin, pupils (and teachers) may find themselves bewildered by an attempt to analyze such words as *duplicate*, *complicate*, and *complex*.

A spelling program can help alleviate some of the uneasiness by introducing pupils to a number of Latin, Greek, and Old English roots and showing how various forms of these roots, coupled with appropriate prefixes and suffixes, produce familiar derivatives. Suppose, for example, that pupils were introduced to the root *spect*, which is of Latin origin with an original meaning of "to look." They might then be provided with an allomorphic spelling of the stem (*spec*) and with some prefixes and suffixes (*in-*, *re-*, *pro-*, *intro-*, *-ful*, *-tion*, *-ing*), and might be asked to build derivatives with the elements.

In carrying out such an exercise, the pupils would be engaged in sophisticated, mature analysis of the orthography, and would be developing a spelling mastery far greater than that usually attainable by traditional means. The authors of this volume suggest, however, that such exercises are most appropriate for the mature pupils in a class. Less advanced pupils should not be penalized if they are unable to perform well in this area.

Chapter Seventeen will show how an eighth-level spelling program should take up such matters as the discovery of patterns in American-English spelling, the effect of machines on spelling, and the feasibility of a world language.

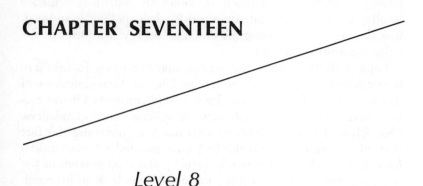

CHAPTER SEVENTEEN

Level 8

In the preceding chapter, it was suggested that a level 7 spelling program should begin with a review of the major phonological, morphological, and contextual characteristics of our language and should then provide pupils with historical information that would lead them to a greater understanding of the orthography. A level 8 program ought to proceed along the same lines, but on a plane adapted to the increased maturity of the pupils.

Spelling patterns

By the time they reach level 8, most pupils will be aware that while the majority of phonemes are rather predictably represented by certain graphemes, some phonemes can be represented orthographically in a variety of ways; /ī/, for example, has 14 possible spellings. The pupils' task is to sort out the various phoneme–grapheme correspondences, to learn the patterns in which they occur in words (taking into account the effect of position, stress, environment, and context), and to determine the correct grapheme to use from a knowledge of these patterns.

Pupils may be interested in learning about various research projects that have been designed to assess how consistently certain spelling patterns occur in the words they are studying. Such information should be included in a spelling program at

levels 7 and 8, supplemented by sufficient statistical evidence
to allay the suspicion that American-English spelling is so irregular that a pupil is wasting his time and energy if he tries to develop a cognitive map of it.

Pupils will likely find it interesting that one study found there
is considerable patterning in the spelling of large numbers of
American-English words — as long as one considers all the factors that can influence phoneme–grapheme correspondences.
(See Chapter Seven.) The class should find intriguing the fact
that when a computer for the first time was fed relevant guidelines, it was able to spell words correctly about 50 percent of the
time, and that when it *did* make mistakes, it made them for much
the same reasons that people do: it did not have available all the
principles and patterns necessary to make correct choices among
alternative graphemes without some error. Many human spelling
errors are *also* the result of failure to consider all the factors that
affect phoneme–grapheme correspondences.

For example, pupils who know that *calf* and *half* were once
pronounced /kalf/ and /half/ should remember to include the *l*
when spelling these words, even though today we say /kaf/ and
/haf/. Similarly, pupils are not likely to forget to spell the final
/m/ in words like *lamb* and *climb* with the two letters *mb* if they
have learned that the *b* once represented /b/. But without proper
briefing, pupils — and a machine — would misspell such words.

Maverick spellings

At level 8, pupils will also find it profitable to examine certain
words long considered spelling demons. In the course of such an
examination, they should discover that most of the sounds in a so-
called demon are actually rather predictably spelled. Therefore,
they should be able to see that they would be well advised to
concentrate only on that part of the word the spelling of which
does not follow a pattern.

For example, consider the word *conscience* (misspelled by the
computer). The *c* spelling of /k/ is regular when one considers
the influence of position (initial) and of environment (*o* follows). In fact, the spelling of the *entire first syllable* (*con*) is
quite predictable. Furthermore, the spellings of the last three
sounds are also predictable (/e/ as *e*; /n/ as *n*; /s/ as *ce*). Therefore, the only truly unexpected spelling is *sci* for /sh/. But even

this is not a completely isolated case: such a spelling of /sh/ occurs in a few other words like *luscious* and *conscious*.

This brings up the fact that the spelling of /sh/ can be extremely troublesome. (See Chapter Fourteen, p. 189.) Pupils may be surprised to learn that /sh/ is spelled *ti* more than twice as often as it is spelled *sh*. The *ti* spelling usually occurs when /sh/ is in initial position in an unaccented syllable (*nation*), but *never* occurs when /sh/ is in initial position in a primary-stressed syllable or in medial position in a syllable. In contrast, the *sh* spelling occurs largely when /sh/ is in initial or final position in a primary-stressed syllable (*shepherd, refreshment*). But pupils will find it necessary to use all available sensorimotor equipment to master the spelling of those relatively few phonemes — such as /sh/ — whose graphemic representations are unpredictable.

The structure of language and of writing

Learning to spell is much like learning to "figure." Once the basic structure of mathematics is grasped and the relationships between numbers and certain processes are understood, it is possible to work out any problem that makes use of this structure and these relationships. Similarly, once the basic structural relationships between speech and writing are grasped, the pupil is well along the path to spelling power.

Pupils might be encouraged to draw a diagram to demonstrate the structure of communication as they see it. Possibly it would resemble the one reproduced in Table 17–1.

Morphology

At level 7, pupils will have been introduced to the term *morpheme*, and a level 8 program ought to increase their understanding of this linguistic unit. The study of morphemes — bound and free — is not nearly so formidable as it might appear to be. In fact, pupils will find that familiarity with morphemes can help them clarify their thinking about language. For example, consider the words *striding, strode*, and *stridden*. One might regard these words as different forms of the verb *stride*; or one might regard each as a separate word. On the other hand, if one thinks of *stride* as a morpheme (a combination of phonemes that has a

Table 17–1

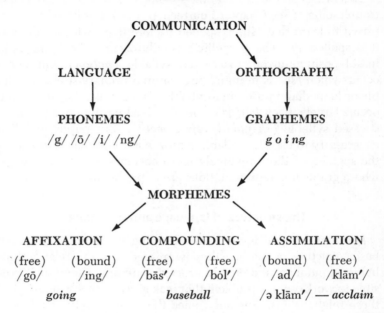

meaning), then one can think of *striding* as a combination of free morpheme (*stride*) plus bound morpheme (*-ing*). (Each addition to a morpheme that changes or alters its meaning is also a morpheme, either bound or free.)

Pupils can develop an interest in the importance of morphology as an aid to building spelling power if they will take the time to study the meanings and the forms of roots, prefixes, and suffixes. For one thing, the meanings of affixes often provide clues to the total meaning of a word. Familiarity with prefixes of Latin and Greek origin will help pupils understand such words as *trilateral* and *macrograph*, for example; and the meaning of words like *symphonic*, *accountable*, and *fluency* will be clearer if the meanings of the suffixes are known.

Pupils sometimes become confused about which suffix to use. Certain generalizations can help in such cases. First of all, the following suffixes are used to create nouns:

1. *-ist, -ant, -ee, -eer*: a person who performs some action or is associated with some belief (*organist, servant, assignee, profiteer*)
2. *-ism*: a condition or belief (*ostracism, patriotism*)
3. *-sis*: an action (*synthesis*)
4. *-ics*: a body of knowledge or principles (*tactics, phonemics*)

The following suffixes are used to create adjectives:

1. *-able, -ible*: capable of (*adjustable, invisible*)
2. *-ive*: showing a tendency toward (*productive, effective*)
3. *-ile*: capable of or liable to (*fertile, hostile*)

The following suffixes are used to create verbs from nouns and adjectives:

1. *-ize*: to render or to make like (*civilize, economize*)
2. *-ify, -fy*: to make or to form into (*certify, clarify, amplify, pacify*)

The following suffixes are used to create adverbs, adjectives, or nouns:

1. *-ful*: full of (*cheerful, cupful*)
2. *-ward*: toward (*skyward, inward*)
3. *-er*: one who has to do with (*worker*); comparative form (*faster*)
4. *-wise*: in a manner resembling, with respect to (*likewise, coastwise*)

Pupils should be encouraged to engage in their own investigations of morphology, since the investment of time can be well repaid by their increased mastery of American-English spelling.

Syllabication

A level 8 spelling program ought to emphasize once again that phoneme–grapheme relationships cannot be fully determined without an understanding of syllabication. At this level, pupils should have learned that each syllable must contain a vowel sound (/ə kròs′/) or a vowellike sound (/kot′ ′n/)[1], and that some may contain several consonant sounds (/prē tend′/).

[1] The /′n/ of *cotton* indicates a syllabic consonant. Some dictionaries prefer to treat such vowellike sounds as a /ə/ + consonant.

To assess the pupil's knowledge of syllabication, the teacher might write the following nonsense words on the chalkboard and ask that they be divided into syllables:

supercalifragilisticexpialidocious[2]
(su per cal i frag i lis tic ex pi al i do cious)

honorificabilitudinitatibus[3]
(hon or if i ca bil i tu di ni ta ti bus)

Pupils can also be asked to write the syllable pattern after each syllable, as for example:

Word 1

su	CV (consonant–vowel)
per	CVC (consonant–vowel–consonant)
etc.	etc.

Word 2

hon	VC (vowel–consonant)
or	VC (vowel–consonant)
etc.	etc.

They may need to be reminded that syllabic patterns are based on *sounds,* not on letters; and that a word's oral syllabication often differs from its written syllabication.

Why teach syllabication when even scholars do not agree on a single set of rules to be followed? One answer to such a question is that *some* form of syllabication is necessary for an understanding of phoneme–grapheme relationships, and that the differences of syllabication in speech and writing are not sufficiently great to warrant "throwing the baby out with the bathwater." Further, there are some guidelines, established by the printing trades, that are extremely useful in determining at what point to syllabify in *writing,* e.g. if a word must be divided at the end of a line.

Rather than ask pupils simply to memorize such guidelines, which are essentially arbitrary, it is probably best to have them make inferences about the rules from syllabified examples such as these:

---

[2] P. L. Travers, *Mary Poppins* (New York: Harcourt, Brace & World, 1962).

[3] William Shakespeare, *Love's Labour Lost.*

1. house' boat, post' man
2. ac' tion, bis' cuit
3. fail' ure, lash' ing
4. gram' mar, at tack'
5. a) leg' end, sav' age
   b) do' nate, pa' per

The use of this kind of inductive approach will probably result in more permanent forms of learning than will dependence on rote memorization. By examining the above list, pupils should arrive at the following rules for *written* syllabication:

1. Compounds: divide between the component words.
2. Two consonants preceded by a short vowel: divide between the consonants.
3. Words with a suffix: divide between the word and the suffix.
4. A single consonant sound, between two vowels, spelled with doubled letters: divide between the doubled letters.
5. a) A single consonant between two vowels, the first of which is short and stressed: divide after the consonant.
   b) A single consonant between two vowels, the first of which is long: divide before the consonant.

After they have done this, the pupils could be directed to divide the following words (or similar ones) into syllables, using the rules they have inferred. They should, of course, check their results against a standard dictionary.

1. football, homeroom
2. fiction, basket
3. trailer, weighing
4. matter, appeal
5. a) tragic, prophet
   b) grocer, tailor

Phoneme position as an influence on spelling

As suggested above, a knowledge of syllabication not only enables us to divide written words into syllables, e.g. at the ends of lines, it also allows us to determine the position of a phoneme in a syllable. This information is necessary for an adequate understanding of phoneme–grapheme correspondences. Pupils should be provided with word lists that illustrate the effect of a phoneme's position on the choice of grapheme to represent it. For example, they might be asked to formulate rules to account for the bold italic spellings in the following sentence:

Those n*o*isy b*oy*s are tr*y*ing to *c*ut a pathw*ay* through some tou*gh* gra*ss*.

Pupils should, with study, be able to infer the following:

1. /oi/ is spelled *oi* when it occurs in the middle of a syllable, but *oy* when it occurs at the end.
2. /ī/ is often spelled *y* when it occurs at the end of a syllable, and always when it is followed by a suffix beginning with /i/.
3. /k/ is spelled *c* before *u* (as well as before *a* and *o*).
4. /ā/ is usually spelled *ay* when it occurs in word-final position.
5. /f/ can be spelled *gh* at the end of a syllable, but never at the beginning.
6. /s/ is usually spelled *ss* when it occurs in final position in a monosyllabic word, or at the end of an accented syllable.

After completing this exercise, the pupils should be urged to check their inferences by first using their rules to spell additional words that have similar sounds and then looking up the correct spellings in a dictionary. Here are some words that could be used for dictation:

chi*c*ken	turm*oi*l	*f*our	curtain	po*ss*ible
l*y*ing	empl*oy*	cube	*oy*ster	d*y*ing
kindred	lo*ss*	j*oy*ful	cameo	con*f*idence

Finally, here are additional words that could be presented for phoneme position and grapheme analysis:

n*ow*	wi*c*ked	lo*u*d	pro*u*dly	po*w*er	bri*ck*

Unstressed syllables

Certain syllables, like certain sounds, are spelled quite predictably. Therefore, if their presence in spoken words could always be identified, pupils would have very little difficulty in spelling them. Unfortunately, however, when such syllables are unstressed, they are often unrecognizable. For example, the prefix *con-* occurs in many words, and it is always *spelled con-*, regardless of how it is pronounced. But in the verb *contract*, it is *pronounced* /kən/, and this is likely to cause confusion.

In fact, one of the greatest spelling difficulties that pupils encounter is caused by the *schwa* sound (/ə/) that appears in most unaccented syllables today, e.g. the /kən/ of *con tract'*. If level 8 pupils have learned a bit about the history of their language, they will probably recognize that although the original vowel sounds of such syllables have been obscured over a long period of time, their *spellings* remain. Thus, the schwa has many different orthographic representations. Compare the unstressed syllables in the following words:

a round'	/ə round'/	*leg' i ble*	/lej' ə bəl/
con tain'	/kən tān'/	*pri' va cy*	/prī' və sē/
fi' nal	/fī' nəl/	*kitch' en*	/kīch' ən/

Since it is unlikely that we will change the orthographic representation of vowel sounds to conform to current pronunciation, pupils must develop various memory aids in order to master such unpredictable spellings. Probably the most practical approach is for pupils to use, *for spelling purposes only,* a spelling pronunciation rather than a normal speaking pronunciation when they are initially confronted with words containing /ə/. For example, when they are studying "kitch*e*n," "rob*i*n," "delic*a*te," "worsh*i*p," "d*e*bate," and "mis*e*ry," they might exaggerate the original vowel sound in the unaccented syllable (in bold italic) rather than using the schwa sound advocated in most standard dictionaries.

Level 8 pupils should recognize, too, that modern dictionaries are *pronouncing* dictionaries whose pronunciation spellings represent the way words are pronounced in ordinary rapid speech rather than serve as a guide to American-English orthography. Therefore, they may *say* /dē' sənt/ but must remember to *write* *decent*; the dictionary may record /kom' it/ or /rō/ bət/, but pupils will need to think /kom' et/ and /rō' bot/ if they are to get full spelling cues for *comet* and *robot*.

Monosyllabic words

The study of spelling usually begins with simple monosyllables, and a level 8 program *also* can include a study of monosyllabic words but in more sophisticated fashion. Pupils will be interested in the fact that according to one study, 344 out of approximately 500 of the most frequently used words in the language are mono-syllabic.[4] While monosyllabic words are generally characterized by simplicity and functionality, some frequently used words contain one or more sounds with quite unpredictable spellings.

Pupils should be encouraged to note the etymology of such words in a dictionary that gives word origins. They will discover that many unpredictable spellings can be attributed to one of the following causes:

1. The word is hundreds of years old, and the pronunciation has changed while the original spelling persists.
2. The original pronunciation is unchanged, but the spelling has been reworked to resemble Latin or French.
3. The word has been borrowed from another language, and has retained either its original spelling or its original pronunciation or both.

Some examples of oddly spelled monosyllabic words are *ache*, *of*, *plaid*, *shoe*, *once*, and *two*. These words look quite unusual in spelling, but on careful examination, pupils will discover that only one of the six has a *completely* unpredictable spelling (*of*). In each of the other words, all but one of the phonemes are spelled as one might expect. The pupils would probably find it interesting to make a list of the monosyllables they use most frequently and to underscore the parts of each word that are not spelled in accordance with the usual patterns of phoneme–grapheme correspondence.

Actually, there are fewer variant spellings of phonemes in words of one syllable than there are in words of more than one syllable. Pupils might test such a statement by making two lists of words from their own writing vocabularies, thus:

1. Monosyllabic words containing various spellings of /ch/ (*crunch*, *hitch*, etc.)
2. Polysyllabic words containing various spellings of /ch/ (*question*, *champion*, *cello*, *future*, *kitchen*, etc.)

---

[4] E. L. Thorndike and I. Lorge, *The Teacher's Word Book of 30,000 Words* (New York: Bureau of Publications, Teachers College, Columbia University, 1944).

Pupils may want to go on to determine whether this situation also prevails in words containing /sh/. If so, they might make similar lists for /sh/, first noting the monosyllabic words that contain various spellings of /sh/ (*sure, chef, schwa, sheep,* etc.) and then the polysyllabic words that contain various spellings of /sh/ (*ocean, crescendo, mission, shield, appreciate, luscious, assure, pension, initiate, sugar,* etc.).

Homographs

Homographs, of which there are very few in American English, represent a decoding (reading) problem more than an encoding (spelling) problem. (See Chapter Fourteen.) As far as spelling goes, the pupil usually only has to remember to associate a particular spelling with two possible pronunciations. For example, if he wants to write about playing the *bass* drum or about catching a 15-inch *bass*, he must remember that both words are spelled exactly alike, regardless of pronunciation; if his pet *dove* is dead, he may write to a friend that his *dove dove* into the fish pond and was drowned. Thus, homographs mainly represent an exercise in recall, and each pupil will master them by using whatever multisensory–multimotor methods of study he finds most effective.

Languages and more languages

The extensive communications facilities in most American homes have made youngsters aware of the distant areas of the world and of the hordes of people who inhabit them; and of the great gaps in communication that are often responsible for misunderstanding between nations. Television programs in particular have made pupils want to learn more about their global neighbors: how they live, what they eat and wear, and what languages they speak and understand.

A spelling program can nurture this interest in people and their languages by providing information about the evolution of language and its written expression. The fact that today there are almost 3,000 languages spoken in the world is impressive, and pupils may be particularly interested in statistics contrasting language usage in the major nations.

They might be told that in addition to official languages, many nations have numerous dialects that are largely comprehensible only to the inhabitants of particular regions. For example, India, a nation one-third the size of the U.S., with a population of over 500 million people, has 14 major language families containing almost 200 different languages — which in turn contain over 700 dialects. Even Belgium, about the size of our state of Maryland with a population of about 10 million, has two different official languages. On the other hand, in the United States, the fourth largest nation in the world geographically and inhabited by over 200 million people, almost everybody speaks and understands *one language,* American English. There is no other nation of comparable size of which this can be said.

Pupils should realize that proliferation of the use of radio, television, and Comsat is making it increasingly possible for people in remote areas to be aware of happenings around the globe; and that international business transactions are breaking down cultural and language barriers that have existed for thousands of years, since in order to trade ideas and material, people must be able to communicate with other people. Pupils might be reminded that when the greatest merchants of the ancient world, the Phoenicians, found it necessary to communicate with many different peoples during the course of their expeditions, they developed a system of encoding that established the alphabetic principle — the basis of most orthographies in the world today. (See Chapter Two.)

A supranational language

As the barriers between nations are eased and people move freely from one national community to another, the need for a supranational language becomes increasingly evident. But this is not a new idea. For hundreds of years, people have been urging statesmen to develop a worldwide official language. For a time, it appeared that French would become the *lingua franca,* since it was accepted throughout Europe and much of the rest of the world as the language of diplomacy, but this no longer seems likely.

Esperanto

Many people and organizations have created various encoding systems that they hoped would be acceptable as instruments of communication. Of these systems, only one — Esperanto — has had any measure of success. It was invented over eighty years ago by a Polish gentleman named Ludovic Lazarus Zamenhof, and it takes its name from Zamenhof's pen name, Dr. Esperanto (literally, "Dr. Hopeful"). The Esperanto alphabet is virtually identical to our own except that it omits *q*, *w*, *x*, and *y*. Most important of all where efficiency is concerned, its spelling consistently reflects its pronunciation and vice versa.

Pupils may want to know why Esperanto has not been proclaimed the supranational language of the world. There are many reasons, not the least of which is simply that Esperanto is an invention, a device, rather than a natural language. A natural language reflects the cultural history of a people, and perhaps most important of all, it possesses a literature. Esperanto, on the other hand, was deliberately manufactured as a convenience item to help a speaker of one language communicate with a speaker of another language, and it has no literature.

However, the fact that Esperanto has not died out like most of its competitors, but is actually gaining in popularity, is impressive. Users of Esperanto have formed clubs in almost every major city of the world. Level 8 pupils may derive a good deal of benefit from extracurricular study of Esperanto — particularly of its orthography — and should be encouraged to determine the languages from which its vocabulary has been derived.

English

Level 8 pupils may wonder what the prospects for achieving a supranational language are, and what this language might be. To arrive at a rational answer, they should be encouraged to study — either through a spelling program or in a reference work such as an encyclopedia — charts that show statistics on language usage throughout the world. (Refer to Chapter Three.) They should try to find answers for the following questions:

1. Which language has the greatest number of speakers? What is the geographical distribution of these speakers?
2. Which language has the second greatest number of speakers? What is their geographical distribution?
3. Which language most nearly approximates the alphabetic principle? How many people speak it? Over what geographical areas?

Pupils will find that at the present time, English is the most widely used language in the world. It is not only the language of commerce, it is also the most widely taught *second* language in the world. Furthermore, its vocabulary is larger than that of any other language, thanks to its long history of word borrowing and its extensive creation of new words to label new ideas and products.

But what are the chances of English becoming truly, and officially, the supranational language of the world? Pupils may find it interesting to survey the opinions of their classmates, friends, and foreign acquaintances with regard to this question. No doubt they will learn that many foreigners regard English as easy to speak, but "impossible" to spell. Some will not hesitate to suggest that a big step toward the acceptance of English as the *lingua franca* would be a revision of its spelling to bring it in line with pronunciation. Pupils should be told that such a proposal is centuries old; and that Benjamin Franklin, Noah Webster, Theodore Roosevelt, and George Bernard Shaw all tried, unsuccessfully, to reform English spelling. But resistance continues to be overwhelming, even to simple changes like eliminating unnecessary letters such as *c* for /s/ and /k/, *q* for /kw/, and *x* for /ks/.

Voice typewriters and spelling reform

In spite of our reluctance to tamper with our language, we may be forced to it by modern developments in electronic technology. Machines are already taking over many of our communication activities, and we ought to be preparing for the imminent arrival of a dictating–transcribing machine so sophisticated that it listens to the human voice dictate a message and promptly produces a typed transcription for the speaker.

If pupils are informed of this, they may ask, "Why should we waste our time learning how to spell? All we will need to know is how to speak." First, pupils should be reminded that the machine has not yet arrived, and that when it does, it may be so expensive that only large companies can afford it. Furthermore, it will be unable to spell without being given directions; people will still have to know what constitutes correct written expression. (Perhaps pupils will suggest other reasons why spelling instruction remains necessary: class notes and grocery lists will continue to be written by hand, for example.)

No doubt some level 8 pupils will be alert enough to raise questions like, "How would the machine know whether to write *not* or *knot*; *lim* or *limb*? Or if I dictate a letter and say something that sounds like 'I'm nut gonna go,' how would the machine know that the sentence should be written as 'I'm not going to go'?" Such questions should lead into a discussion of the desirability of making our spelling conform to pronunciation — or vice versa. Some pupils may want to try to devise a way to simplify the orthography; others may be motivated to make their pronunciation more precise; still others may develop a new respect for spelling instruction.

CHAPTER EIGHTEEN

Evaluating Pupil Growth
in Spelling Mastery

Modern spelling programs differ from traditional ones in two fundamental ways. First, the orthography is viewed as language-based and systematic. Second, study words are chosen for their ability to demonstrate orthographic principles as well as for their potential usefulness to the individual writer. These two character-istics of a modern spelling program affect the way in which a pupil's mastery of the orthography is measured.

First of all, it needs to be recognized that although enabling the pupil to spell correctly any word he wants to write is the aim of all spelling instruction, the *means* to this objective are mark-edly different in traditional as opposed to modern spelling cur-riculums. From a traditional viewpoint, each word in one's writ-ing vocabulary is stored there largely through an individual act of rote memorization. Therefore, mastery of the orthography is measured by the pupil's ability to spell those words he has specifically studied.

In a modern spelling program, however, the principles and processes that undergird our writing system are crucial ingredients in the development of spelling power, since these principles and processes make any word in the pupil's speaking vocabulary a potential candidate for his writing vocabulary. Thus, in modern programs, spelling ability is measured not only in terms of the pupil's ability to spell study words correctly, but also in terms of his ability to apply orthographic principles in new spelling situations.

Although commercial spelling tests are useful for measuring a pupil's spelling progress in traditional terms, they are at present not constructed to assess his progress in mastering orthographic principles. Therefore, language-based spelling programs must themselves provide this type of measurement, both through the teacher's informal observation of the pupil in daily spelling activities and through more formal assessment of his ability to apply orthographic principles to unfamiliar words. Let us examine some of the ways in which such an assessment can be made.

Measuring a knowledge of phonological cues

From the outset of a language-based spelling program, pupils are led to observe that our orthography is alphabetically based. They learn that some phonemes have highly predictable spellings regardless of where they occur in words; /p/, for example, is almost always spelled *p* (e.g. *pink, spin, kept, flip*) except in those relatively few instances in which *pp* is used (*apple, appear*). These highly predictable phonemes ordinarily do not present spelling difficulties. But there are many other phonemes whose spellings are not so easily determined. In order to choose the correct spelling for these phonemes, the pupil must use additional phonological clues such as those provided by position, stress, and environment. Familiarity with these factors and their effect on spelling is an important ingredient of spelling mastery and should be evaluated whenever the child's growth in spelling ability is measured.

Position

Numerous phonemes whose spellings would otherwise not be very predictable can be dealt with once their position in syllables is noted. Modern spelling programs therefore help the pupil to discover and use positional cues when appropriate; and his abilities in these areas should be tested by the presentation of new words as well as familiar ones which contain the orthographic principle.

For example, suppose that the teacher wants to measure the pupil's mastery of the principle that /oi/ is nearly always spelled *oy* at the end of a syllable, but *oi* in other positions. A typical spelling lesson presenting this principle might include the following words:

boil	join	point	spoil
broil	joy	voice	oily
noise	toy	enjoy	moist
toil	coil	choice	soil

Asking the pupil to write the words on this list merely shows whether or not he knows how to spell *these particular words*. But if he is asked to spell new words such as *ointment, void, poise, rejoin, destroy*, and *employ*, his ability to *apply* the /oi/ principle can be assessed.

Stress

Since syllable stress often provides important clues to spelling, an assessment of pupils' understanding of stress effect on spelling certain phonemes needs to be made also. For example, pupils may have learned that final /k/ is commonly spelled *ck* in stressed syllables (*black, attack*) and *c* in unstressed syllables (*attic, tonic*). The following study words might be used to illustrate this principle:

basic	stock	public	phonic
music	picnic	pluck	traffic
thick	wreck	stack	flock

After appropriate study, the pupil's ability to apply the principle could be assessed by asking him to spell words such as *trick, sonic, comic, quick, civic*, and *slack*.

Environment

Modern spelling programs round out the pupil's knowledge of phonological influences on the orthography by leading him to observe the effect of *environment:* the fact that the spellings of certain phonemes can be affected by adjacent sounds and/or adjacent spellings. For example, he may be led to discover that final /j/ is spelled *dge* when preceded by a short vowel, but *ge* when preceded by a long vowel or a consonant. The following words might be used to illustrate this point:

badge	edge	dodge	gouge
bridge	budge	age	barge
oblige	strange	gorge	cringe

In order to test the pupil's final mastery of this principle, he might then be asked to spell the following words: *tinge*, *merge*, *wedge*, *nudge*, *rage*, and *wage*.

Measuring a knowledge of morphological cues

To be able to select the correct grapheme when there are several alternatives, the pupil must not only be alert to phonological cues. He must also be familiar with the morphological features of our language and how they are reflected in writing. If he knows, for example, how most nouns and verbs are inflected and the relevant orthographic principles for adding suffixes to roots, he has at his command a way of spelling thousands of words which otherwise would have had to be memorized individually. Modern spelling programs therefore provide substantial instruction in such word-building skills. They should also provide a means to assess the pupil's competency in applying those skills in new spelling situations.

The word list below, for example, might be presented to illustrate how nouns are made plural. By examining the list, pupils would be able to infer that most nouns in English are made plural by adding /s/ or /z/ spelled *s*, or /əz/ spelled *es*. They would also see that when nouns end with *e* or *y*, certain spelling changes must be made during the pluralization process: *e* must be deleted before *es* is added (*wedges*) and *y* must be changed to *ie* before *s* is added (*spies*).

branch	wedge	rope	product
gem	creek	spy	cough
enemy	surface	goal	recess

But to make sure that a pupil really understands the principles involved in pluralizing nouns, he should be asked to spell not only the plurals of the study words, but also the plurals of other nouns whose singular forms he already knows how to spell, e.g. *energy*, *ridge*, *march*, *cap*, and *frog*.

Similar methods can be used to test the pupil's ability to apply the spelling principles involved when certain derivational affixes are added to root forms. Suppose, for example, he has inferred from a list of study words that when a root ends in unstressed final *y*, the *y* must be changed to *i* before a suffix is added (cf. *empty* and *emptily, emptiness*; *busy* and *business, busily*; *merry* and *merrily, merriment*). He should then be asked to form derivatives from similar, but new, words such as *worthy, accompany*, and *kindly* to demonstrate that he can apply the principle correctly.

Such assessments of the pupil's familiarity with morphological — as well as phonological — influences on spelling shed light on his growing cognitive map of the orthography and thus permit the attentive teacher to guide his learning in productive ways.

The analysis of spelling errors

A language-based approach to the teaching of spelling requires that an analysis be made of the *kinds* of errors a pupil makes in test situations and in his daily writing. To judge his degree of competency merely on the basis of the number of words he misspells is to overlook vital diagnostic information.

First of all, a careful analysis of a pupil's spelling errors can reveal the specific things that he needs to review or to be retaught. Second, such an analysis can reveal *degrees* of spelling difficulty: for example, to spell /lam/ as *lam* when *lamb* is meant is not as serious as to write /sent′ ə mənt/ as *sediment*, since the latter error clearly indicates that the pupil is identifying the wrong morpheme. Three of the commonest types of spelling errors are discussed below.

Errors caused by mistaken analogy

Although the spellings of most phonemes are quite predictable when phonological, morphological, and contextual factors are considered, maverick spellings do occur. For example, /e/ is spelled *ie* in *friend*, /a/ is spelled *ai* in *plaid*, /u/ is spelled *oo* in *blood*. Exceptional spellings like these must ordinarily be learned by the most effective sensorimotor means available, not excluding rote memorization.

Pupils who write — for example — *frend, plad*, and *blud* indicate that they obviously know how /e/, /a/, and /u/ are *typically* spelled but that they have erroneously applied this knowledge to exceptional cases. They should be reminded to check against the dictionary the spelling of words that they are using for the first time in writing.

Errors of an oral–aural nature

Unlike the errors of analogy in which the pupil identifies a phoneme but chooses the wrong grapheme to represent it, oral–aural errors are based on a failure to identify phonemes correctly. If the word *pin* is misspelled as *pen*, for example, this suggests that the pupil has not distinguished between /i/ and /e/. Although inability to differentiate between or among phonemes may be caused by physiological and developmental as well as dialectal factors, this type of spelling error is often responsive to oral–aural exercises *for spelling purposes only.*

Errors caused by misunderstanding orthographic principles

Some spelling errors occur because the pupil has not mastered orthographic principles completely. For example, if *hedge* and *huge* are misspelled as *hege* and *hudge*, it can be seen that the pupil is aware of the variant spellings of final /j/ but does not yet know when to use *ge* and when to use *dge*. Therefore, he may need to review the relevant principles and practice applying them to unfamiliar words.

Summary

It should be apparent that viewing spelling as language-based requires careful teaching. But the teacher should remember that pupils will profit considerably for the rest of their writing lifetimes if, during the formative school years, they are helped to understand how our orthography functions and how to apply their knowledge in writing situations.

To measure the kind of spelling ability developed in a modern program also requires care, since it is extremely important to know whether children are approaching a functional understanding of the orthography that will work for them in and out of school. An examination of the *kinds* of errors made is essential, for it is from such errors that one can determine what the pupils' spelling difficulties are and how they might be resolved.

EPILOGUE

With Chapter Eighteen the authors bring to a close Part Two, which describes the scope and sequence that a modern spelling program for the schools might have and some strategies for organizing such a program.

Part One presents the basic research in linguistics and learning theory on which the rationale for teaching spelling is built today. It includes the type of information and frame of reference which have too long been omitted in the preservice and in-service education of classroom teachers and language-arts specialists.

As we have noted, it was previously believed that American-English spelling is so unpredictable, the learning of each word must largely be a separate memory act. With this as the basic assumption, a minimum number of words would be selected for pupils to memorize by rote each week. Spelling experts spent a great proportion of their time and effort researching which 3,000 words were most frequently used, whether a teach-test or test-teach sequence was more productive, and what the best strategies for rote-memorizing the standard spelling of each word were.

Today most spelling programs start with a very different set of basic assumptions. Spelling is viewed as the graphic representation of the sounds we say and hear in the words we use. It is believed that the alphabetic principle, which is the foundation of most writing systems in the world today with American English no exception, is grasped by the beginning school child as he is presented familiar objects to name that have the same beginning or ending sounds. He is helped to identify these phonemes in their position in various words that are spelled in much the same way. He is then taught which graphemes he should use to represent the sounds that he has identified in the words under analysis.

By planning a sequential program of such experiences for the first few levels, or grades, the teacher enables the child to construct the beginnings of a cognitive map that gives him the power to spell correctly many of the more consistently spelled words through familiarity with their pattern of phoneme–grapheme correspondences.

As the pupil advances through the levels, he is introduced to a language-based model of the orthography, including the phonological, morphological, and contextual elements of language. In each of these systems of encoding patterns, he encounters aspects of our orthography that are not included in traditional spelling programs. To the basic sound-to-letter strategies he has learned are now added increasingly sophisticated spelling patterns in which the phonemes and graphemes surrounding the particular phoneme under analysis and the stress of the syllable in which the phoneme occurs help determine which grapheme out of the several options will represent the phoneme. The program spirals and expands over the school years to include additional experiences with word-building through compounding and affixation.

In the upper levels, much attention is given to helping students understand some of the unique characteristics of American-English orthography through a look at the history of the English language, particularly the borrowings and coinage of new words and phrases. This is a story that not only is fascinating in itself but helps pupils understand why we spell many words as we do.

Some words in American English seem to lack a reason for their peculiar spellings, particularly on first look. But to the maturing pupil it becomes clear upon deeper and more careful examination during the course of his years of involvement in a well-designed and well-taught spelling program that almost every seemingly difficult word has highly predictable, graphemic representations for most of its phonemes. His knowledge of the spelling patterns of the predictably spelled parts of a word — patterns which he has formulated into rules, or generalizations — opens up to him the possibility of applying those patterns to thousands of additional words that he may wish to use to express his ideas and feelings. This strategy, of course, calls for a frequent check with a dictionary so he can make sure that in following his cognitive map of spelling patterns he has navigated a standard course. When he finds that his map has not given him adequate cues for correctly spelling a particular syllable or phoneme, he can then use his "study steps" to fix, perhaps by rote memory, the less predictable part of the word and thereafter spell the word without error.

Such a modern program of spelling should produce a writing vocabulary composed of three to five times the number of words that traditionally have been considered an adequate accomplishment at school. It seems likely that the pupil who has experienced such a sequence of language-based content and multisensory–multimotor method, a program that stresses "pupil discovery" rather than "teacher telling," will develop a power to spell that will greatly enrich his written expression in the decades ahead.

GLOSSARY OF LINGUISTIC
AND PSYCHOLOGICAL TERMS

The basic purpose of this glossary is to help the reader flesh out his understanding of 1) the linguistic and psychological concepts on which the new spelling programs rest; and 2) the new teaching–learning strategies, which are designed to help pupils develop the ability to spell an unlimited number of words.

Because of space limitations, it has been necessary to simplify many definitions. Recognizing that a fuller discussion often would both clarify seeming inconsistencies and permit a deeper understanding of the subtle issues that interest linguists, the authors refer those readers who wish additional information to the bibliography.

Throughout this glossary, virgules (slash marks) are used to indicate a phoneme: e.g. /d/; and bold italic type is used to indicate a grapheme: e.g. *d.* The method herein of explaining the linguistic terms is used to help show the reader how the comprehension and application of each term can lead to a more effective spelling program.

ABBREVIATION: A shortened form of a word or phrase used chiefly in writing, such as *Mt.* for *Mount, mph* for *miles per hour,* and *N.Y.C.* for *New York City.*

ACCENT: The stress with which a certain syllable is pronounced, in comparison with that of other syllables of the same word. See STRESS, PRIMARY; STRESS, SECONDARY; UNSTRESSED SYLLABLE.

ACRONYM: A word formed by combining the first letter or two of each word in a group of words. For example, *scuba* originates from *s*elf-contained *u*nderwater *b*reathing *a*pparatus.

AFFIX: A bound morpheme, such as a *prefix, suffix,* or *infix,* which is attached to or inserted in a root or stem. See INFIX; PREFIX; SUFFIX; MORPHEME, BOUND; ROOT; STEM.

AFFIXATION: A process of building new words or forming inflected or derivative words by adding a prefix (*re-* + *enter* = *reenter*), a suffix (*look* + *-ing* = *looking*), or an infix (American English does not use true infixes). See IN-FIX; PREFIX; SUFFIX.

ALLOMORPH: One of two or more forms of the same morpheme. For example, in English /z/ represented by *s* in *boys,* /s/ represented by *s* in *cats,* and /əz/ represented by *es* in *boxes* are all members of the set of sounds that signal plurality when attached to nouns. In other words, /z/, /s/, and /əz/ are all forms, or allomorphs, of the "plural" morpheme. See MORPHEME.

ALLOPHONE: A variant of a class of similar speech sounds that constitute a phoneme. For example, the sound represented by *p* in *pin* is produced slightly differently from the sound represented by *p* in *spin;* yet both sounds are recognized by English speakers as the "same." Thus, /p/ in *pin* and /p/ in *spin* are allophones of the phoneme /p/.

ALPHABET: A system of written symbols representing the phonemes of speech; American English has 26 such symbols.

ALPHABETIC ORDER: An arrangement of words which follows the order of the letters of the alphabet: A, B, C, D, etc.; for example, the listings in a telephone directory or a dictionary. See ALPHABET.

ALPHABETIC PRINCIPLE: The principle of using graphemes to signify phonemes which underlies many written forms of languages. Ideally, each phoneme would be represented by its own distinctive grapheme. In American English, the alphabetic principle is approximated. See PHONEME; GRAPHEME; PHONEME–GRAPHEME CORRESPONDENCE.

ALPHABETIC WRITING: A system of encoding spoken forms of a language into written forms by using graphemes to represent the phonemes in a word, in contrast to writing systems in which a grapheme represents a *morpheme* (as in Chinese) or a *syllable* (as in Old Persian cuneiform). See MORPHEME; SYLLABLE.

AMERICAN ENGLISH: The kind of English spoken in the

United States, as compared with British English, Canadian English, Australian English, etc.

ANTONYM: A word whose meaning is opposite to that of another word. For example, *kind* and *unkind, violent* and *nonviolent,* and *short* and *tall* are three pairs of antonyms. See SYNONYM; THESAURUS.

APOSTROPHE: A graphic mark (') used 1) to indicate the omission in words of one or more sounds and their graphic representations, as in *we'll* for *we will;* 2) to indicate the possessive form of a noun, as in "the *pup's* mother" (singular possessive) or "the *pups'* mother" (plural possessive); 3) to indicate the plural of a few nouns, as in "the two *d's* in *add*" and "the three *4's* in *444.*" See CONTRACTION; POSSESSIVE.

ARTICULATION: The act of forming sounds by means of the vocal organs; in particular, the movements of these organs in producing distinct speech sounds.

ASSIMILATION: A process whereby one of two adjacent phonemes adopts partially or wholly to the sound and/or form of its neighbor. For example, *affair* is derived from Latin *ad-* + *faire* (to do). Over time, the /d/ of *ad-* was "absorbed" by the /f/ of *faire.* In many such cases, the spelling of the "lost" sound is changed to the same spelling as the surviving sound. See SYNTHESIS.

AUDITORY: Relating to or experienced through the sense of hearing, a basic sense involved in learning to encode phonemes into graphemes in alphabetic writing systems. See AURAL; HAPTICAL; ORAL; MULTISENSORY–MULTIMOTOR; SENSORIMOTOR; VISUAL.

AURAL: Relating to the detection of spoken sounds (phonemes) by the ear. Ascertaining phonemes in running speech for purposes of spelling involves aural abilities. See PHONEME; GRAPHEME; ALPHABETIC PRINCIPLE; AUDITORY.

BLEND: 1) A word formed by combining parts of other words. Sometimes called a *portmanteau* word. *Motel* is a blend of *motor* and *hotel; smog* is a blend of *smoke* and *fog.* 2) A term often erroneously assumed to be a synonym of *cluster.* See CLUSTER.

BORROWING: The process of taking a word from one language and using it in another. Sometimes both the pronunciation and spelling of the borrowed word are preserved, as in *parfait* /pär fā′/, taken from the French. In other instances, the spelling is kept but the pronunciation is modified to make the word more like the host language style of speaking, as in **bonnet** from Old French *bonet* /bō nā′/, later spelled **bonnet.** See DRIFT; ETYMOLOGY.

BOUND MORPHEME: See MORPHEME, BOUND.

CLIPPED FORM: The shortening of a word to save energy, time, or writing space, eventually resulting in general acceptance, as **taxicab** and then **taxi** for **taximeter cabriolet;** and *oleo* for *oleomargarine.* See CONTRACTION; ABBREVIATION; ACRONYM; BLEND; DERIVATIVE.

CLOSED SYLLABLE: See SYLLABLE, CLOSED.

CLUSTER: A sequence of two or more consonant phonemes in a syllable. The word *bran* contains a consonant cluster /b/ + /r/ represented by **br.** However, not all consonant phonemes can be clustered in American English; for example, the following nonsense syllables contain impermissible initial clusters: *tlop, sbat, vrog.* See BLEND; CONSONANT PHONEME; CVC PATTERN; POSITION.

COGNITIVE MAP: The stable, clear integration and organization of a learner's subject-matter knowledge in a given discipline. The synthesis of all learning on a subject through the sensorimotor modalities, which produces in the central nervous system a meaningful set of patterns and principles to which the learner refers when he must act. See MODALITY; MULTISENSORY–MULTIMOTOR; SENSORIMOTOR.

COMMUNICATION: Sharing information, generally by means of speech or graphemically encoded speech (writing).

COMPOUND: Two or more free morphemes combined to produce a single unit. Compounds may be written as a single word (*baseball*), as separate words (**high school**), or as words connected by a hyphen (*air-condition*). See MORPHEME, FREE; PHRASE WORD.

COMPREHENSION VOCABULARY: See VOCABULARY, COMPREHENSION.

CONSONANT PHONEME: One of two groups of sounds found in every language (the other being *vowel phonemes*) produced when outgoing breath is constricted, or halted and then released, somewhere between the throat and the lips. In American English there are approximately 24 consonant phonemes. See VOWEL PHONEME.

CONSTRAINT: The restrictions placed upon the occurrences of phoneme–grapheme correspondences within syllables by other phonemes and/or graphemes in the *same* syllable. For example, /f/ is always spelled *ph* following /s/, as in *sphere*. See ENVIRONMENT.

CONTEXT: The parts of a written or spoken statement that surround a given word and can throw light on its meaning; a fundamental aid in spelling a word which has one or more homonyms. See HOMONYM; CONTEXTUAL ENVIRONMENT.

CONTEXTUAL ENVIRONMENT: The overall meaning of the words preceding and/or following a given word, which determines the correct spelling of it. See HOMONYM; CONTEXT.

CONTRACTION: A word or word group shortened in speaking by the omission of certain phonemes. When a spoken contraction is encoded, the graphemes representing the omitted phonemes are also omitted; an apostrophe is inserted to represent the omitted sound or sounds; e.g. the contraction *he'll* is the shortened form of *he will,* and the apostrophe (') represents the omitted phonemes /w/ and /i/. See APOSTROPHE.

CORRESPONDENCE: See PHONEME–GRAPHEME CORRESPONDENCE.

CVC PATTERN: A formula to describe the makeup of a syllable in terms of its sequence of consonant phoneme, vowel phoneme, and consonant phoneme, as in *pit.* Some variations of this formula are CV (*boy*), CCVC (*spell*), CVCC (*books*), V (*eye*), VC (*it*), VCC (*its*).

DECODING: The process of rendering written or printed symbols (alphabetical letters, syllabary, ideograph, rebus, or pictograph) into the speech forms that were originally recorded. Decoding is part of the *reading* process and is the reverse of *encoding* (spelling). See ENCODING; READING; SPELLING.

DERIVATION: The process whereby the grammatical function of a root or stem is changed by the addition of an affix. See AFFIX; AFFIXATION; DERIVATIVE; ROOT; STEM.

DERIVATIONAL AFFIX: A suffix or prefix which not only permits a root to be used in an extended way, but also changes its grammatical function; i.e. *tight*, an adjective, can be altered by the following derivational suffixes:

> *tight*   (adjective)
> *tight* + *-ness* = *tightness* (noun)
> *tight* + *-en*   = *tighten*   (verb)
> *tight* + *-ly*   = *tightly*   (adverb)

See DERIVATIVE; ROOT; AFFIX; INFIX; PREFIX; SUFFIX.

DERIVATIVE: A word formed by adding one or more derivational affixes to a stem. For example, *friendliness* is a derivative formed by adding the suffixes *-ly* and *-ness* to the stem *friend*. See DERIVATIONAL AFFIX; STEM.

DIACRITIC MARK: A mark added to a grapheme to indicate the pronunciation of the phoneme which the grapheme represents. Thus, in *āble* the mark over the *a* indicates that *a* stands for /ā/, the so-called long-*a* sound. Dictionaries always have a key for interpreting diacritic marks. See PRONUNCIATION KEY.

DIALECT: A variety of a language that is distinguishable from other varieties of the same language by differences in phonology, grammar, and vocabulary. A dialect can set off one group of speakers from another geographically, socially, ethnically, or occupationally. The variations may be so slight that only a specialist in linguistics can detect them. See DRIFT; PHONEME; DIALECT ATLAS.

DIALECT ATLAS: Maps of a geographic area showing the distribution of various phonological, grammatical, and lexical features of the different dialects of that area. See DIALECT; MORPHOLOGY; PHONOLOGY.

DICTIONARY: See LEXICON; SPELLER DICTIONARY; STANDARD DICTIONARY; UNABRIDGED DICTIONARY; THESAURUS.

DIGRAPH: Two letters representing a single phoneme, or speech sound; for example, *ch, th, sh.*

DIPHTHONG: A sequence of two vowel or vowellike sounds within the same syllable and pronounced as a single vowel phoneme. In the word *about,* the grapheme *ou* represents the phoneme /ou/, which technically is composed of the vowel /ä/ and the semi-vowel /w/.

DRIFT: The gradual, unplanned change that takes place in the character of a language commonly resulting in a dialect that would probably be unintelligible to the speakers of the earlier period. One example is the gradual but significant change that transformed Old English into modern English. Drift is a continuous process.

ENCODING: The process of recording spoken communication through graphic marks or symbols. "Word" writing, syllabaries, and alphabetic writing are the major means man has invented to encode the spoken word. Most modern languages use alphabetic writing to encode (spell) the sounds (phonemes) uttered in speech. See ALPHABET; ALPHABETIC PRINCIPLE; PHONEME; GRAPHEME; READING; DECODING; ALPHABETIC WRITING; ORTHOGRAPHY; PICTOGRAPH; SYLLABARY; IDEOGRAPH.

ENUNCIATION: The pronunciation or articulation of speech sounds (phonemes) in words, especially distinct pronunciation. In spelling, careful enunciation augments the opportunity to select correct graphemes for phonemes in words that are to be written. See ARTICULATION; SPEECH, FORMAL; PRONUNCIATION, FORMAL.

ENVIRONMENT: The position in which a phoneme occurs in syllables *in relation to* other phonemes within the same syllable. For example, /j/ in *ledge* is in final position following a short vowel phoneme. Environmental factors often have a strong bearing on how certain phonemes are spelled in American English. The /j/ as in *ledge* generally is spelled *dge* following a short-vowel phoneme. See CONSTRAINT.

ESPERANTO: An artificial language invented for use as a world language. Made up of derived words most commonly used throughout Europe and the Americas.

ETYMOLOGIST: A linguist who specializes in tracing the origins and history of words. See LINGUISTICS; ETYMOLOGY; DRIFT; DERIVATION; BORROWING.

ETYMOLOGY: The study of the history of a word from its earliest recorded form and meaning to its present status.

FINAL POSITION: The occurrence of a phoneme at the end of either a syllable or a word. The /g/ in the first syllable of *bighorn* is in syllable-final position. The /g/ in the last syllable in *catalog* is in word-final position. See PHONEME-GRAPHEME CORRESPONDENCE; INITIAL POSITION; GRAPHEMIC OPTION; SYLLABLE; WORD; WORD-FINAL POSITION.

FORMAL PRONUNCIATION: See PRONUNCIATION, FORMAL.

FORMAL SPEECH: See SPEECH, FORMAL.

FREE MORPHEME: See MORPHEME, FREE.

GEMINATE CONSONANTS: Term used to denote a doubled consonant grapheme; e.g. the *dd* in *add* or the *ff* in *off.*

GLOSSARY: A list of special or technical terms used in discussing a particular topic or subject or field; usually arranged in alphabetic order. See DICTIONARY; LEXICON.

GRAPHEME: A unit of writing which in alphabetic systems represents a spoken sound. Thus, the graphemes which represent the word /boi/ are *b* and *oy,* whereby *b* represents /b/ and *oy* represents /oi/. In this volume a grapheme is shown in boldface italic type.

GRAPHEMIC OPTION: One of the graphemes which may represent a given phoneme. The phoneme /oi/, for example, can be represented by the letters *oi* or *oy* (as in *oil* or *boy*); /f/ can be represented by *f, gh, ph, ff* (as in *foot, cough, phone, gruff*). Graphemic options for many sounds in American-English words are determined by certain principles of the writing system.

GUIDE WORDS: The words in heavy faced type at the top of each page of a dictionary, used to indicate the first and last words on that page. For example, *bracket* and *bread* inform the reader that all words falling in alphabetic arrangement between these two entries will be found on this page if they are included in the dictionary. See DICTIONARY; ALPHABETIC ORDER.

HAPTICAL: Relating to the combined tactile (touch) and kinesthetic (muscular) responses involved in writing; one of the multisensory–multimotor processes involved in mastering the spellings of words. See AURAL; ORAL; MULTISENSORY–MULTIMOTOR; VISUAL.

HIEROGLYPHIC: A system of writing that largely employs pictographs and ideographs and was used by early Egyptian priests. See PICTOGRAPH; IDEOGRAPH; LINGUISTICS.

HOMOGRAPH: One of two or more words that are spelled alike but differ in derivation, meaning, and sometimes pronunciation; a homonym. The boldface italic words in the following sentences are homographs: Why do you *object* to my plan? What is the *object* of this game? Similarly: A *tear* ran down her cheek. She has a *tear* in her new dress.

HOMONYM: One of two or more words that are alike in spoken and/or written form but different in meaning. When homonyms are alike in speech, they are *homophones;* when alike in writing, they are *homographs.* A term sometimes used synonymously for *homophone* and/or *homograph.* See CONTEXTUAL ENVIRONMENT; HOMOGRAPH; HOMOPHONE.

HOMOPHONE: One of two or more words that are pronounced alike but differ in meaning, derivation, and often in spelling; a homonym. The boldface italic words in the following sentences are homophones: The water in the *pool* is cold. He is an expert *pool* player. The *meat* was well done. I'll *meet* you at 3 P.M.

IDEOGRAPH: A graphic character or symbol that refers to an idea or thing without necessarily representing spoken words. Classical Chinese manuscripts are examples of ideographic writing. See PICTOGRAPH; SYLLABARY; GRAPHEME; ALPHABETIC WRITING; ALPHABET.

INFIX: An inflectional morpheme placed *within* a stem, as distinguished from a prefix or suffix. American English does not employ true infixes. See AFFIXATION; PREFIX; SUFFIX.

INFLECTIONAL SUFFIX: A suffix that alters or extends the use of words without altering their grammatical function or basic meaning; e.g. the suffix /əd/ spelled *ed* attached to *add* makes *added;* the suffix /ėr/ spelled *er* attached to *fast* makes *faster.* See DERIVATIONAL AFFIX.

INFORMAL PRONUNCIATION: See PRONUNCIATION, INFORMAL.

INFORMAL SPEECH: See SPEECH, INFORMAL.

INITIAL POSITION: The occurrence of a phoneme at the beginning of a word or syllable; e.g. /a/ is in initial position in the word *advice;* /v/ is in initial position in the second syllable of *advice.* See WORD-FINAL POSITION; CONSTRAINT; ENVIRONMENT.

INTERIOR PHONEME: A phoneme occupying other than the initial or final position in a syllable. The typical English syllable pattern is CVC (consonant, vowel, consonant), e.g. /bed/. In this case a vowel is the interior phoneme, while in a CCV pattern, e.g. /stā/ (*stay*), a consonant is the interior phoneme. See CVC PATTERN; PHONEME; GRAPHEME; INITIAL POSITION; FINAL POSITION.

LANGUAGE FAMILY: A group of clearly related languages that can be traced to a "parent" language. There are approximately 3,000 languages in the world which can be traced to a few language families: primarily Indo-European, Semitic, Sino-Tibetan, Austronesian, Bantu. American English is a branching of the Indo-European language family.

LETTER: An alphabetic symbol; one of 26 such symbols used in encoding American English. See ALPHABET.

LEXICOGRAPHER: One who writes or compiles dictionaries. See LEXICON; SPELLER DICTIONARY; STANDARD DICTIONARY; UNABRIDGED DICTIONARY.

LEXICON: 1) All the morphemes in a language; 2) an alphabetically arranged list of terms used in a field of endeavor or study. See MORPHEME.

LINGUA FRANCA: Any common and commercial language spoken by people of different language communities and made up of a mixture of the vocabularies and grammars of the several languages within the larger language community. See WORLD LANGUAGE; ESPERANTO.

LINGUISTICS: The scientific study of language. Not to be confused with *philology*, the study of written records chiefly from a historical point of view; historical linguistics. (Persons trained in linguistics who conduct various studies of language are known as *linguists.*)

MEDIAL PHONEME: See INTERIOR PHONEME.

MEDIAL POSITION: See INTERIOR PHONEME.

MODALITY: Any one of the several major categories of sensori-motor mechanisms by which the central nervous system receives messages for sorting and storing. The main modalities for spelling are oral, aural, visual, and haptical. See AURAL; HAPTICAL; MULTISENSORY–MULTIMOTOR; ORAL; VISUAL.

MONOSYLLABIC WORD: A word containing only one syllable. ***Man, boy, girl, school, book, spell, house, through, strength*** are all monosyllabic words. See SYLLABLE; POLYSYLLABIC WORD.

MORPHEME: The smallest meaningful unit of language. A morpheme may be a complete word, as ***boy;*** or it may be a speech sound that has no meaning when pronounced by itself but contributes to the meaning of words; e.g. the sound /z/ represented by *s* in *boys.* See WORD; MORPHEME, FREE; MORPHEME, BOUND; MORPHOLOGY.

MORPHEME, BOUND: A morpheme which cannot be used as a word but must be combined with one or more other morphemes to form a word. The sound added to ***pin*** to produce the plural ***pins*** is a bound morpheme. See MORPHEME; MORPHEME, FREE; PREFIX; SUFFIX; WORD.

MORPHEME, FREE: A morpheme which can be used independently as a word; e.g. ***pin.*** See MORPHEME, BOUND; MORPHEME; WORD.

MORPHOLOGY: The study of the arrangement and interrelationships of morphemes in words; the "word building" properties of a language. See COMPOUND; MORPHEME; MORPHEME, BOUND; MORPHEME, FREE; DERIVATION.

MULTISENSORY–MULTIMOTOR: A term referring to the process of learning through the simultaneous use and reinforcement of such modalities and motor mechanisms as eye, voice, ear, muscle, and touch. Spelling is considered a multisensory–multimotor activity. See AUDITORY; ORAL; HAPTICAL; SENSORIMOTOR; AURAL; SPEECH ORGANS; MODALITY; VISUAL.

NEOLOGISM: 1) A new word or phrase (*robot*); 2) a new meaning or new word from an old word or words (*know-how*).

ONOMATOPOEIC WORD: A word whose sound suggests its meaning, as the *hiss* of steam or the *buzz* of a bee.

OPEN SYLLABLE: See SYLLABLE, OPEN.

OPTION: See GRAPHEMIC OPTION.

ORAL: A term referring to the production of speech by vocal tract and breath. One aspect of the multisensory–multimotor apparatus used in learning to spell. See SPEECH ORGANS; MULTISENSORY–MULTIMOTOR; SENSORIMOTOR.

ORTHOGRAPHY: A set of rules, principles, standards, and conventions by which spoken forms of language are transcribed into written forms; spelling. In English the orthography is largely a set of rules for transcribing phonemes into graphemes. See WRITING CONVENTIONS.

PHONEME: The smallest meaningful unit of sound whereby the substitution of one for another changes the meaning of a morpheme as in the following two sentences: I'll *bat* you on the head. I'll *pat* you on the head. See MORPHEME.

PHONEME CLUSTER: See CLUSTER.

PHONEME–GRAPHEME CORRESPONDENCE: The relationship between a phoneme and a graphemic option representing the phoneme. In the word *fish,* comprised of the phonemes /fish/, /f/ is represented by *f*, /i/ by *i*, /sh/ by *sh;* in *phone* /fōn/, /f/ is represented by *ph*, /ō/ by *o-e*, and /n/ by *n*. See ALPHABETIC PRINCIPLE.

PHONEMICS: The study, analysis, and classification of phonemes; a special study in phonology, a branch of linguistics.

PHONETICS: The study of the production, transmission, and reception of human speech sounds; a branch of both physiology and physics.

PHONICS: A method of teaching reading in which the pupil is taught to assign the correct speech sound to a grapheme; "sounding out." The opposite of teaching spelling in which the pupil is taught to select the correct grapheme to represent a particular phoneme. See GRAPHEME; PHONEME.

PHONOLOGY: The study of the sound structure of a language including phonetics and phonemics; a branch of linguistics. See PHONEMICS; PHONETICS.

PHRASE WORD: A group of words that forms a unit of meaning; e.g. *well-meaning, has-been, ten-year-old.* The separate words of a phrase word are commonly joined in writing by the use of hyphens (-). See COMPOUND.

PICTOGRAPH: The pictorial representation of an object; probably the earliest form of recording events, such as drawing pictures on the walls of caves. See ALPHABETIC WRITING; SYLLABARY; IDEOGRAPH.

PLURAL: The form of a noun (or other part of speech) denoting more than one. The plural of a noun is usually formed by adding *s* (/s/), e.g. *cats, s* (/z/), e.g. *dogs,* or the syllable *es* (/əz/), e.g. *churches,* to the singular noun. Some nouns, however, have only one oral and written form for singular and plural, as in *moose* or *sheep;* and some singular nouns change their form internally, as in *mouse/mice.* See MORPHOLOGY; DERIVATIVE.

POLYSYLLABIC WORD: A word containing two or more syllables. *Woman, about, textbook, spelling, represent, unmarketable* are polysyllabic words. See SYLLABLE; MONOSYLLABIC WORD.

PORTMANTEAU WORD: See BLEND.

POSITION: See FINAL POSITION; INITIAL POSITION; INTERIOR PHONEME; DERIVATIVE.

POSSESSIVE: Expressing or signifying ownership. A possessive noun is a "shortcut" way of expressing ownership. One can say, "The marbles belong to the tall boy," or "The tall boy's marbles." Thus, merely by adding the *'s* to *boy,* one expresses the idea of ownership. See APOSTROPHE; DERIVATIVE.

PREFIX: An affix that precedes the root or stem to which it is added, e.g. the **un-** of **unalike,** the **con-** of **context.** See AFFIX; MORPHEME, BOUND; SUFFIX.

PRIMARY STRESS: See STRESS, PRIMARY.

PROGRAMMED SPELLING SERIES: A set of spelling textbooks, or textbook–workbooks, with a master plan for enabling pupils to observe in a systematic way the spelling patterns which constitute American-English orthography. As illustrated in Part Two of this book, such a scope and sequence master plan can be built on the phonological, morphological, and contextual principles which govern the standard spelling of the vast majority of words in use and includes useful psychological principles for teaching and learning spelling. See SCOPE AND SEQUENCE.

PRONUNCIATION, FORMAL: The careful enunciation of the sounds in words. Formal pronunciation is a useful and recommended *spelling practice* because it provides many precise cues for observing phoneme–grapheme correspondences. For example, in formal pronunciation, we would pronounce *debate* as /dē bāt′/, not /di bāt′/, thus reinforcing the fact that the vowel in the first syllable is spelled *e.* See ENUNCIATION; SPELLING PRONUNCIATION.

PRONUNCIATION, INFORMAL: The casual pronunciation of the sounds in words. This style of speaking is acceptable in conversation and is sufficient for communication. However, informal pronunciation often obscures many useful phoneme–grapheme correspondence cues that can help the speller. See PRONUNCIATION, FORMAL; PHONEME–GRAPHEME CORRESPONDENCE; PRONUNCIATION.

PRONUNCIATION KEY: A system of graphic symbols used in dictionaries to show the reader how to pronounce written words and to help the speller determine sound values of graphemes. See DIACRITIC MARK.

PROOFREADING: To read a piece of handwritten, typed, or printed material to detect and correct errors made either during the original composition of the piece or during the copying, typing, or printing. Proofreading is an important element of general spelling ability.

READING: The process of comprehending the meaning of

written or printed communication. See DECODING; ENCOD-
ING; ALPHABETIC PRINCIPLE; SPELLING.

REBUS: A written statement composed of pictures and regular
graphemes whose names suggest the sounds of the words
or syllables they represent; e.g.   " 👁 'll 🐝 8 🐝 4
👁 C U again" is rebus writing, signifying "I'll be
eight before I see you again."

ROOT: The element of a word that remains after all affixes
have been removed. Also called a *base.* A root may be a
free morpheme or a bound morpheme; e.g. *like* of *unlikely,*
cept of *unacceptable.* See MORPHOLOGY; DERIVATIVE; AF-
FIX; PREFIX; SUFFIX; ETYMOLOGY; MORPHEME, BOUND; MOR-
PHEME, FREE; STEM.

SCHWA: An indistinct, "neutral" vowel sound used in unaccented syllables; e.g. *a* represents schwa in *about; u* represents schwa in **circus.** Shown in phonemic transcription
as /ə/.

SCOPE AND SEQUENCE: The range of material to be presented and the development of this material from level to
level (grade to grade) in a curriculum.

SECONDARY STRESS: See STRESS, SECONDARY.

SENSORIMOTOR: Having to do with both sensory and motor
activities. The identification of sounds in words and the
simultaneous transcription of these sounds into written
symbols ("going from sound to letter") is a sensorimotor
spelling activity. See MULTISENSORY–MULTIMOTOR.

SIMPLIFIED SPELLING: Proposed systems for reducing the
number of spellings of phonemes represented in American-
English orthography. Typically, proposed schemes would
eliminate 1) *c,* using *k* for /k/ and *s* for /s/; 2) *x,* using
ks for /ks/, as in *eksersize* for *exercise;* and 3) *qu,* using
kw for /kw/, as in *kween* for *queen.* Graphemes that are
not essential in the spelling of a word would also be
dropped, as in *det* for *debt.*

SINGULAR: The form of a noun (or other part of speech)
denoting only one. *Man* is a singular noun; *men* is a plural
noun. See PLURAL.

SLASH MARKS: See VIRGULES.

SOUND-SPELLING KEY: See PRONUNCIATION KEY.

SPEAKING VOCABULARY: See VOCABULARY, SPEAKING.

SPEECH, FORMAL: That style of oral communication in which the speaker makes an effort to use precise vocabulary and correct grammar and to enunciate clearly, etc., in contrast to informal speech, in which the speaker is interested primarily in getting his message across quickly and exerts little effort to be precise. Formal speech enhances phoneme–grapheme correspondence cues in spelling. See SPEECH, INFORMAL; ALPHABETIC PRINCIPLE; ENUNCIATION; ACCENT; AMERICAN ENGLISH; COMMUNICATION; DIALECT; PRONUNCIATION; VOCABULARY.

SPEECH, INFORMAL: That style of speaking ordinarily used in conversation, as distinguished from platform or broadcast speech. See SPEECH, FORMAL.

SPEECH ORGANS: Any part of the human vocal tract — tongue, teeth, palate, lips, nasal passage, velum, diaphragm, larynx, lungs — that helps, actively or passively, voluntarily or involuntarily, in the production of speech sounds. See ORAL; MULTISENSORY–MULTIMOTOR; SENSORI-MOTOR.

SPELLER DICTIONARY: A special dictionary incorporated into a spelling textbook and containing the words appropriate to the lessons and the grade level. A speller dictionary serves the specific purpose of teaching pupils over a period of time how to make full use of the standard dictionary. See STANDARD DICTIONARY; UNABRIDGED DICTIONARY; LEXICON.

SPELLING: The process of encoding, or of rendering spoken words into written symbols. See ENCODING; READING; DECODING.

SPELLING PRONUNCIATION: The careful enunciation of speech sounds (phonemes) in words to reinforce association between them and their graphemic representations. See PRONUNCIATION KEY; PRONUNCIATION, FORMAL; PRONUNCIATION, INFORMAL.

SPIRAL PROGRAM: A spelling program that starts at level 1 with the most predictable and consistent phoneme–grapheme correspondences and periodically includes less consistently spelled but previously presented phonemes in order to furnish additional phonological, morphological, and contextual information to help the pupil select from the various graphemic options the correct spelling of these phonemes in newly introduced words.

STANDARD DICTIONARY: A conventional, unabridged or desk-sized dictionary, as opposed to a bound-in-text speller dictionary. A standard dictionary has many more entries; more definitions for each entry; more information on derivatives, antonyms, synonyms; more information on etymology, etc. See SPELLER DICTIONARY; UNABRIDGED DICTIONARY; LEXICON.

STEM: Any morpheme or combination of morphemes to which an affix can be added. For example, *friends* contains the stem *friend* plus the plural affix spelled *s*. See MORPHEME; AFFIX; ROOT.

STRESS: The relative force or intensity with which a sound or syllable is pronounced. See ACCENT; STRESS, PRIMARY; STRESS, SECONDARY; UNSTRESSED SYLLABLE.

STRESS, PRIMARY: The strongest stress given to a sound or syllable (or syllables) in polysyllabic words. Thus, the first syllable in *neigh' bor hood* receives the primary stress, which is indicated by an accent mark ('). See ACCENT; STRESS, SECONDARY; UNSTRESSED SYLLABLE.

STRESS, SECONDARY: Stress of a sound or syllable which is greater than that given to unstressed syllables but not so great as that given to primary-stressed syllables. Thus in *math' e mat' ics,* the third syllable receives a primary stress, the first syllable a secondary stress, and the second and last syllables are unstressed. The secondary-stressed syllable is often indicated by an accent mark that is lighter (') than the mark (') for primary stress. See ACCENT; STRESS, PRIMARY; UNSTRESSED SYLLABLE.

STUDY LIST: A set of words selected for spelling study with particular phonological, morphological, or contextual features in common. See MORPHEME; PHONEME; CONTEXT; PHONEME–GRAPHEME CORRESPONDENCE; ALPHABETIC PRINCIPLE.

SUFFIX: An affix that follows the root or stem to which it is added. Suffixes may be inflectional, e.g. the sound represented by *s* in *boys,* or derivational, e.g. the *-ly* of *friendly.* See AFFIX; DERIVATIONAL AFFIX; INFLECTIONAL SUFFIX; MORPHEME, BOUND; MORPHEME, FREE; PREFIX.

SYLLABARY: An orthography in which graphic symbols stand for syllables rather than for phonemes. See ENCODING; IDEOGRAPH; PHONEME; PICTURE WRITING; SYLLABIC WRITING.

SYLLABIC WRITING: A writing system in which graphemes represent syllables instead of phonemes. See SYLLABARY; ALPHABETIC WRITING.

SYLLABLE: A unit of sound composed of a vowel phoneme or a phoneme with vowellike quality and usually one or more consonant phonemes. Not to be confused with a "sound." The word *through,* for example, is made up of one syllable, three sounds or phonemes, and seven letters or graphemes. See MONOSYLLABIC WORD; POLYSYLLABIC WORD; CVC PATTERN.

SYLLABLE, CLOSED: A syllable ending in one or more consonant phonemes. The first and last syllables of *ransom* and the last syllable of *secret* are closed syllables. See SYLLABLE, OPEN.

SYLLABLE, OPEN: A syllable ending in a vowel phoneme. The first syllable of *table* and the last syllable of *window* are open syllables. See SYLLABLE, CLOSED.

SYLLABLE PATTERNS: See CVC PATTERN.

SYNONYM: A word that has a meaning similar to that of another word. *Imitate* and *mimic* are synonyms. See THESAURUS.

SYNTAX: The arrangement of words in a language to form phrases, clauses, and sentences. See CONTEXT; CONTEXTUAL ENVIRONMENT.

SYNTHESIS: A process whereby a combination of sounds produces a new sound; usually associated with the addition of suffixes to roots and stems. For example, the suffix *-ion* by itself is pronounced /yən/. However, when *-ion* is added to *act* to produce *action,* the /t/ of *act* and the /y/ of /yən/ combine to form /sh/, as in /ak′shən/. See ASSIMILATION.

THESAURUS: A dictionary of synonyms and antonyms; a storehouse of organized vocabulary. See SYNONYM; ANTONYM.

UNABRIDGED DICTIONARY: A dictionary that is nearly complete; one that is comprehensive, not condensed. Dictionaries come in many sizes and vary greatly in number of entries and completeness of information. Unabridged dictionaries are considered to be the most complete record of the lexicon of a language. See SPELLER DICTIONARY; STANDARD DICTIONARY; THESAURUS; LEXICON.

UNSTRESSED SYLLABLE: In polysyllabic words, unstressed syllables are those which are pronounced with least force; they are unmarked in the pronunciation entries of a dictionary. See STRESS, PRIMARY; STRESS, SECONDARY.

VESTIGIAL LETTER: A letter that does not represent a sound value of its own but did at one time. The *k* of *knight* and the *b* of *lamb* are vestigial letters that once represented /k/ and /b/ respectively. See DRIFT; BORROWING; ETYMOLOGY; SPEECH, FORMAL.

VIRGULES: Graphic characters sometimes called slash marks, / /, used in linguistic writing to indicate phonemes as distinguished from graphemes. For example, the first sound in *cup* is /k/ spelled *c.*

VISUAL: Related to or experienced through the sense of sight. One of the senses involved in the development of spelling ability. See AUDITORY; AURAL; HAPTICAL; MULTISENSORY– MULTIMOTOR; ORAL.

VOCABULARY: The stock of words that comprise a language. See VOCABULARY, COMPREHENSION; VOCABULARY, SPEAKING; VOCABULARY, WRITING; LEXICON.

VOCABULARY, COMPREHENSION: The set of words an individual understands when he hears or sees them but does not necessarily use in his speaking and writing. See VOCABULARY; VOCABULARY, SPEAKING; VOCABULARY, WRITING.

VOCABULARY, SPEAKING: Those words which an individual can use appropriately in speaking. A speaking vocabulary is usually larger than a writing vocabulary but smaller than a comprehension vocabulary. See VOCABULARY; VOCABULARY, COMPREHENSION; VOCABULARY, WRITING.

VOCABULARY, WRITING: Those words which an individual can use appropriately in writing. A writing vocabulary usually is smaller than both speaking and comprehension vocabularies. See VOCABULARY; VOCABULARY, COMPREHENSION; VOCABULARY, SPEAKING.

VOICE TYPEWRITER: A dictator–transcriber; a machine capable of receiving a spoken message and encoding that message automatically into written or typed form.

VOWEL PHONEME: In every language, one of two groups of sounds (the other being *consonant phoneme*) produced by the vibration of the vocal cords with no restriction on the outgoing air between the throat and lips. American English has approximately 22 vowel phonemes (including simple vowels and diphthongs). See CONSONANT PHONEME.

WORD: The smallest unit of speech which has independent meaning. See MORPHEME; MORPHEME, FREE.

WORD-FINAL POSITION: The occurrence of a phoneme at the end of a word. In *trough* the phoneme /f/ is in word-final position; the grapheme *gh* is used to represent the /f/ in this word-final position. See INITIAL POSITION; CONSTRAINT; FINAL POSITION.

WORLD LANGUAGE: A language suitable for common and commercial use throughout the world and officially recognized as such by the major language communities of the world.

WRITING CONVENTIONS: Stylebook rules, traditions, or customs followed as the accepted form in written expression; such conventions may have nothing to do with the alphabetic sequence in an accepted spelling pattern. Failure to adhere to a writing convention is traditionally tantamount to "incorrect" spelling. Thus, to omit the apostrophe when writing a contraction or possessive results in a "misspelled" word. Other writing conventions apply to the use of capital letters, punctuation marks, and abbreviations. See ORTHOGRAPHY.

WRITING VOCABULARY: See VOCABULARY, WRITING.

BIBLIOGRAPHY

AMERICANA CORPORATION. *The Encyclopedia Americana.* New York: Americana Corp., 1957.

ANDERSON, GEORGE K. *The Literature of the Anglo-Saxons.* New York: Russell & Russell, 1962.

ANDERSON, VIRGIL A. *Improving the Child's Speech.* New York: Oxford University Press, 1953.

ATKINS, J. W. H., ED. *The Owl and the Nightingale.* Cambridge, England: Cambridge University Press, 1922.

BAUGH, ALBERT C. *A History of the English Language,* 2nd ed. New York: Appleton-Century-Crofts, 1957.

BERGQUIST, SIDNEY R. "A Comparative Index for the Linguistic-Based Patterns of American-English Spelling." Unpublished, two-volume doctoral dissertation, Stanford University, 1966.

BETHEL, JOHN P., ED. *Webster's New Collegiate Dictionary,* 6th ed. Springfield, Mass.: G. & C. Merriam Co., 1961.

BLOOMFIELD, LEONARD. *Language.* New York: Henry Holt & Co., 1941.

BLOOMFIELD, LEONARD, AND BARNHART, CLARENCE L. *Let's Read: A Linguistic Approach.* Detroit: Wayne State University Press, 1961.

BLOOMFIELD, MORTON W., AND NEWMARK, LEONARD. *A Linguistic Introduction to the History of English.* New York: Alfred A. Knopf, 1963.

BOLINGER, DWIGHT. *Aspects of Language.* New York: Harcourt, Brace and World, 1968.

BREASTED, JAMES H. *The Conquest of Civilization.* New York: Harper & Brothers, 1926.

BROWN, ROGER. "Language: The System and Its Acquisition," pp. 246–349 in *Social Psychology, Parts I and II.* New York: Free Press, 1965.

BRUNER, JEROME S. "Individual and Collective Problems in the Study of Thinking," pp. 22–37 in *Fundamentals of Psychology: The Psychology of Thinking.* New York: Annals of the New York Academy of Sciences, Dec. 23, 1960.

BRUNER, JEROME S., ED. *Learning About Learning: A Conference Report.* Cooperative Research Monograph No. 15, OE–12019. Washington, D.C.: U.S. Department of Health, Education, and Welfare, 1966.

BRUNER, JEROME S.; GOODNOW, JACQUELINE J.; AND AUSTIN, GEORGE A. *A Study of Thinking.* New York: John Wiley & Sons, 1956.

BRYANT, MARGARET M. *Modern English and Its Heritage,* 2nd ed. New York: Macmillan Co., 1962.

CARROLL, JOHN B. *Language and Thought.* Englewood Cliffs, N.J.: Prentice-Hall, 1964.

――――. "Language Development," pp. 744–752 in *Encyclopedia of Educational Research,* ed. Chester W. Harris. New York: Macmillan Co., 1960.

CLYMER, THEODORE. "The Utility of Phonic Generalizations in the Primary Grades," *The Reading Teacher* (January, 1963), pp. 252–258.

CORSA, HELEN STORM. *Chaucer: Poet of Mirth and Morality.* Notre Dame, Ind.: University of Notre Dame Press, 1964.

DALE, EDGAR, AND EICHHOLZ, GERHARD. *Children's Knowledge of Words.* Columbus, Ohio: Bureau of Educational Research and Service, Ohio State University Press, 1960.

DEWEY, GODFREY. *Relative Frequency of English Speech Sounds.* Cambridge, Mass.: Harvard University Press, 1923.

DIRINGER, DAVID. *The Alphabet: A Key to the History of Mankind,* 2 vols., 3rd ed. London: Hutchinson and Co., 1968.

――――. *Writing.* London: Thames and Hudson, 1962.

DOLBY, JAMES L., AND RESNIKOFF, HOWARD L. *The English Word Speculum: Volume I — Random Word List.* Sunnyvale, Calif.: Lockheed Missiles & Space Co., 1964.

――――. *Notes on Written English.* Palo Alto, Calif.: Lockheed Missiles and Space Co., 1963.

DOWNING, JOHN. *Experiments with an Augmented Alphabet for Beginning Readers in British Schools.* London: Reading Research Unit, University of London Institute of Education, 1963.

DRAKE, WILLIAM D. *The Way to Spell.* San Francisco, Calif.: Chandler Publishing Co., 1967.

EISENSON, JON, AND OGILVIE, MARDEL. *Speech Correction in the School.* New York: Macmillan Co., 1957.

EMERY, DONALD W. *Variant Spellings in Modern American Dictionaries.* Champaign, Ill.: National Council of Teachers of English, 1958.

ENCYCLOPAEDIA BRITANNICA, INC. *Encyclopaedia Britannica.* Chicago: William Benton, 1959.

ERVIN, SUSAN M., AND MILLER, WICK R. "Language Development," *Child Psychology,* ed. J. W. Stevenson. 62nd Yearbook of the National Society for the Study of Education, Part I, Chap. 3. Chicago: University of Chicago Press, 1963.

EVANS, BERGEN. *Comfortable Words.* New York: Random House, 1962.

FERGUSON, CHARLES W. *The Abecedarian Book.* Boston: Little, Brown & Co., 1964.

FERNALD, GRACE M. *Remedial Techniques in Basic School Subjects.* New York: McGraw-Hill Book Co., 1943.

FIELD ENTERPRISES EDUCATIONAL CORP. *The World Book Encyclopedia.* Chicago: Field Enterprises Educational Corp., 1968.

FITZGERALD, JAMES A. *A Basic Life Spelling Vocabulary.* Milwaukee, Wis.: Bruce Publishing Co., 1951.

FRANCIS, W. NELSON. *The English Language: An Introduction.* New York: W. W. Norton & Co., 1965.

————. *The Structure of American English.* New York: Ronald Press Co., 1958.

FRAZIER, ALEXANDER, ED. *New Directions in Elementary English.* Champaign, Ill.: National Council of Teachers of English, 1967.

FRIES, CHARLES C. *Linguistics and Reading.* (See Chapters 5, 6, and 7.) New York: Holt, Rinehart & Winston, 1963.

————. *The Structure of English.* New York: Harcourt, Brace & Co., 1952.

FUNK, WILFRED. *Word Origins and Their Romantic Stories.* New York: Grosset & Dunlap, 1954.

GARVIN, PAUL L., ED. *Natural Language and the Computer.* New York: McGraw-Hill Book Co., 1963.

GATES, ARTHUR I. *A List of Spelling Difficulties in 3,876 Words.* New York: Bureau of Publications, Teachers College, Columbia University, 1937.

GELB, I. J. *A Study of Writing,* rev. ed.   Chicago: University of Chicago Press, 1963.

GLEASON, H. A., JR. *An Introduction to Descriptive Linguistics.* New York: Holt, Rinehart & Winston, 1961.

————. *Linguistics and English Grammar.* New York: Holt, Rinehart & Winston, 1965.

GOVE, PHILIP B., ED. *Webster's Third New International Dictionary of the English Language,* Unabridged. Springfield, Mass.: G. & C. Merriam Co., 1961.

GREENBERG, JOSEPH. *Essays in Linguistics.* Chicago: University of Chicago Press, 1957.

GREENE, HARRY A. *The New Iowa Spelling Scale.* Iowa City: Bureau of Educational Research and Service, State University of Iowa, 1954.

HALL, ROBERT A., JR. *Introductory Linguistics.* Philadelphia: Chilton Co., 1954.

————. *Linguistics and Your Language.* Garden City, N.Y.: Doubleday & Co., 1960.

————. *Sound and Spelling in English.* Philadelphia: Chilton Co., 1961.

HANNA, PAUL R., AND HANNA, JEAN S. "The Teaching of Spelling," *National Elementary Principal* (November, 1965), pp. 19–28.

HANNA, PAUL R.; HANNA, JEAN S.; HODGES, RICHARD E.; AND RUDORF, ERWIN H., JR. *Phoneme–Grapheme Correspondences as Cues to Spelling Improvement.* OE–32008. Washington, D.C.: U.S. Department of Health, Education, and Welfare, 1966.

HANNA, PAUL R., AND HODGES, RICHARD E. "Spelling and Communications Theory: A Model and an Annotated Bibliography," *Elementary English* (May, 1963), pp. 438–505, 528.

HOCKETT, CHARLES F. *A Course in Modern Linguistics.* New York: Macmillan Co., 1958.

HODGES, RICHARD E. "An Analysis of the Phonological Structure of American-English Orthography." Unpublished doctoral dissertation, Stanford University, 1964. (Condensed in Hanna, Hanna, Hodges, and Rudorf, U.S. HEW publication No. OE–32008.)

————. "Another Look at Those 'Spelling Demons,'" *The Elementary School Journal* (October, 1967), pp. 31–34.

————. "The Case for Teaching Sound-to-Letter Correspondences in Spelling," *The Elementary School Journal* (March, 1966), pp. 327–336.

————. "Linguistics, Psychology, and the Teaching of English," *The Elementary School Journal* (January, 1966), pp. 208–213.

HORN, ERNEST. "Spelling," pp. 1337–1354 in *Encyclopedia of Educational Research,* ed. Chester W. Harris. New York: Macmillan Co., 1960.

HORN, THOMAS D., ED. *Research on Handwriting and Spelling.* Champaign, Ill.: Committee of the National Conference on Research in English, National Council of Teachers of English, 1966.

HORN, THOMAS D. "Spelling," pp. 1282–1299 in *Encyclopedia of Educational Research,* 4th ed., ed. Robert L. Ebel. New York: Macmillan, 1969.

HUCKLEBERRY, ALAN W., AND STROTHER, EDWARD S. *Speech Education for the Elementary Teacher.* Boston: Allyn & Bacon, 1966.

INTERNATIONAL PHONETIC ASSOCIATION. *The Principles of the International Phonetic Association, Being a Description of the International Phonetic Alphabet and the Manner of Using It.* London: International Phonetic Association, 1949.

KENYON, JOHN S., AND KNOTT, THOMAS A. *A Pronouncing Dictionary of American English.* Springfield, Mass.: G. & C. Merriam Co., 1953.

KLEIN, ERNEST. *A Comprehensive Etymological Dictionary of the English Language.* 2 vols. Amsterdam, N.Y.: Elsevier Publishing Co., 1966.

KURATH, HANS. *A Phonology and Prosody of Modern English.* Ann Arbor, Mich.: University of Michigan Press, 1964.

LAIRD, CHARLTON. *The Miracle of Language.* Cleveland: World Publishing Co., 1953.

LANDER, HERBERT J. *Language and Culture.* New York: Oxford University Press, 1966.

LANGACKER, RONALD. *Language and Its Structure.* New York: Harcourt, Brace and World, 1968.

LEFEVRE, CARL A. *Linguistics and the Teaching of Reading.* New York: McGraw-Hill Book Co., 1964.

LLOYD, DONALD J., AND WARFEL, HARRY R. *American English in Its Cultural Setting.* New York: Alfred A. Knopf, 1956.

LOBAN, WALTER. *The Language of Elementary School Children.* Champaign, Ill.: NCTE Research Report No. 1, National Council of Teachers of English, 1963.

LODWIG, RICHARD R., AND BARRETT, EUGENE F. *The Dictionary and the Language.* New York: Hayden Book Co., 1967.

MacGINITIE, WALTER M. "Language Development," pp. 688–699 in *Encyclopedia of Educational Research,* 4th ed., ed. Robert L. Ebel. New York: Macmillan, 1969.

MARCKWARDT, ALBERT J. *American English.* New York: Oxford University Press, 1958.

————. *Linguistics and the Teaching of English.* Bloomington: Indiana University Press, 1967.

MARKWARDT, WILLIAM, ED. *Linguistics in School Programs,* pp. 215–228 in 69th Yearbook of the National Society for the Study of Education. Chicago: University of Chicago Press, 1970.

MATHEWS, MITFORD M. *A Dictionary of Americanisms.* Chicago: University of Chicago Press, 1956.

MENCKEN, H. L. *The American Language,* rev. ed. New York: Alfred A. Knopf, 1960.

————. *The American Language: Supplement One.* New York: Alfred A. Knopf, 1945.

MILLER, GEORGE A. "Information and Memory," pp. 104–109 in *Contemporary Readings in General Psychology,* ed. Robert S. Daniel. Boston: Houghton Mifflin Co., 1959.

————. "Speech and Language." pp. 789–810 in *Handbook of Experimental Psychology,* ed. S. S. Stevens. New York: John Wiley & Sons, 1951.

MILLER, G. A., GALANTER, E. AND PRIBRAM, K. A. *Plans and the Structure of Behavior.* New York: Holt, Rinehart and Winston, 1960.

MILLIKAN, CLARK H., AND DARLEY, FREDERIC L., EDS. *Brain Mechanisms Underlying Speech and Language.* New York and London: Grune and Stratton, 1967.

MOORE, JAMES THOMAS, JR. "Phonetic Elements Appearing in a Three-Thousand-Word Spelling Vocabulary." Unpublished doctoral dissertation, Stanford University, 1951.

MOORHOUSE, A. C. *The Triumph of the Alphabet: A History of Writing.* New York: Henry Shuman, 1953.

MYERS, L. M. *The Roots of Modern English.* Boston: Little, Brown & Co., 1966.

NEILSON, WILLIAM A., ED. *Webster's New International Dictionary of the English Language,* 2nd ed., Unabridged. Springfield, Mass.: G. & C. Merriam Co., 1957.

NIDA, EUGENE A. *Morphology: The Descriptive Analysis of Words.* Ann Arbor, Mich.: University of Michigan Press, 1956.

NIST, JOHN A. *A Structural History of English.* New York: St. Martin's Press, 1966.

OGG, OSCAR. *The 26 Letters.* New York: Thomas Y. Crowell Co., 1948.

O'NEIL, WAYNE. "The Spelling and Pronunciation of English," pp. XXXV–XXXVII in *The American Heritage Dictionary of the English Language,* ed. William Morris. Boston and New York: American Heritage Publishing Co. and Houghton Mifflin Co., 1969.

ONIONS, C. T. *The Oxford Dictionary of English Etymology.* Oxford: Clarendon Press, 1966.

———, ED. *The Shorter Oxford English Dictionary.* Oxford: Clarendon Press, 1955.

ORNSTEIN, JACOB, AND GAGE, WILLIAM W. *The ABC's of Language and Linguistics.* Philadelphia: Chilton Books, 1964.

PARTRIDGE, ERIC. *Origins: A Short Etymological Dictionary of Modern English.* London: Routledge & K. Paul, 1966.

PEI, MARIO ANDREW, ED. *Language Today: A Survey of Current Linguistic Thought.* New York: Funk & Wagnalls Co., 1967.

———. *The Story of the English Language.* Philadelphia: J. B. Lippincott Co., 1967.

PENFIELD, WILDER, AND ROBERTS, LAMAR. *Speech and Brain Mechanisms.* Princeton, N.J.: Princeton University Press, 1959.

PETERS, ROBERT A. *A Linguistic History of English.* Boston: Houghton Mifflin Co., 1968.

PETTY, WALTER T., ED. *Research in Oral Language.* Champaign, Ill.: National Conference on Research in English, 1967.

PINTO, V. DeSOLA. *The English Renaissance.* London: Cresset Press, 1966.

PORTER, DOUGLAS. *An Application of Reinforcement Principles to Classroom Teaching.* Cambridge, Mass.: Harvard University Cooperative Research Project No. 142, Office of Education, U.S. Department of Health, Education, and Welfare, 1961.

PYLES, THOMAS. *The Origins and Development of the English Language.* New York: Harcourt, Brace & World, 1964.

———. *Words and Ways of American English.* New York: Random House, 1952.

RINSLAND, HENRY D. *A Basic Vocabulary of Elementary School Children.* New York: Macmillan Co., 1945.

RUDORF, ERWIN H., JR. "The Development of an Algorithm for American-English Spelling." Unpublished doctoral dissertation, Stanford University, 1964. (Condensed in Hanna, Hanna, Hodges, and Rudorf, U.S. HEW publication No. OE–32008).

SAPIR, EDWARD. *Language: An Introduction to the Study of Speech.* New York: Harvest Books, 1949.

SAPORTA, SOL, ED. *Psycholinguistics.* New York: Holt, Rinehart & Winston, 1964.

SHIPLEY, JOSEPH T. WADELL. *Dictionary of Word Origins.* Ames, Iowa: Littlefield, Adams & Co., 1957.

SMITH, FRANK, AND MILLER, GEORGE A., EDS. *The Genesis of Language.* Cambridge, Mass.: MIT Press, 1966.

SMITH, ROBERT W. L. *Dictionary of English Word-Roots.* Totawa, N.J.: Littlefield, Adams & Co., 1966.

SOFFIETTI, JAMES P. "Why Children Fail to Read: A Linguistic Analysis," *Harvard Educational Review* (1955), pp. 63–84.

SOLOMON, HERBERT, AND MACNEILL, IAN. "Spelling Ability: A Comparison Between Computer Output Based on a Phonemic–Graphemic Algorithm and Actual Student Performance in Elementary Grades," *Research in the Teaching of English* (Fall, 1967), pp. 157–175.

STEIN, JESS. *The Random House Dictionary of the English Language.* New York: Random House, 1966.

STEVICK, ROBERT D. *English and Its History: The Evolution of a Language.* Boston: Allyn and Bacon, 1968.

TATLOCK, JOHN STRONG PERRY. *The Mind and Art of Chaucer.* Syracuse, N.Y.: Syracuse University Press, 1950.

TAYLOR, HENRY OSBORN. *The Classical Heritage of the Middle Ages.* New York: Macmillan Co., 1929.

TAYLOR, STANFORD E. *Listening.* Washington, D.C.: Department of Classroom Teachers and American Educational Research Association of the National Education Association, 1964.

THORNDIKE, EDWARD L., AND LORGE, IRVING. *The Teacher's Word Book of 30,000 Words.* New York: Bureau of Publications, Teachers College, Columbia University, 1944.

TIEDT, IRIS M., AND TIEDT, SIDNEY. *Readings on Contemporary English in the Elementary School.* Englewood Cliffs, N.J.: Prentice-Hall, 1967.

VALLINS, G. H. *Spelling.* Revised by D. G. Scragg. London: Andre Deutsch, 1965.

WALLIN, ERIK. *Spelling: Factorial and Experimental Studies.* Stockholm: Almqvist & Wiksell, 1967.

Webster's New World Dictionary of the American Language. Cleveland: World Publishing Co., 1953.

WIJK, AXEL. *Regularized English: An Investigation into the English Spelling Reform Problem with a New, Detailed Plan for a Possible Solution.* Stockholm: Almqvist & Wiksell, 1959.

WILSON, JOHN W. *The Mind.* New York: Time, Book Division, 1964.

ZIPF, GEORGE KINGSLEY. *Human Behavior and the Principle of Least Effort.* Cambridge, Mass.: Addison-Wesley Press, 1949.

INDEX

ABCDEFGHIJ— RM —76543210